A SPOONFUL OF SUGAR

A SPOONFUL OF SUGAR

A NANNY'S STORY

Brenda Ashford

DOUBLEDAY

NEW YORK LONDON TORONTO SYDNEY AUCKLAND

Book design by Pei Loi Koay
Jacket design and illustration © Jessica Hische

LIBRARY OF CONGRESS CATALOGING-IN-PUBLICATION DATA

Ashford, Brenda, 1921–
A spoonful of sugar : a memoir / Brenda Ashford. — 1st ed.
p. cm.
1. Ashford, Brenda, 1921–   2. Nannies—Great Britain—Biography.
3. Child care—Great Britain—History—20th century.   I. Title.
HQ778.7.G7A84 2013
362.70941—dc23
2012022432

ISBN 978-0-385-53641-7

MANUFACTURED IN THE UNITED STATES OF AMERICA

1 3 5 7 9 10 8 6 4 2

First Edition

To my mother and father,

for giving me the most wonderful gift ever:

a long and gloriously happy childhood

Contents

ᴀ𝒸ᴋɴᴏᴡʟᴇᴅɢᴍᴇɴᴛꜱ

ᴛʜɪꜱ ʙᴏᴏᴋ ᴄᴀᴍᴇ ᴀʙᴏᴜᴛ (out of the blue), via the Norland College, at a time when I was getting very tired of being confined to my flat following a hip operation. I was asked if I was interested in writing about my time as a Norland nurse before and after World War Two. My immediate reaction was one of excitement, but I also felt very daunted at the prospect. I needn't have worried. Kate Thompson, whose help has been invaluable, came to see me soon afterward, bringing her six-week-old son, Stanley. I had the privilege of giving him a bottle throughout our first meeting. Right from the start Kate and I got along so well together. My sincere thanks go to her for the hard work, research, and dedication to the making of the book. I am truly indebted to her.

I am grateful to my two brothers Christopher and David, who have been so encouraging all along, and to the friends who have allowed me to write about the time I spent with them and their families. We have changed names and some locations for confidentiality.

My sincere thanks go to my agent, Diane Banks; the editors at Doubleday/Random House; and also to the Norland College, for all their help, encouragement, and friendliness throughout the writing of this book. Without them it would never have made it into print.

Last but not least, I would like to thank the warden Julia and my friends in sheltered accommodation where I now live, and also my many friends in the Baptist church where I worship, for their prayers, encouragement, and support.

Above all, I thank God for his love and care for me throughout my ninety-two years.

—*Brenda Ashford*

A SPOONFUL OF SUGAR

PROLOGUE

CLIFTON COURT RESIDENTIAL HOME
OLNEY, BUCKINGHAMSHIRE, ENGLAND
[2011, AGE NINETY]

Sunday Schedule

7:30 AM: Wake up, wash, and dress.

8:30 AM: Eat breakfast of cereal with banana and cream.

9:00 AM: Receive my daily call from my little brother David.

9:00 AM TO 1:00 PM: I used to get out and tend the residents' communal garden until I suffered a fall, after which I could no longer tolerate the physical strain of gardening. The morning is punctuated by visits from the warden or friends from the church who pop in for coffee. If fine, I always try to get out for a walk. When people hit ninety they seem to stop walking. Well, that's not going to happen to me. I shall never give up; and even if it's a small walk in the garden, I try to get out every morning.

1:00 PM: Eat hot lunch, followed by a pudding in the residents' lounge.

2:00 PM: Watch the news on the television.

3:00 PM: Bake a chocolate cake or biscuits.

5:00 PM: Take phone calls from former charges, asking after me, or from church members.

6:00 PM: Have a light supper of homemade sausage and mash or chicken casserole.

7:00 PM: Watch television. I love *One Born Every Minute*, a real-life documentary about babies and childbirth; *Downton Abbey*; and *Upstairs, Downstairs*.

9:00 PM: Wash and undress slowly. Read proverbs from the Bible, then lights out by 10 PM.

The time is 7:30 am; the date is Christmas Eve, 2011.

I smile as I pull back my bedroom curtains. A little warm glow that starts in my toes soon tingles up the length of my spine. I simply adore Christmas Eve. No other day on the calendar promises quite so much joy and magic.

Right on cue a light dusting of snow falls from the white skies and settles on the chimney tops outside. A breath of wind picks up a white feather from the ground and I watch transfixed as it dances, floats, and flutters into the air.

"A white Christmas," I murmur. "How perfect."

I know it will never be as cold or snowy as the winters of my past. I will never forget the snows of 1940. Do you know, that was the coldest winter on record? The snowfall buried cars and we had to travel by sled everywhere. But still, even now aged ninety, nothing thrills me like the sight of a white Christmas.

Hugging my dressing gown tight around me, I potter to my little kitchen, flick the kettle on, and spoon tea leaves into a pot. While I wait for the kettle to boil I reflect on the day ahead.

With any luck my tiny one-bedroom flat will be filled with a steady stream of well-wishers, from family and friends to members of my church. I expect my kettle shall barely be off the boil as people pop in to share a cup of tea, drop off a card, or simply pass on their season's greetings. I shiver with excitement. It really doesn't matter how old you are, the magic of the buildup to Christmas never fades.

I've baked, of course. Just a few mince pies, a pudding, and a fruitcake. My shelves are also groaning with chocolate biscuits for eager little hands. Well, I have to have something to share with my guests, young and old, don't I? Besides, I do so adore the rich, warm, spicy smell that fills a home when you bake.

On Christmas evening nothing says welcome better than a warm mince pie and a piping hot mug of tea.

And I want my home to be as toasty warm, open, and inviting as possible because what else is there in life?

After I have dressed and said my prayers, the warden Julia, who looks after all the residents at the sheltered housing where I live, knocks on the door.

"Only me, Brenda," her cheerful voice calls out.

I fling open the door and shake my head. Even after all these years I still find it a surprise to be called *Brenda* and not *Nanny*.

"Merry Christmas," I cry, giving her a warm hug. "And what have we here?"

"I swear you get more cards each year." She chuckles, placing a thick wodge of cards on my coffee table. "You could give Santa Claus a run for his money, dear."

"Oh thank you." I smile. "You will stop for a cup of tea, won't you?"

We share tea and swap stories, and after Julia has left I pick up my cards and start to open them.

Soon my eyes are filled with grateful tears.

Card after wonderful card is from all my "babies." They come from all over Britain, but they all have one thing in common, they were all looked after by me, Nanny Brenda.

"Dear Nana, we can't wait to see you at Christmas, hope you are taking care of yourself as much as you did us. . . . Love, Felix."

And another . . .

"Dear Nana, we can't wait to see you. . . . Love, Susanna."

And another . . .

"To my favorite nana, merry Christmas. . . . Love, Jemima."

Gently I pin each card to the wall on a length of red velvet ribbon. Soon the walls of my little flat are covered with colorful cards from all my former charges, each expressing gratitude and festive wishes.

But it is I who should be thankful, thankful that I am in their thoughts. Each card is truly a joy to behold. For each and every single one of the one hundred plus children I have cared for over the past sixty-two years is very much in my heart. It is they, beautiful children who have blossomed into wonderful adults with lovely families of their own, who have filled my heart and life with love.

Being a nanny—some might say Britain's oldest and longest-serving nanny—has been a privilege and an honor for which I count my blessings daily.

Opening the last card, I smile as I read: *"To our oldest recruit, Merry Christmas, Nurse Ashford. Love from everyone at the Norland Institute."* Norland is now known as Norland College, but back when I first started training, it was known as the Norland Institute, changing its status in 1946 in order to sound more modern.

The Norland Institute is where it all began, where I took my first nervous steps as a fledgling nanny back in 1939. What a wondrous journey of discovery I have been on since then.

Pinning the card up with the rest, I turn my gaze back to the window and I am spellbound by the falling snowflakes. Suddenly, I find myself transported back to the magical winters of my blissful childhood. . . .

Here I am with my siblings, left to right: Michael,
Kathleen, Christopher, David, me, and Basil.

Home Is Where the Heart Is

HALLCROFT HOUSE
SURREY, ENGLAND
[1930, AGE NINE]

Lullaby, hushaby, hasten away
Little pink pilgrims, till dawn of the day.
Slow swings the cradle, but swift is the flight.
Lullaby, hushaby, baby, good night

—NINETEENTH-CENTURY ENGLISH LULLABY

Sunday Schedule

7:00 AM: Woke up and dressed in our special church clothes.

8:00 AM: Took turns helping Mother make the beds.

8:30 AM: Ate breakfast of boiled eggs and toast soldiers, the toast all placed in a rack and the eggs with little cozies on top.

9:15 AM: Politely asked if we may leave the table, which Mother insisted we do at the end of every mealtime.

9:30 AM: Washed faces and brushed teeth.

9:45 AM: Mother popped potatoes to bake in the oven so they'd be ready for our return, and then we set off for the four-mile walk to church.

1:00 PM: Home for lunch, which was always leftover cold meat, salad, and baked potatoes.

3:00 PM: After lunch Mother and Father always insisted on having a couple of hours alone, and we children were expected to entertain ourselves.

5:00 PM: Had afternoon tea of jam sandwiches and a glass of milk.

6:00 PM: We always got round the piano Sunday evenings without fail, Father playing and Mother singing. We were all encouraged to join in.

7:00 PM: Bedtime started at 7:00, but bedtimes were staggered with the youngest going up first. Boys were always washed together and then Kathleen and me. You never had boys and girls in the bath at the same time: always separate baths, for decency's sake.

7:30 PM: Father read us all *Rupert Bear* as a bedtime story.

8:00 PM: Said our prayers before Mother and Father tucked us up and kissed us good night.

I HAVE SUNG THE LULLABY that begins this chapter thousands of times throughout my life and each time is as sweet as the last.

In sixty-two years of being a nanny I have lost count of the number of children I have cared for, but it must be approaching one hundred. Which means I am inordinately proud to say that, despite never having given birth, I have one hundred children and my families are spread far and wide.

Children are born uniquely vulnerable and with a need for love that they never outgrow. A baby has a special way of adding joy every single day and can flood your heart with love like nothing else. How strange I find it that some people claim you can never truly love a child that is not your own. This defies every instinct that runs through me, for I have loved children born to other women all my life, and never had my own family.

Even the little terrors (which every spirited child can be at times) I have adored with all my heart. Many I would have laid down my life for; in fact, on some memorable occasions, when I have had to flee to air raid shelters clutching my charges to my chest, I nearly have.

The outbreak of World War Two catapulted me headlong into some of the most bewildering, exhausting, frightening, and challenging moments of my career; but I, like every sensible British woman I knew, never allowed terror to take hold. We had no choice but to go about our business—running the home, shopping, cooking, and keeping the nation's children happy, healthy, and as well fed as rations allowed—while chaos erupted around us.

There is little I haven't come up against in the years since I began my training as a Norland nanny in 1939. Colic, bed-wetting, bullying, absent mothers, sick children, freezing winters, disease, adultery, deserters, scandal, inspiring evacuees and their memorable cockney mothers, all have conspired to make my life interesting. I know that few people get to experience the adventures I've had in my life, and I'm very grateful for the cards that were dealt to me.

When you've trained in Britain's oldest nanny school and by draconian matrons of 1930s hospital wards, Hitler and his army hold no fear. Every fiber of my being was focused on the welfare of the children in my care.

Nothing was more important than being the most loving and professional nanny that I could possibly be.

Much has changed since World War Two ended, and the dangers facing our children today have drastically altered. Back then, it was bomb blasts and malnutrition. Now there are threats posed by the Internet—things we could never have imagined. But I believe the fundamentals for bringing up happy children haven't changed.

I don't intend this book to be a child care manual. I doubt I should even have the brains to qualify as a Norland nanny today and I haven't a clue which child care trends are in vogue. I do know this: if your heart sings with love for little children, you can't go far wrong.

Where did this all-consuming love come from in my case? I have asked myself this on many an occasion, and I think it stemmed from the moment I met my baby brother when I was nine years old.

THE SENSE OF EXCITEMENT WAS TANGIBLE in the air at Hallcroft House in Lower Farm Road, Effingham, Surrey.

Every corridor, nook, cranny, and crevice in the vast house hummed with anticipation. Our cleaner, Winnie, an ageless, round woman who sang as she worked, had come up from the village and polished and scrubbed the house until every surface sparkled like a new penny.

Winnie was flushed red from her efforts. "Got to get everything just right for the new arrival," she'd said, winking, when she'd spotted me watching her.

Winnie had done us proud. The oak floors gleamed like freshly churned butter. Every room smelled of lavender polish and carbolic soap, the leather thong handles on the doors glistened with beeswax, and pretty pink roses had been picked from the garden and dotted round the house in glass vases.

King George V himself, who was on throne at the time, wouldn't have gotten such a rapturous reception had he showed up at Hallcroft that sunny spring morning. Little wonder the birth of my baby brother or sister was more exciting than every birthday and Christmas rolled into one.

My poor mother. From the moment she first told me she was expecting, I had pestered her daily. "Is the baby coming today? Where is she? She's taking so long."

I said *she* because I was certain the baby would be a girl, a real-life doll for me to dress up in pretty clothes and push around in my pram alongside my favorite actual doll, Constance.

And now the great moment was here.

I had been sent off to stay with my aunt Jessie. My elder sister, Kathleen, and my younger brothers, Michael, Basil, and Christopher, had been packed off to various other relatives, but now, finally, the call had come to say the baby had arrived and my mother, Doris, was at last ready for our return home.

My father, Arnold, was duly dispatched to collect us all and bring us home.

As was customary in 1930, my mother was expected to give birth at home. That was quite the norm in those days. The poorest of the poor right up to aristocracy and royalty made their entry into the world in the surrounds of their own home, attended by a local maternity nurse.

If that sounds backward to you, I should put it in context. The Midwives Act had been passed only in 1902, after a group of inspiring women fought to have midwifery and antenatal care recognized as a profession. Prior to that, any woman, or for that matter man, could deliver a baby.

Usually babies were delivered by a woman from the local community called the handy woman. Some were good at their job, others less so. Some were apparently prostitutes who were reputedly paid in gin.

Fortunately the act became law, the Royal College of Midwives was born, birthing standards soared, and infant deaths dropped.

My mother was extremely lucky not to have died giving birth to me, since I came four weeks early. There was no time for pain relief for her, not that it would have helped that much in any case. The only respites from the agony of childbirth were chloroform and forceps to speed things up if the baby got stuck.

Goodness only knows what pain my mother suffered giving birth. Not that she would have discussed it with us or anyone else. What went on in her bedroom remained strictly between herself and the maternity nurse, with Father banished downstairs to avoid the gruesome reality and us children packed off to stay with a relative.

Back in those days, women were confined to bed for at least ten days after giving birth. This was known as the lying-in period. I still find it hard to believe that some women are now discharged from hospital just forty-eight hours after giving birth. Don't they deserve more time to rest?

After ten days' bed rest and recuperation for Mother, we were finally allowed to come home.

The door to my parents' bedroom swung open as I pushed it, and my excitement bubbled over. "Where's the baby?" I gasped in a fever pitch of emotion.

An angry face loomed into view: Nurse Evans, the maternity nurse. She was a short, dumpy woman in her fifties, wearing an apron and hat, and radiating disapproval. "Hush, child," she hissed. "You'll wake him up."

But her words were lost on me.

Because there, nestled in his wicker Moses basket, lined in mauve cotton and organza with delicate mauve bows, was quite simply the most exquisite thing I had ever set eyes on.

"Oh," I breathed in wide-eyed wonder.

"She is a he," said my mother, smiling, when she spotted my face. "Meet your baby brother, David."

The world turns on tiny things. It's not so much the outstanding events that have influenced my life. It may sound absurd but, though hearing we were at war with Germany, witnessing the devastation of the blitz, and the jubilant crowds on VE-day were all moments I shall never forget, the most life-altering of all was when I set eyes on baby David.

I swear my heart skipped a minute's worth of beats.

My other brothers' births simply hadn't made the same impact on me because I had been too young to remember them or to help out. But now I was old enough to see clearly what a miracle I was witnessing.

Dressed in a white cotton gown, David was just a tiny little scrap of a thing, no bigger than a porcelain doll.

Any lingering disappointment I may have had over not having a baby sister melted away when he snuffled and sleepily opened his eyes. The little creature fixed his dark blue eyes on mine and I was done for, hook, line, and sinker.

"Can I hold him?" I asked, utterly mesmerized.

A thunderous voice piped up from the corner of the bedroom.

"*No!* He's not to be woken," Nurse Evans muttered through thin lips.

But even a cranky old nurse couldn't stem the unspeakable joy that flooded through me. Was it his delicate fair lashes that swept over creamy cheeks, the little murmurs and sighs he made when he slept?

Or was it the way his tiny fingers curled round mine and the beautiful musky smell that filled my nostrils when I kissed his soft, downy hair?

No, the thing I loved most about David, and every baby I cared for after him, was his heartbreaking innocence and vulnerability.

Adults are complicated, contrary beings, capable of hurting or betraying you. But babies are simple, sweet, and full of love.

Many great things were invented, created, or begun in 1930, the year David was born: helicopters, FM radio broadcasting, the jet engine, and construction on the Empire State Building, to name but a few; but to my mind the greatest creation ever was my baby brother.

That "baby" may now be eighty-three but we still share a bond that I know was created in those precious early days.

From that moment on, I cared for David as if my life depended on it. My mother had only to issue a simple request and I was there. Nothing was too much trouble.

I fed him his bottles, helped bathe him, changed his cloth nappies, sterilized his glass feeding bottles, and spent hours singing him lullabies.

When he cut his first tooth, I helped ease the pain of teething by giving him an ivory ring to chew on or dashing to the shops to buy him Allenburys rusks. When he was ready to be weaned, it was usually me gently feeding him gruel, or porridge, as we call it now.

Most of all, I loved gently picking him up out of his warm, cozy nest to feed him his evening bottle. He was so sweet and drowsy that his little rosebud lips would begin sucking before the bottle was anywhere near them. Then, like a little lamb, he would hungrily latch on and suckle. I witnessed a small miracle every evening at 6:00 PM.

That little boy flooded my heart with love every time he nestled into my chest and fell asleep on me; and when I gently put him on my shoulder to wind him and he gave a soft milky burp, it did so make me chuckle.

Those days exist in my memory as a warm and rosy glow,. Little did I know it then, but they sparked a lifelong love for children.

Every day was filled with magic and promise. . . .

If home is where the heart is, then at the heart of my home were my parents. You'd be hard-pressed to find a more devoted couple than Doris and Arnold Ashford. I often wonder what the secret to their success was, but all I know is that in forty-five years of marriage they could hardly bear to leave each other's side.

My mother was a gentle soul, a quiet, loving woman devoted to her husband and six children. Women had only won the right to vote in 1928, seven years after my birth, and traditional attitudes toward women still prevailed. Married women were not expected to work. It never occurred to any of us that Mother should leave the home and actually get a job—nor to my mother either, I suspect.

She was never happier than on the Saturday afternoons we spent sitting round a crackling coal fire in the sitting room, with Henry Hall's BBC Dance Orchestra playing on the gramophone accompanied by the clicking of her knitting needles.

My mother had six children pretty much one after the other, so she seemed to me to be constantly either pregnant or nursing a baby. But every so often my father would insist on sweeping my mother to her feet so they could dance round the sitting room.

"Dance, Bobby?" he'd inquire, gathering her in his arms.

I often wondered why he called her Bobby. It was only years later I discovered that Mother had contracted Spanish flu before she had us children and was really rather ill. The flu hit England in 1918, just after the end of World War One. It was a worldwide pandemic and fifty million people died, making it one of the deadliest natural disasters in human history.

Poor Mother was so ill all her hair fell out, and after that it never grew past her shoulders so she always wore it in a bob, hence the nickname. I thank goodness she was strong enough to survive. She was one of the lucky ones.

Maybe this made Father love and cherish my mother all the more. Their eyes would lock and they would smile tenderly at each other, a secret little smile of understanding that left me breathless with wonder.

It saddens me a little to think that I never found that love for myself, but I don't dwell on it. I prefer to think instead that the love they gave to me enriched my whole life. Besides, I was too busy with my babies.

Doris and Arnold were so potty about each other they insisted on having every Sunday afternoon by themselves, with us children packed off to the garden. We knew better than to try to disturb them. I wasn't short of playmates, though. Besides me there were my elder sister by thirteen months, Kathleen, and my four younger brothers: Michael, Basil, Christopher, and baby David.

The whole essence of my childhood and, in my opinion, the key to any happy childhood is simplicity.

BECAUSE MY DAYS WEREN'T FILLED WITH television, computer games, and constant activities, my siblings and I learned to use our imaginations. Sometimes children need to be bored in order to stimulate themselves. Except with five siblings for company, life was anything but boring.

Michael was the musical one, always tinkering around on an instrument. His hard work paid off, as in later life he became a stage manager for the musical *Oliver!*

Poor Christopher and Kathleen always suffered with their health, so they seemed to spend a lot more time inside, with Mother fussing over them. I did so feel for my siblings. They were wrapped in cotton wool and had cod-liver oil rubbed on their chests daily by Mother. It seemed like a simply horrible thing to be so weak. I was so robust and untroubled by illness; and looking back, I'm sure I took my good health for granted.

That left me, Basil, and, as soon as he could run, David to charge around the garden with. I begged my only sister to join us in our adventures, but she always had her head stuck in a book.

"Oh, do come outside," I urged one day. "We've got a wizard game of hide-and-seek going on."

Kathleen stared at me from over the top of *What Katie Did Next*. "Can't you see I'm busy reading?" she said with a sniff.

"Suit yourself," I said, and grinned, galloping out the door and down the stairs. I couldn't for the life of me see what was more fun than hide-and-seek. Books were dull. The real adventures were to be found outside in the fresh air.

Try as I might I just never could apply the same tight restrictions and self-control that Kathleen governed her life with.

Books and study weren't my bag, oh no. If there was a tree to be climbed, a stream to be waded through, or a field to be explored, you could bet I'd be flushed with excitement in the thick of it with my brothers. Why should boys get to have all the fun?

While Kathleen was losing herself in literature, I was usually to be found tearing through the vegetable patch wearing a headdress, whooping at the top of my voice, and pretending to be an Indian or a cowboy. Kale, cabbages, and carrots were trampled underfoot as I ran hollering after my little brothers.

I loved our house, but as a child the garden was one giant adventure playground, designed to feed my vivid imagination.

The rockery in the front garden, which was usually ablaze with color, was not simply a place to cultivate alpine flowers. To me it was a mountain to be scaled, an ideal lookout for a surprise enemy attack. The kissing gate at the end of a lavender-lined path was the perfect spot to launch an ambush on an unsuspecting little brother. The rose garden in the back garden? Why, a training camp for spies, of course. And the fields, or roughs as we called them, which backed onto our house, were a wild territory to roam for hours on end, with streams to dam, blackberries to pick, and frontiers to conquer.

My mother never worried about us when we played out there, sometimes for a whole day. In fact, she made us some cheese sandwiches and packed us off out to the roughs. Out there, we could be anyone we wanted to be—an explorer, a nurse, a train driver. . . .

It's so different for children today. I daresay most poor parents are simply too frightened to let their children out unsupervised, what with the ever-present threat of strangers. I do so feel for modern parents and the constant pressures they are under. Stranger danger simply wasn't there in my day.

But the delicious smell of Mother's homemade Queens of Pudding, my favorite confection of bread crumbs baked with jam and covered with meringue, crept out from the kitchen, over the fields, and soon had us haring for home. . . . It's funny how a recipe from childhood can stick in your mind so much. I still make that pudding today and enjoy every mouthful just as much as I did back then.

I've always recommended that parents cook the recipes from their childhood for their own children. Dig them out and serve them up. Children get such a thrill knowing their parents ate it as a child and the parents love going on a trip down memory lane.

Poor Mother. Six grubby children tore into the kitchen like a giant whirlwind, clutching all manner of treasures, from sheep's wool we'd collected from the fences to acorns and sticks.

"Eurgh!" she cried when she spotted the wool. "Dirty things full of maggots and lice."

I did little to trouble my mother; we left that to Basil, the naughty daredevil of the family. If there was mischief to be found, Basil would be there, in the thick of it.

I have found there is always a spirited child in every family, keeping everyone on their toes, and that is exactly just as it should be. Wouldn't it be dull if every child were just the same?

It was Basil who coined the rhyme for little Bobby Penfold, the washerwoman's son, who brought back our freshly laundered clothes each week, wheeling them up the drive in a baby's pram:

> *Washing's in the pram,*
> *Baby's in the bath,*
> *Bobby pushes it up the hill,*
> *How it makes us laugh.*

It was also Basil who wrote "bomfers" on the coal house door. *Bomfers* was just a silly word that made us children roar with laughter, as we imagined it to be something rather naughty. Whatever it meant, it earned Basil a clip round the ear. If you heard a distant cry of alarm from somewhere in the house, you could bet Basil had jumped out, shouted "boo," and run away laughing.

We once had a French au pair for a summer. I didn't know her name; we just called her Mademoiselle. She was terribly lazy and often when she should have been tending us, she sat reading the paper.

On one memorable occasion she was sitting by the gas fire, reading, with Basil at her feet. I looked up to see her engrossed in an article on sewing, flames licking up the bottom of the paper.

"Fire," I gasped.

She looked up, startled, then . . .

"Le feu, le feu!" she screamed, leaping to her feet with a red-hot copy of the *Telegraph* burning in her lap. Adds a new meaning to "hot off the press."

Mother dashed in and put her out with a wet cloth and no harm done, but Mademoiselle pointed the finger at Basil. He could be a bit mischievous at times, but I never thought him capable of setting fire to a French au pair. She left shortly after.

I'm glad Basil was never severely punished for his largely harmless acts. To suppress a child's sense of mischief is to crush the joy out of his life. While caring for children I am always mindful not to be too strict and be tolerant of their short attention spans!

Nowadays they'd label Basil and children like him as having attention deficit disorder or some such nonsense. I like to think he was just high-spirited.

Hallcroft, our childhood home, was a beautiful idyll that Father had worked hard to create.

Arnold Ashford was a six-foot-tall bear of a man, with a cheeky crooked grin, pointed ears, and striking blue eyes that sparkled with fun. I worshipped him. His slight stutter and lisp just endeared him to me more.

From Monday morning to Saturday afternoon Father worked in Regent Street in London, running a business selling ladies' and children's knitwear to grand stores like Harrods. With six mouths to feed he was no stranger to hard work, but he earned enough to design and have built his dream home.

Father was typical of many men of his era. During World War One he was a lieutenant in the army. He was even awarded the Military Cross for his courage and skill in leading his platoon at one of the bloodiest battles of the war, at Hill 60, or as it was nicknamed, "Hell with the lid off."

My father may have talked to those comrades that survived Hill 60, but he never uttered a word to me about the horrors he must have witnessed or what he did to earn his Military Cross. Part of me wishes I knew what his exact role was, but maybe he was right not to divulge it to us. He wanted to keep our childhoods as innocent as possible, hoping that we wouldn't be touched by the horrors of war.

Mother was certainly no shrinking violet when it came to war efforts either. Because of her love of children she had always longed to train as a Norland nanny, but in the early 1900s, child care wasn't considered a respectable career for a young woman of the upper middle classes. There were really only two options for a woman of my mother's social rank: teaching as a governess or nursing. Like me, my mother showed no academic prowess, so she opted to train as a nurse, which was thought less intellectually demanding.

Before she began her training, Mother was confined by the Victorian belief that a woman should know nothing of a man but his face and clothes until marriage, so her work tending wounded soldiers must have been an eye-opener. I read later that she would have witnessed amputations and deaths and cleaned up rivers of blood.

Mother and Father rarely mentioned the awful things they had seen, nor would they ever dream of discussing in front of us children any problems or disagreements they may have had. In forty-five years of marriage I didn't hear a single word uttered in anger between them. They set a marvelously good example by never, ever quarreling in front of us. They exercised extreme self-control and courtesy. You must remember—and this is something my parents knew, of course—that in little ones the imitative faculties are highly developed. A child's character will receive lasting impressions from those with whom they interact.

In later life, if I ever heard people in a family I worked for bickering I was horrified. Why would you fill your home with anger and subject your children to disharmony? It remains a mystery to me today.

Maybe this is another reason I never married: how could any relationship match up to my parents'? My father's eyes shone with love whenever he talked of my mother, and she in turn devoted her life to him and us children. This intense love just made the tragedy that occurred later all the more painful.

Work may have claimed my father for most of the week, but come midday Saturday he was all ours. As soon as we heard his key in the lock, we ran to the door and jumped all over him like excited puppies. His smart tailored navy wool suit, tie, trilby, and briefcase would soon be discarded in favor of fawn flannels and a cotton shirt . . . then the fun would begin.

"What have you brought for us, Daddy?" we cried.

"Close your eyes and hold out your hands," he said in a voice rich with fun and laughter.

Eagerly, I squeezed shut my eyes and stuck out my hands.

Just the rustling of a brown paper bag was enough to make my mouth water.

"No peeking," he warned. As if I'd want to spoil the magic of the moment.

Seconds later a pear drop or some other tasty morsel was deposited in our outstretched palms. Mother was always rewarded with a bag of sugared almonds and a kiss on the cheek.

For taste buds unaccustomed to really sweet things, the tangy, acidic burst of sugar on my tongue was like nectar. Pear drops were my favorite and always made a Saturday; but if it weren't those it was bull's-eyes, which we'd take out to the roughs and suck until our tongues were purple. Sometimes Father brought Pontefract cakes, small licorice disks, but I never understood how anyone could like licorice.

In the 1930s, sweet shops were all the rage and popping up all over London. It was a very productive decade for Rowntree's. For a small child, imagining where the sugary delights came from was a constant source of wonder. After continual begging from us children, Father finally told us.

"There's a little place I go to just off Regent Street," he said, his voice dropping to a whisper, "with a bell on the door that jingles as you enter and a lady older than your mother wearing a dressing gown who appears with a metal scoop to weigh out your sweets—"

"Tell us about the sweets, Daddy," I interrupted.

Father smiled and paused for dramatic effect.

"Row upon row upon row of shiny glass jars crammed with sweets," he said eventually.

My eyes were as a big as bull's-eyes as he went on.

"Every kind of sweet you can imagine . . . lollipops, licorice bootlaces, gobstoppers, peanut brittle, toffees, walnut whips, cherry lips, coconut mushrooms, Uncle Joe's Mint Balls, pineapple chunks."

I glanced over at Basil. He was nearly drooling.

"And on the counter, chocolate, glistening fudge, gingerbread men, sugared plums."

It was almost too much. Our palates weren't much troubled by unusual flavors in those days; and food largely consisted of some sort of meat, potatoes, and vegetables such as turnips or carrots from the garden, with suet or steamed sponge pudding for dessert. To hear about these exotic sounding treats was to be transported to food nirvana. It's no wonder sweet o'clock, midday Saturday, was the most hotly anticipated time of the week.

I must confess, Father's treats left me with a lifelong sweet tooth. If you were to visit me in my flat today, you would find a good number of chocolate biscuits stacked in my cupboards. One bite of heavenly chocolate and, if I close my eyes, I am transported back to my childhood.

Our Saturday fun didn't stop there. While some fathers may have retired to the study with a paper and strict instructions not to disturb, ours adopted a more hands-on approach.

We loved sitting at his feet as he read *Rupert Bear* to us and sipped stout from a large brown bottle. For us children it was a cup of hot cocoa in winter or a glass of the milk that was delivered weekly by a milkman on a horse-drawn float and sold by the jug from a stainless steel milk churn.

On one day I'll always remember, Father spent hours in the garden plotting a surprise. When we children were finally allowed outside, the suspense was killing us.

With a smile a mile wide, Father stood in the middle of the lawn to the side of the house that had always been earmarked for use as a tennis court.

"What is it, Daddy?" I piped up, puzzled.

"Look down," he said, and winked.

Father had mowed lines in the garden to look like railway tracks, and up and down the tracks he'd placed signals that he'd made in the shed and that he operated with a string pulley system.

"Who wants to play trains?" he bellowed.

Did we ever! Every Saturday afternoon after that was spent hurtling up and down the tracks on our trains, which to the untrained eye might have looked like bicycles.

Looking back at the childhood my parents had, it is nothing short of a miracle that they turned out so full of love.

My mother's mother, Granny Brown, was from the Victorian era and clung to the rigid discipline of her day. She certainly didn't share our father's hands-on approach to child rearing. Not for Granny Brown the sugary delights of hidden pear drops and running amok in the vegetable patch. Like most Victorian people, she believed that children should be seen and not heard and expected docility and obedience at all times.

I dreaded our annual visit to her home in Norfolk. Our days there were rigid in their routine. After fresh air on the beach and a lunch of boiled cod and junket, we had to lie very still on the floorboards and rest. To an excitable child who just wanted to be running free, this was nothing short of agony.

The only time a frenzied burst of activity was acceptable was when the national anthem came on the wireless and we were expected to leap to our feet, with the command "show some respect and stand to attention." It was ghastly!

It's no wonder that the end of the Victorian period coincided almost exactly with the invention of psychoanalysis. I'm fairly sure that my parents never went in for any of that, but perhaps they made an unconscious decision not to replicate their own childhoods in the way they brought up their offspring.

Mother and Father's unashamed love of children, enthusiasm for life, and sense of fun made our childhood that much richer. Thanks to their efforts, I realized subsequently that becoming a mother or father doesn't automatically make you a good parent. You have to learn and work hard at family life, a lesson I hope I have instilled in my many charges.

One tradition that was most certainly passed down was that of a boarding school education. In 1932, at age eleven, I was sent to Courtfield Gardens School for girls in Bognor Regis.

The boys were all sent to the same boarding school on the Isle of Wight, and Kathleen had gone to Courtfield Gardens the year before me. Having been duly equipped with the correct green school uniform, I prepared to set off with my father, who was to drive Kathleen and me down to Bognor.

It was only fifty miles, but I may as well have been traveling to the moon. Apart from our trips to Norfolk to see Granny Brown, I had scarcely left Hallcroft. I was desolated at leaving David, who was coming up to two, but I accepted my fate. Girls from my background were always sent to boarding school to be educated.

Nevertheless, it was a big change for an eleven-year-old. Parting from the warmth and security of my family was agony.

As Father loaded our trunks into the car, Mother stood on the doorstep, clutching David to her chest. His chubby little arms pumped with excitement when he saw the car. He loved cars almost as much as he loved my kisses. Already I knew big changes would take place in my absence. Every day he'd pick up a new word, toddle that bit farther up the garden, embark more boldly on life's journey . . . and I wouldn't be there to witness any of these new milestones.

Sadness gripped my heart.

"Be good, my little angel," I whispered in his ear, as I planted a soft kiss on his jam-smeared face.

Mother scooped me into her arms.

"I'm so proud of you, Brenda. Now you do me proud."

She kissed me, and my cheek tingled where her soft, downy cheek had touched mine. Her skin was as warm as toast and she smelled of lemony soap.

I gulped back my tears and nodded my head vigorously. "I will, Mother," I whispered.

In the car Kathleen stared out the window, lost in her own thoughts, so I was left quite alone in my misery. By the time we pulled up in front of Courtfield Gardens, my head was spinning.

The driveway was full of parents unloading trunks, excited girls babbling away ten to the dozen, anxious mothers and fathers checking their watches. You could spot the new girls a mile off: they looked as bewildered as I did.

Father crouched down to our level.

"D-do—do me proud, my darlings," he stuttered, hugging us both close.

My lip wobbled as I watched him turn and stride to the car.

Don't cry, Brenda, don't cry, not here, not now.

And then he was gone, and I was sucked into the regime that is boarding school life.

Courtfield Gardens was a rambling old mansion house with ten dormitories sleeping five girls each.

Our routine was similar to most boarding schools. The day started at 7:30 AM, when the deputy matron came to wake us. We washed, dressed, and stripped our beds.

We waited for the bell to ring, which was the signal for quiet while we said our prayers, then filed to the dining room for breakfast.

Then we trooped to our classrooms for a day of lessons. Formal education in those days was focused on the three R's: reading, writing, and arithmetic.

Occasionally I saw Kathleen in the dining hall, but our lives were still very separate. She had her friends and I had mine. Mind you, she still managed to have an impact on my life.

One morning, during a particularly complex lesson on algebra, I found myself completely dumbfounded. No matter how hard I tried, I just couldn't grasp it. The letters and numbers swam in front of my eyes like a foreign language.

"Why can't you get it, Brenda?" snapped the teacher. "Your sister, Kathleen, can do it."

Annoyance prickled inside me. I was hopeless, totally hopeless at numbers; and as soon as the teacher started making comparisons to Kathleen, something inside me just shut down even more.

I wasn't Kathleen. I was me. Brenda Ashford.

That moment lodged in my mind. Throughout my career I have never, ever drawn comparisons between children in order to humiliate them. Each child is a unique individual with his or her own skills and talents.

There was a strange sense of comfort in the unchanging daily routine, but even so, boarding school was a bewildering place with many unspoken rules to learn and observe.

I was greatly relieved therefore when summer term ended and Father collected us for the hotly anticipated summer holidays. I couldn't wait to get home and tore up the drive like a tornado.

"Mother, David!" I shouted. "We're home."

Mother came rushing into the hall. I noticed her slight hands were nervously ringing a tea towel. She had faint black circles under her eyes and a vein twitched in her temple.

What had gone on since I was at school?

And then I noticed. *Everything* was different. The hall was piled up with brown packing boxes, the windows had no curtains, and even the ceiling lights were just bare bulbs.

I ran from room to room, tears blurring my eyes. Every room had been stripped bare of its belongings. The bedroom we had all been born in looked vast and empty. Even the air felt thinner.

Shivering, I returned to the hall where Kathleen and Mother stood looking bewildered.

"I'm afraid we are moving, girls," said Mother.

And that was all that was said on the matter. Neither Mother nor Father elaborated any further.

Years later I learned the truth about why we had to leave Hallcroft that fateful summer morning. Father's business partner had done the dirty on him.

For years my father had been asking to see the books, and his partner had been fobbing him off. When Father finally got his hands on them, he was horrified to see the company was in debt—bad debt that his unscrupulous partner had run up against the business. Then the scoundrel did a runner to America, leaving Father to face the music. The wholesale ladies' and children's knitwear business with its grand premises was forced into bankruptcy.

Mother's brother, our uncle Jeffrey, came to the rescue and gave Father enough money to rent a small bungalow in Bookham in Surrey, but the business was closed and Hallcroft had been sold.

Can you imagine the shame of bankruptcy for a man like my father—a man with high morals, decorated for his bravery during the war? He had survived the trenches only to be destroyed by an enemy closer to home.

It must have been a savage blow.

Father had a hand in everything that had gone into Hallcroft, right down to those leather thong door handles. He had designed it and overseen the building of it. It was the pinnacle of everything he had achieved, and his lifeblood pulsed through every oak staircase and floorboard. He had been so proud of that house.

But the human spirit is nothing if not resilient, and to us children it was merely a blip. We might no longer have our glorious home to run through, but we still had each other. Mother and Father were the heart of the home, and to me it didn't matter where we slept at night as long as I had them. So in the summer of 1933 we found ourselves living at Amberley bungalow in Bookham.

Over the eighty years since we left Hallcroft House I have moved many times, and I do so without a backward glance.

Trading down taught me an important lesson: never let a house define you. You can make a home anywhere, from an air raid shelter to a shed, if you have to. Riches and wealth don't matter a jot. You can be happy anywhere so long as you have love and family in your life. I may never have had much money but I have always been rich in love.

That first night, as I snuggled down in the room I shared with Kathleen and listened to the boys' soft breathing in the room next door, I looked forward to the next adventure in my life.

Nanny's Wisdom

A HOUSE IS JUST A BUILDING.

A house is just four walls filled with material items. It's not the house and the price of the items in it that count—it's the occupants who really matter. Whether you live in a castle or a shack, you can find true and lasting happiness only if the house in which you live is filled with family and love. Only then, when a house is ringing with laughter and people you worship, can it become a home. So next time you find yourself wishing you lived in a bigger house with more space and rooms, think again. I enjoyed just as many happy memories crammed into that bungalow with my family as I did in our big house. Wealth, riches, and a fancy kitchen don't matter. It's the people that count.

SURPRISE YOUR CHILDREN.

Every now and again why not do what my father did and surprise your children with some wonderful sweets in a brown paper bag. Watch their eyes light up when you pull it out of your pocket—not too often, mind you. . . .

CHAPTER 2

THE CALLING

THE RAVENSHERE FAMILY
BYFLEET, SURREY, ENGLAND
[1937, AGE SIXTEEN]

One, two, buckle my shoe
Three, four, knock at the door
Five, six, pick up sticks
Seven, eight, lay them straight
Nine, ten, a big fat hen
Eleven, twelve, dig and delve
Thirteen, fourteen, maids a-courting
Fifteen, sixteen, maids in the kitchen
Seventeen, eighteen, maids in waiting
Nineteen, twenty, my plate's empty

—ENGLISH NURSERY RHYME

Schedule

7:00 AM: Woke up, washed, and dressed.

7:30 AM: Fixed boys breakfast of cereal and hot buttered toast.

8:00 AM: Got boys' satchels and their coats on so they were ready for their father to drive them to school.

9:00 AM TO 1:00 PM: Washed up, made boys' beds, and tidied their rooms. Did chores dictated by Mrs. Ravenshere, from washing and ironing to cooking and baking.

1:00 PM: Ate homemade soup and bread roll for lunch with Mrs. Ravenshere.

2:00 PM: Did more chores, such as washing, mending, and sewing.

3:00 PM: Helped muck out and feed Mrs. Ravenshere's ponies.

5:00 PM: Fixed the boys ham sandwiches and milk on their return from school, then supervised two hours of homework.

7:00 PM: Helped with the bedtime routine. Got out boys' pajamas and drew their bath. Watched Mrs. Ravenshere tuck them up and kiss them tenderly good night.

8:00 PM: Ate supper, then bed by 9:30 PM.

THE WIND OF CHANGE WAS heady in the air. King George V had died and his heir to the throne, Edward, was causing shock waves throughout the country with his determination to marry the scandalous American divorcée Wallis Simpson.

To a fifteen-year-old girl not schooled in the ways of love, this seemed simply outrageous. How could he court a woman who had cheated on her husband, then expect us to accept her as our queen? Preposterous. It wasn't only schoolgirls who felt that way, mind. I didn't meet a single person who didn't think it was wrong. Looking back, the vilification of Wallis Simpson was probably over the top, but in those innocent yet judgmental times their love seemed destined to fail. In the end, Edward chose love over duty, whereas I have always chosen duty over love. Would I have been happier had I opted for marriage rather than life as a nanny? I very much doubt it.

There was change in my life, too, albeit on a smaller scale. Our reversal of fortune meant no more smart boarding school for me. Instead, the local county school in Epsom beckoned.

As for my brothers, Father had made a gentlemen's agreement with the headmaster of their boarding school on the Isle of Wight that they could stay on; and eventually all four would be schooled there, on the proviso he could have two boys educated for the price of one. It was only later when the bill for the school fees came in that he realized the headmaster had rescinded on his agreement and charged the full cost for all their board and education. This was a fresh blow for my father, who was struggling financially.

In many ways Father was naive: he just accepted what everyone told him as gospel. He simply saw the best in people and never had a bad word to say about anyone. I hope I have inherited these traits and I hope I have done my best to pass them along to my charges. Sadly, people with personalities such as ours will never grow rich, but at least we know we will always do right by others.

It was with this attitude that I marched into my first day at my new school.

As I walked into the classroom, I felt all eyes swivel and turn to rest on me. I could see all the girls taking in my freshly pressed and starched uniform, gleaming white socks, and plimsolls. We may not have had much money then, but my mother was a proud woman and wouldn't have dreamed of having her children leave the house looking anything less than immaculate.

Nervously I took my seat as the others girls tittered and nudged one another. Listening to them talk, I was amazed. I had led a sheltered life and these girls were street-smart.

"'Ere," hissed the girl next to me, elbowing me sharply in the ribs. "Ainchya that girl what lost all 'er money?"

I swallowed back my tears and tried to ignore her.

In playground at lunchtime it was more of the same. They turned their noses up and marched past me, cackling.

"Stuck up cow," one said with a laugh. "Who does she fink she is?"

I didn't think I was anyone. I just wanted friends to play with.

It was a miserable time and I hated it. My old, safe, comfortable world seemed a million miles away. By the time the first school term ended, I was in a state of despair. I had made no real friends, showed no aptitude for learning, and was at a loss to know what to do with my life. Why couldn't I be a clever bookworm like Kathleen?

"I don't belong," I wailed to Mother and Father one night as they attempted to explain a mathematical formula for what felt like the hundredth time. "I don't understand it and I hate school."

My head slumped into my hands as I sobbed. "I'm just a stupid, stupid dummy."

Mother was horrified. "Of course you're not, my darling," she soothed. Gently she cupped my face in her hands and looked me right in the eyes. "You are different from Kathleen, it's true, but you are just as clever as her in different ways. You have very good practical skills."

I loved my mother for trying so hard to console me, but her assurances did nothing to ease my loneliness and sense of isolation.

I've purposely clung to this memory and the agony of feeling so desolate to remind myself what it is to be a child and feel out of your depth. All children, even those from the most secure and happy of households, feel low at times; and we must remember that their fears, however irrational, are very real to them. If any of my charges were miserable about something,

I made sure never to dismiss their pain but instead to listen to their worries and to do whatever I could to ease their burden.

I've always made a point to ask my charges at the end of the day if there is anything that troubled them or worried them. Chances are, something will have and it will be something that can be so easily sorted.

Some children have a funny habit of holding on to little moments, pockets of pain, or irrational worries and storing them away to be worried over at a later day. Take time to dig out their fears and soothe them away.

I realize now that in some ways I was sad that my idyllic childhood was coming to an end. I was in that funny land straddling childhood and adolescence. Adulthood seemed like a bewildering, frightening place to be.

It was all right for Kathleen. She had just left home in a flurry of excitement to train as a midwife in London. But what was to be my purpose in life? What did my future hold?

Of that I wasn't yet sure, but there was one thing I was certain of: I was going nowhere fast at the local county school. I was sick of feeling like the dummy, of being compared to my clever older sister, and tired of Father having to explain my homework to me over and over. By spring of that year I had made up my mind. I had turned sixteen by now; surely that meant I could decide my own fate?

I strode into school on Monday morning with fire in my belly.

Knocking on the headmistress's door I politely requested a meeting.

I sat down and drew in a deep breath. "I think it's time I left school," I said.

The headmistress looked at me through her half-moon glasses and not unkindly replied, "But you have to take your exams, Brenda."

Sitting up straight, I coughed nervously. "But what is the point? I don't think I'll pass."

Headmistress sighed and removed her glasses. "Well," she said finally, "I have to agree with you."

What a blessed relief.

It was decided there and then that I should leave school with immediate effect. Walking out of the building, I felt an enormous burden lift from my shoulders.

Back at home, Mother wasn't cross, just concerned about what I would do with my life.

"Oh darling," she said with a sigh, "I wish you'd stayed on to take your exams, but I can't say I'm surprised. We need to find you a job."

Mother had seen my despair building, and I half wonder if a tiny bit of her wasn't relieved. She was practical and good with her hands like me, and she could see I was drowning under all that homework.

But if I had thought I could sit around at home while I worked out what to do next, it seemed Mother had other ideas.

"I can stay here and help you look after David," I protested.

"No," she insisted, her voice turning a shade firmer. "You need to work."

All too soon she had lined me up with a job, one that was to alter the course of my life forever. I was to be a mother's help to Mrs. Ravenshere, who lived not far from us in a smart home in Byfleet in Surrey. She had two sons, aged eight and eleven, who attended Dulwich School as day boys. My duties included helping her to keep house, run errands, and help look after the boys when they returned from school. For that I was paid the princely sum of ten shillings a week. A pittance, really. I have never earned much money throughout my life, but then you don't go into child care for the money, do you?

Mrs. Ravenshere didn't work. I don't suppose it occurred to anyone that she should, and while her husband was at work in the city and her children at school, every fiber of her being went into making that house a home. She was the very epitome of a homemaker. Every room in that house was immaculate. She would never have dreamed of letting her husband come home from work without finding his slippers laid out next to his pipe, a newspaper, and a glass of whiskey in the drawing room.

She poured her whole heart into that family and they loved her for it.

The boys adored it when they came home from school and found a fresh-baked sponge cake cooling on the countertop or clean socks warmed by the fire for them to change into. After she'd poured them milk, they would all sit round the kitchen table and she'd ask them what they'd learned that day. Her eyes never left theirs as they eagerly told her of cricket matches won and tricks played.

"Oh, you are quite brilliant boys." She laughed gaily when they told her once about the time they'd been asked to captain their respective rowing teams or how nervous they'd been when they had to recite in front of the rest of the class. Her eyes shone with love as they chattered and wolfed down her cake. Of course, they never asked her about her day; it never occurred to them, nor to her to tell them about it. She just wanted to know every detail of their lives.

The man of the house never said more than he had to and locked himself away in his study as soon as he returned home. In many ways he was absent from their lives, so the boys looked to their mother for light and love.

I felt like a fly on the wall, watching this family play out their daily lives and interact with one another, but just studying them was teaching me so much.

I already knew from my own family how important a mother was to a home, but watching Mrs. Ravenshere and the huge daily effort she made to connect with her boys and the way she worshipped and loved them made me realize just how influential a mother is. How, with just one word or a smile, she had the power to bolster their egos and turn their worlds around. Because of her unrelenting love she made them feel like men ten feet tall.

"You have a natural ability with those boys," I told her one morning after she'd waved them off to school.

"Do I?" she said, looking surprised. "I don't think I do very much at all. I'm only their mother."

Only their mother!

Throughout the rest of my career I heard that come from so many women's mouths. It's always said in an apologetic tone, as if all of the million things they do daily for their offspring happen quite by chance.

I wish mothers would stop putting themselves down so much. All mothers are quite brilliant in my eyes and nine times out of ten don't realize the sacrifices they undertake or the powerful contributions they make. And, of course, life is ten times harder now than for the mothers I used to work for. Mothers today juggle work, child care, paying bills, ferrying their children around, and keeping their children, bosses, and husbands happy in a climate of constant fear over crime and economic instability. Quite honestly, I don't know how they do it; they are all amazing.

Please, I urge all mothers to remember that. They provide the very foundations upon which a house is built; they are the linchpins of their families. Mothers today are quite, quite brilliant.

Aside from loving her boys unconditionally, Mrs. Ravenshere had a number of ponies, including one mischievous little Shetland pony by the name of Jelly, who often escaped and rampaged through the neighbors' gardens, causing chaos.

After we had spent one afternoon chasing Jelly round the neighborhood, Mrs. Ravenshere and I sat down to tea.

"You know, Brenda, I've been thinking," she said. "Have you ever thought of training to be a Norland nanny? You're good with children; they love you."

Of course I had heard of Norland nannies. Everyone had. They were famous for taking on only smart young ladies of genteel birth, and schooling them to achieve the highest standards of child care for the offspring of the wealthy. Everyone knew it wasn't easy to earn the right to push those big coach prams round London's smartest postcodes. Coach prams are the original and, in my eyes, best prams ever invented. With big, old-fashioned wheels, high sides, and a beautiful roomy interior lined in pure cotton, they are quite simply the Rolls-Royce of prams. Modern prams simply don't compare, and Norland nannies pushed the coach prams with pride.

I had seen pictures of Norland nannies in my mother's *Nursery World* and *Good Housekeeping* magazines and admired their beautiful uniforms and capes, but it was all far too grand for sixteen-year-old Brenda Ashford from Surrey. I was just a country girl.

Besides, Father had no money now; there was no way he could afford to send me to train at the Norland Institute. There was an entrance fee of one guinea, and a year's tuition was £132. On top of that, those beautiful uniforms cost £16 10s. It all added up to a small fortune, one I knew my father simply didn't have.

"But there could be a way round it," insisted Mrs. Ravenshere. "Let me talk to your father."

"No, please," I pleaded. "I don't wish to trouble him."

Since the bankruptcy, Father was struggling to find work and set up in business again. I didn't want to add to his load by reminding him that he could no longer afford to have his children educated.

Besides, I couldn't move all the way to London by myself.

But the conversation left me feeling even more fretful about my future. What was my calling in life?

The answer came via a large black horse.

Later that day Mrs. Ravenshere said she was sending me to the local stables, owned by a friend of hers, for a riding lesson round Byfleet common. As a horse lover, especially one for whom riding lessons had been consigned to my old life as just another unaffordable luxury, I was thrilled at the prospect. Mrs. Ravenshere's friend even gave me a new pair of cream jodhpurs and a beautiful pair of shiny brown leather boots. They must have cost a small fortune. I hesitated to take such kind gifts, but she insisted.

Then, out of the stables the instructor led the most magnificent horse I had ever seen. Jet was sixteen hands high; and his well-chiseled head, long neck, and high withers told me he was a young and spirited Thoroughbred. His black coat gleamed as he trotted round the yard, tossing his mane this way and that.

I felt a ripple of excitement run through me as the instructor gave me a leg up. Soon Jet and I were trotting happily along the common. Didn't I feel grand and grown-up, riding on such a beautiful creature in my new leather boots.

But as we trotted under a railway tunnel a train thundered overhead. Jet took fright, flared his nostrils, and started to dance all over the path.

"Hold on tight, Brenda," warned the instructor. "I think he's going to bol . . ."

Her words were lost on the wind as Jet bolted. Hedges and trees flashed past in a blur of green as we galloped flat out over the common.

I clung on for dear life, my heart in my mouth, as we dashed down the path. Using all my might, I tried to pull his head up, but it was to no avail.

"Please stop," I whimpered.

My weedy arms were no match for his powerful neck.

Just then I realized, *We were heading for the road.*

My knuckles were white with terror as we galloped full tilt toward the traffic.

No way was this horse going to send me flying into the path of a motorcar.

With an almighty grunt and a superhuman show of strength I pulled his head up, and at the last minute we swerved out of the way of the road and slowed to a halt by a tree.

It was hard to say who was trembling more—me or Jet. His flanks were coated in sweat, and my hands were shaking so hard I could barely hold the reins.

Suddenly, I experienced something else. Pure exhilaration. Grappling with a runaway horse had sent my blood racing. By the time the instructor caught up with me, I was laughing.

"I thought I was a goner," I said breathlessly.

"So did I," she said, panting.

When we arrived back at the stables and Mrs. Ravenshere heard of my adventure she was obviously impressed with my ability because she rewarded me with a cup of hot sweet tea and a slice of cake.

My brush with death made me appreciate something: there were no second chances in life and perhaps we should grab all that is put in our way.

"I was thinking," I said between sips of tea. "Perhaps you could speak to Mother about Norland?"

"If you handle children as well as you handle that horse, you will make an excellent nanny," said Mrs. Ravenshere, with a smile.

AND SO IT WAS THAT MY mother and I found ourselves some months later boarding a train bound for London Victoria.

The Norland interview, which my mother had arranged over the phone, had put me in a state of heightened excitement for weeks, and the night before I had barely slept a wink.

"Now remember, Brenda," advised my mother as the train hurtled toward London, "don't talk too much. Listen, nod your head politely, and sit up straight."

I don't recall much about that journey, what I wore, or what I'd eaten for breakfast—just that my destiny was unfolding and everything hinged on this interview.

In London my senses were assaulted. I'd never been to the big city before and I was bewildered and excited by everything I saw.

Mother decided we should walk from Victoria to Norland in Pembridge Square in London's Notting Hill. There was intense noise everywhere. Red buses whizzed past, belching out clouds of smoke; the road seemed to be clogged up with motorcars and electric trolleybuses. We even passed an underground station, and Mother told me there was a train there every ninety seconds. Unimaginable.

Suddenly, I felt so small. Everyone seemed to be marching about with real purpose and a sense of determination.

I spotted a sweet shop much like the one Father must have bought our Saturday treats from. The glass jars lined up in the window glittered tantalizingly close. But then I remembered, I was on a mission, too. There was no time to dawdle.

Soon the crowded cobbled streets gave way to wider pavements and smart leafy squares. The Notting Hill and Ladbroke Grove areas—which today are buzzy multicultural places filled with bars, shops, restaurants, and a yearly carnival—were very different seventy-three years ago.

Elegant, stuccoed white mansions looked out on a slow-moving world. Calm, peace, and prosperity prevailed. Norland nannies and smart mothers pushed their fashionable black coach prams serenely in front of the imposing mansion houses. Little girls in smart smock dresses walked in a crocodile to school; boys in sailor suits ran along, clutching boats to sail on the Serpentine in Hyde Park.

My mother stopped in front of one of the grandest homes I'd ever seen. It was far bigger than our little bungalow, bigger even than Hallcroft.

Numbers 7, 10, and 11 Pembridge Square, London, W2, were home of the Norland Institute Nurseries Ltd.

Suddenly, I felt like a tiny mouse on the doorstep. I'd never crossed the threshold of somewhere so grand.

Mother knocked on the imposing black door.

Looking back, it must have been a strange moment for her. She, too, had longed to train at the Norland, but Grandpa Brown didn't consider it to be a suitable career choice for a young lady and forbade it. Times had changed, and now I was about to have the interview she had always longed to have.

Mother turned to me with a faraway look in her eyes. Excitement and something else, sadness perhaps, flickered over her beautiful face. "I can't tell you how much I would love to have been a Norland nanny, Brenda," she said softly. "I loved babies just as much as you."

I didn't doubt it. She would have made a wonderful nanny; no one knew more about children than my mother.

She shook herself a little, as if to shrug off the ghosts of unchased dreams. "Listen to me," she said, as the door swung open. "I'm so thrilled for you, darling. Let's show them what you're made of."

She straightened out my coat and smoothed down a stray hair, then pushed me gently inside the impressive hallway.

A few chairs lined the black-and-white tiled corridor. Mother and I sat down nervously. A large clock ticked ominously on the wall.

Finally a door was flung open, and a tall, imposing woman who I guessed was in her forties towered over us. She was dressed in a dark-colored dress with collar and cuffs trimmed in white lace.

Miss Ruth Whitehead—the principal, and to my young mind, a truly terrifying sight—held the key to my future.

On the wall above her head was a black-and-white photo of a regal-looking lady, underneath the Norland motto, *Love never faileth*. She seemed to be staring straight at me.

"I'll have a word with you now," she said.

Mother and I leaped to our feet, scraping our chairs back and nervously straightening our skirts.

"Not you," she said, fixing my mother with a penetrating gaze. "You stay here."

Mother sat down, well and truly put in her place.

My heart hammering, I followed Miss Whitehead into her office and sat down opposite her on the other side of a grand mahogany desk.

I listened intently as she filled me in on the history of the Norland. The institute was founded in 1892 by Emily Ward. Inspired by the alternative theories of teacher Friedrich Froebel, who likened children to plants that needed nurture and love in order to flourish, she set up a training institute for ladies "of genteel birth" to become nannies. Her aim was to overthrow the tyranny of the Victorian nursery and train nannies who rejected the need for spanking and used love and encouragement instead to raise children.

On hearing the inspiring story of Emily Ward's life's work, my heart felt like it was about to burst. I practically shot out of my seat as excitement bubbled over.

But this was me . . . this was the way I felt about children.

I felt like the sun had just come out from behind the clouds. The world was suddenly a far, far bigger place than Bookham. Sitting in this smart London house, I had an epiphany, a lightbulb moment if you like.

This was my calling in life.

I wasn't clever enough to be a teacher or a nurse like Kathleen, but I did love babies and children. If Norland was a glove, then it fit me perfectly. I, too, could help bring the dreams of children to life.

Suddenly, I felt better about the fact that I could no more do what Kathleen was doing than fly to the moon. To learn how to deliver a baby, change dressings, administer medicines, and tend the sick was out of my league—my head spun at the mere thought—but place a baby in my arms and, well, that was another matter. I could love, cherish, protect, and care for a baby with more heartfelt passion than anyone I knew. To nurture a baby into a child and then help it on its journey into adulthood was an honor and a privilege as far as I was concerned.

I thought of my poor mother, sitting outside in the corridor, willing me on. She never got the chance to follow her dreams, but I could do this. I could do this for me and for her.

Ignoring my mother's advice not to talk, I started to chatter away ten to the dozen. When I get nervous I start to babble, and I was very, very nervous.

"I love children, Miss Whitehead, I really do," I blurted. "I've helped raise my brother. I was no good at school, not at all clever . . . not like you. My father has no money, well, he did have, but he lost it all, you see. Then I nearly fell off a horse. . . . We got the train up, you know . . . terribly nervous."

On and on I rambled.

Miss Whitehead raised one eyebrow a fraction and finally my voice trailed off to a whisper.

" . . . and so here I am."

Silence.

"I see," said Miss Whitehead in a clipped voice. "We'll be in touch."

That signaled the end of the interview. I slunk out the room to rejoin my mother.

"Well?" she said, on the edge of her seat.

"I don't suppose I shall get in," I whispered, biting my lip to stop myself from crying.

I'd well and truly fluffed it.

The journey back to Amberley seemed to last forever. I gazed out the window so Mother couldn't see the tears threatening to spill down my cheeks. Despair gripped my heart. I'd let Mother and Father down. I'd let Mrs. Ravenshere down.

But worst of all, I could see my dreams crumbling to dust. . . .

Nanny's Wisdom

*ENCOURAGE CHILDREN'S STRENGTHS AND
NOT THEIR WEAKNESSES.*

While I was floundering at school and feeling so inferior to Kathleen, my mother, quite rightly, explained that I was just as clever as my sister but that I had different talents and skills. Hers lay in academic pursuits; I was more practical and better with my hands. Don't focus on what your children can't do. Instead, find out what they *are* good at or enjoy and encourage them in that.

MAKE TIME TO TALK.

Put aside thirty minutes out of every day to sit and ask your child how her day was and then listen to what she tells you. It's not long, but that thirty minutes spent with your attention focused solely on her will have an enormous effect on her life. Mrs. Ravenshere did, and her boys grew up to be confident and happy individuals. They loved her for it.

REPORT from the INSTITUTE { Domestic Period of Training (3 months).

Subjects.	Term's Work.

Domestic Science.

	Written.	Practical.
Needlework		Very Good.
Cookery	Fairly Good.	Very Good.
Laundry Work	Good.	Very Good.
Housewifery	Good.	Excellent.

Educational Subjects.

Nursery Management	Very Good.
Hygiene	
Practice of Education	Good.
Child Psychology	Very Good.
Nature Study	Very Good.
Story Telling...	Good.
Handwork	Very Good.
Children's Games	Very Good.

Moral Qualities

Punctuality	Very Good.
Neatness	Excellent.
Personal Neatness	Very Good.
Tact	Very Good.
Interest in her Work	Very Good.
General Tone	Very Good.
General Capability	Very Good.

Signature _Ruth Whitehead_

Principal

Date _June 7 1939_

$\mathcal{N}$ANNY $\mathcal{B}$OOT $\mathcal{C}$AMP

NORLAND INSTITUTE

PEMBRIDGE SQUARE, NOTTING HILL, LONDON, ENGLAND

[1939, AGE EIGHTEEN]

A wise old owl lived in an oak.
The more he saw, the less he spoke.
The less he spoke, the more he heard.
Why can't we all be like that wise old bird?

—NURSERY RHYME

Schedule

7:00 AM: Woke when the bell rang. Washed, and dressed in our uniforms. Made our beds perfectly with corners tucked down, and checked our dorms were squeaky clean. Placed slippers under the bed; wiped toothbrushes clean with no trace of toothpaste anywhere.

8:00 AM: Breakfast of cereal, bread and butter, and tea.

9:00 AM: Lectures—either on housewifery, child care, moral tone—or ironing and washing in the laundry room.

1:00 PM: Lunch. All the children came in to join us for lunch with the other more advanced nurses and their charges. You ate everything on your plate whether you liked it or not.

2:30 PM: More lectures. Afternoon lectures were more practical: sewing, smocking, darning.

5:00 PM: Students' tea. Bread, butter, and pudding, washed down with milk.

6:00 PM: Two-hour homework revision in lecture room, or sometimes we were given tasks such as making toys for the children.

8:00 PM: Free time in our dorm. We changed into our own clothes, read, wrote letters home, or chatted with our set. It felt a bit like boarding school and there was a lot of giggling.

9:00 PM: Washed, changed for bed, and said our prayers.

10:00 PM: Lights out and bedtime.

IT WAS MOTHER WHO OPENED the letter.

For days I'd been moping round the house like a wet weekend, utterly desolate and quite convinced I'd fluffed my interview.

We were sitting at the breakfast table, drinking tea, while Mother sifted through the morning's mail. I looked up when I noticed that she had frozen in her seat, staring intently at the letter in her hand.

"You've done it, Brenda," she cried, nearly knocking her teacup over with excitement. "You've been accepted by the Norland."

Father's face paled. "But how, darling? There's no money to train."

"It's all right," Mother went on, reading excitedly from the letter. "Says here that at first you were considered for the maiden's scheme, but upon reflection you are suitable to start immediately as a student, and the training will be funded with a bursary."

"A what?" I asked, puzzled.

"It means they pay the cost of your training, darling."

I later found out what the maiden's scheme was. In 1904 Norland introduced the scheme with the intention of helping those girls who were eligible but could not afford the fees. They were to give their services in the domestic work of the house for a year, and in return for cooking, cleaning, and housework they would receive the training and uniform for free. During their year of maiden's work, they were required to forfeit their Christian names and be known under the name of Honour, Mercy, Prudence, or Verity; wear a special uniform while on duty; and sleep in a cubicled dormitory on the top floor.

This may seem strange and perhaps even a bit offensive, but the thinking was that when girls had completed their year of service, they could then enter as a student, revert to their Christian name, and be accepted on an equal footing by their fellow students. It was so popular a scheme that there was a waiting list.

Turns out I had narrowly escaped being named after a Victorian virtue, after Miss Whitehead decided I was suitable enough to qualify for a bursary from the Isabel Sharman Fund. This was set up after the death of the institute's first principal with the intention of helping fund training for suitable ladies of slender means.

Euphoria fizzled up inside me. I'd done it. I'd really, really done it. I wasn't a complete dummy after all. I'd been accepted! I clutched the letter to my heart and felt so happy I could burst. I was so grateful to the Norland. I knew if it took me the rest of my life I would pay back every penny.

"Oh, thank you, oh, thank you." I laughed, dancing round the kitchen, kissing everyone in sight.

There was much rejoicing in the Ashford household that day. Mother walked around with a little smile on her face and Father just looked thrilled to bits.

"Just think," he said, kissing me on the head, "our Brenda's going to be a Norland nanny. I'm proud of you."

If he felt any shame at having his daughter's education means-tested and funded, he kept it to himself. He was a proud man, but he only ever wanted the best for his children and could see I was over the moon.

THREE WEEKS LATER, THE MORNING OF March 23, 1939, dawned bright and clear. My first day at the Norland Institute. Today was the first day of the rest of my life, and of one thing I was certain: I was going to be the best nanny I could possibly be.

Upon our reporting to Pembridge Square, Mother left me at the doorstep. I could scarcely believe it. The last time I stood on these steps I was certain I was destined for failure. Now here I was. An actual Norland nurse. Well, a nurse in training.

My stomach was in knots.

"Well, darling," said my mother, briskly drawing herself upright, I suspected, to stop herself from crying. "This is it. Do me proud."

"Oh, I'll try, Mother. I really will," I said.

"I know you will, darling."

She gave me a sweet, sad little smile, kissed me on the cheek, and then was gone.

Mother had the softest velvety down on her cheek, and as she turned and walked up the road I could still feel its sweet sensation on my face. The smell of the Lux soap that she washed with hung in the air, and I felt a lump form in my throat. Suddenly, the enormity of my situation hit me. I was eighteen years old and all alone in the Big Smoke. I knew no one here except the terrifying Miss Whitehead.

I crept upstairs and nervously pushed open the door to my modest dorm room.

A girl stood unpacking.

"Hello," I said timidly. "I'm Brenda."

"Mary Rutherford's the name," barked the tall, confident brunette, bounding over to shake my hand enthusiastically.

"That's your bed over there. Look lively, we've to report to Miss White-head in the lecture room in five minutes."

"Oh . . . oh, right," I said, impressed at Mary's efficiency. Wouldn't do to be late on our first day.

On my bed was an immaculately starched and folded bundle of clothes: my Norland uniform.

I changed into the fawn long-sleeved dress with stiff detachable white collar and cuffs, a white apron, petersham belt, and brown petersham bow to tie at my neck.

I hung up my wool cloak and felt hat in the small wardrobe beside my bed. My real pride and joy, though, was a beautiful blue silk dress with a cotton apron with lace insertion across the bib and round the hem. The lace was especially made in Belgium. It was exquisite. No wonder the dress was for use on formal occasions only and children's parties.

"Rather special, isn't it?" said Mary, beaming as she watched me.

I took it out of the tissue paper like it was made of butterfly wings and hung it up carefully.

As I was smoothing down my skirt, two more girls came in as shyly as I had.

"Hi, I'm Joan," said a young girl, blushing. "I'm from Devon, my first time in London."

Instantly I warmed to Joan. She was followed by a beautiful Scottish girl. Her kind green eyes twinkled beneath a halo of fiery red hair.

"I'm Margaret from Dumfries."

Her warm Scottish accent endeared me to her instantly.

Margaret was followed by Yvonne. Yvonne was a very well-to-do French lady, which made her incredibly exotic in my eyes. Her dark eyes and expertly styled shiny black hair spoke money. She had the most exquisite clothes, all arranged beautifully in her leather case.

As she started slowly removing her things I noticed that she was utterly bewildered. She held up clothes like they were foreign objects and tugged at her bedside drawer like she'd never unpacked before.

It was then that I realized. She probably never had unpacked.

"We have servants who do this for us," explained Yvonne, when she spotted me watching her.

"Here," I said, smiling. "I'll help."

Helping Yvonne to unpack her clothes, I reflected on what a mixed bunch we were, all from different backgrounds and with very different characters. I resolved there and then to try my hardest to get on with everyone as best as I could. In later life I always advised my charges to do the same. Put aside your prejudices and always accept people at face value. Don't listen to their accents or obsess about their clothing. Try to get to know the person beneath, for only then will you find true friendship.

Many different friends from all walks of life will enrich your life far more than people you assume to be "just like you." That belief has paid off in my life as today I count myself lucky to have a very mixed and wide range of friends.

Poor Yvonne was a good person; just because she had servants didn't mean that her heart wasn't in the right place.

"Thanks, Brenda," she said with a smile, as we folded away the last of her clothes. "You're spiffing."

"Come on, girls," ordered Mary, rounding us all up. "We can't keep Miss Whitehead waiting."

We all hurried downstairs to the main lecture room. The arctic blast of air hit us all at the same time.

"Gosh," I said with a shiver. "It's freezing in here."

"Aye, not a patch on Dumfries," said Margaret, grinning, "but perishing all the same."

Wanting to ingratiate myself with the twenty or so girls assembled in the room, I hurried over and shut the window.

Minutes later, Miss Whitehead marched into the room.

Some people have an air of authority about them that commands respect. As soon as she strode purposefully to the front of the hall, twenty heads snapped to attention and you could have heard a pin drop.

Miss Whitehead, wearing a navy dress with a white apron and white, pleated cap, put down her books and looked long and hard at each of her trembling new recruits.

She took off her navy cloak lined in red silk and carefully and deliberately placed it over the back of her chair.

"Stand, please," she ordered.

The sound of scraping chairs filled the room as we jumped to attention. Her lips pursed disapprovingly.

"Your first lecture will be on hygiene," she barked. "Will the student at the back please open the window?"

I wanted the ground to swallow me up. Trust me to do the wrong thing on the first day.

Mary dashed over and flung open the window.

"Fresh air makes for healthy living," announced Miss Whitehead.

Never again would any of us dare to close a window.

Miss Whitehead quickly became a legendary figure in our eyes. She had been appointed principal four years previously in 1935, after working as a trained nurse and midwife, but was fast making her mark as a draconian guardian of the uniform. She was adamant that her nurses would be seen as superior nannies only if they were dressed and behaved impeccably at all times.

Gone with the Wind was playing at the cinema and was captivating audiences. All over the Western world, women clamored to dress like Scarlett O'Hara with romantic full-length skirts over crinolines. Others raised temperatures with silk stockings or were prone to lift one perfectly groomed eyebrow from under a little velvet hat tipped over one eye, à la Greta Garbo in *Romance*. To get the Hollywood look, women flaunted their assets by wearing brassieres that pushed their breasts up and out under tight sweaters and finished the look off with a slick of pillar-box red lipstick.

No such daring for us Norlanders. Miss Whitehead would have had a blue fit if we'd sauntered in wearing any such feminine outfits.

Inside these hallowed walls there was no room for silk stockings or makeup. Cosmetics were strictly banned from the nursery, and stockings were made of sensible and comfortable lisle fabric.

"I am a stickler for a properly worn uniform," she went on, surveying us all as she spoke.

Immediately I looked down at my own and tried discreetly to straighten my skirt and smooth out the material under my belt.

"Mrs. Ward once said, 'It's such a pity that we could not give only the good nurses a uniform and take it away from the others,' and I do endorse this. In fact," she said, her voice rising an octave, "I might think of having a roll of honor of the nurses who really do wear a properly kept uniform, but I am afraid it would not require a large frame."

She paused to let her words sink in.

"You are given the uniform, having promised to wear it that you may demonstrate to the world that you are a member of this institute, which has the highest ideals. Among them is an awareness of the great responsibility it is to bring up little children to be true and good, to enable them to be men and women of the highest character."

Quite what Miss Whitehead would have made of today's nannies' wearing jeans and sweatshirts I can't even imagine! I'm not sure I would relax the uniform to such an extent. A smart day dress or smart trousers and blouse speaks volumes and says that you are the person in charge and also that you take care of your appearance and respect the position of authority that you are in. Having said that, I do feel the uniform back then was possibly over the top. At least nannies today in jeans can get down on the floor and play easily, something we always struggled to do.

What you wear speaks volumes about you, and sadly people can make snap judgments about you purely based on your clothing. In later life I found people made unflattering assumptions about my nannying based on my uniform. Some assumed that Norland nannies were above their station or didn't want to get their hands dirty. Nonsense of course, but such is the power of clothing.

Ultimately I think it comes down to this—you must feel comfortable with what you are wearing, otherwise how else can you concentrate first and foremost on being the best nanny you can possibly be?

After Miss Whitehead's monologue we all breathed a sigh of relief. But she wasn't finished with us yet.

"The rules for all Norlanders are these . . ." she went on.

We braced ourselves.

"You will have one afternoon a week off. Outside of these four walls you are a representative of this institute, which means no smoking or gossiping on street corners like a park nurse, especially when with your charges. I have been known to cycle around these streets to ensure there are no Norlanders on parade, engaging in these unsavory activities.

"And no male visitors to this establishment under any circumstances."

I wondered briefly what the penalty was for any nurse caught smuggling a man into a dorm, but looking at Miss Whitehead then, I found it hard to believe anyone would dare try.

"Bedtime is ten PM prompt, and your dormitories are to be spotless at all times."

This was one doyenne not to be messed with! Every student in the room shifted uncomfortably.

"Finally," she said shrilly, "I would like to remind you that none of you are training to be nannies."

Every face in the room looked utterly baffled.

"You are nurses. The word *nanny* embodies the status and standards that Mrs. Ward was determined to rise above."

I don't remember much more of the rest of the lecture, but when Joan, Margaret, Mary, Yvonne, and I returned to our dorm we sank onto our beds quite exhausted. Just as well that it was supper, evening prayers, then lights out 10:00 PM prompt, as my head was swimming with exhaustion.

THE NEXT MORNING WE WERE PRESENTED with our black leather-bound testimonial books. I opened mine gingerly, as if it were made of the most fragile lace, marveling at the beautiful gold-embossed cover and marbled endpapers. I gasped. There was my photograph on the inside cover, followed by page after page of subjects to be studied, just waiting for a grade to be marked against them. I swallowed hard. There was a lot of work ahead.

I read through the institute's definition of my working conditions. Do not ask your nurse to eat with your servants nor to eat meals in her bedroom. She should not be expected to carry coal or scrub floors. She should be given time off to worship and take exercise.

I hardly minded if they did ask me to carry coal or eat with the servants, so pleased was I to even be here!

Half a day off a week doesn't seem like much, but throughout most of my career those are the hours that I worked.

I rose when the children rose, usually at 6:00 AM, and my day wasn't finished until they were all asleep and all my jobs were done, usually at 10:00 PM. I was always promised weekends off, but more often than not the mothers would get a curious headache as my time off drew near. I barely had much time off at all, much less time to read a novel, socialize, listen to the radio. My life was within the nursery and with the children, full stop. Just as well I love children as much as I do.

Today, a nanny's schedule would be very different. I believe they work shorter hours and get evenings and weekends off, but then they have to do things that were never expected of me, like driving children all over the place for playdates, sports, and extracurricular activities. It sounds like a hectic pace of life for nanny and children. I'm not sure if I could have coped with that. I never even had a car when I was a nanny.

I think nannies, and mothers, too, could benefit by simplifying their lives. Does it matter if your child doesn't have French and violin lessons followed by swimming and dancing? He or she will learn just as much by being around the home with you or their caregiver.

People are constantly running around these days. We didn't do those sorts of things simply because they weren't available. What's wrong with just letting a child be a child? Of course you can encourage extracurricular activities, but don't give your child a regimented timetable.

Childhood is over so quickly nowadays anyway; just slow things down and hold on to it for as long as you can! There's plenty of time for schedules when children grow older and have to get a job! Keep childhood as innocent, pure, and carefree as possible, that's my motto.

We were to have three months' training at the Norland Institute, followed by three months' experience of living and working in a London hospital, after which we returned to Pembridge Square for another three months of lectures and practical domestic work. At the end of this we were to take written exams and our certificate was deferred until twelve months' satisfactory work had been completed in our first post.

"Your employers will be required to write you a written reference in your testimonial book," our lecturer informed us. "Forgery is an offense which will result in instant dismissal."

AFTER A PUNISHING DAY OF BACK-TO-BACK lectures we returned to our dorm to prepare for supper.

No sooner had we stepped inside than Yvonne gasped. Her dark eyes flashed with anger.

"*Mon Dieu,*" she said, dropping her books on the floor with a thud.

All her bed linen had been stripped off, her drawers emptied, and their contents placed on the floor in a neat pile.

"Who has messed up my bed?" she demanded. "I made it this morning."

It was a complete mystery.

"Bally cheek," blasted Mary. "Who would do such a thing?"

All was about to be revealed.

In marched a senior lecturer, who turned on Yvonne.

"Your bed was a complete mess, child. Most irksome. You will learn to make your bed properly with the crease of the sheet to run in a straight line down the middle. The corners will be neatly tucked in. Your eiderdown will be turned down and drawn tight and neat. Otherwise there will be a mark against your name," she snapped. "You will be required to make it again properly this time and every day from here on in."

Yvonne's mouth was still flapping open and shut in shock as the lecturer disappeared in a cloud of disapproval.

Poor Yvonne. Servants had made her bed every morning. She had never learned quite simply because she never had to. I doubted that she had ever made her own cup of tea or cleaned a toilet in her life, either. At that moment I was so grateful to my mother for teaching me the importance of housewifery.

Later in my career I always made sure my charges made their beds when they were old enough, or at least we all helped make them together.

When my siblings and I were growing up, Mother insisted we took it in turn to help her make all the beds in the house, boys one day and girls the next. She was the fairest person I know and it really instilled in us a sense of duty, not to mention housewifery!

This practice taught us that if we weren't slapdash about even the smallest tasks, then we would not be encouraged to become slapdash in other areas of our lives.

Children shouldn't be brought up to believe it's not their job to help keep a house tidy or clean. Those responsibilities lie with everyone who lives in a house and contributes toward making the mess. How else will they learn when they've moved out of home? Making a bed would come as a pretty big shock if you haven't had to do it until you're twenty-one.

It certainly was for poor Yvonne!

In the coming years I would have many children who led a privileged life, and I always tried to imbue them with a sense of hard work.

"It's like being in the army," grumbled Yvonne.

I offered to help her redo her bed and showed her how. "Let's all muck in together."

From then on, dorm inspection became a daily occurrence. Our rooms, beds, and belongings had to be spotless, with not a thing out of place. Even our toothbrushes weren't allowed to have a trace of toothpaste on them!

But Yvonne wasn't the only student shamed by the institute. The next day Margaret rushed into the room, her eyes red and puffy and her face as white as flour. She threw herself onto her bed, sobbing.

"Whatever is wrong, Margaret?" I asked, alarmed.

"They want me to have elocution lessons," she cried in her beautiful, soft, lilting Scottish accent. "I have to learn to speak the Queen's English so employers can understand me better. I dinnae know there was anything wrong with the way I speak. They cannae do that . . . can they?"

It seemed that if Margaret wanted to be a Norland nurse, they could and they would.

Poor Margaret. I felt so desperately for her and was quite certain that at some point I, too, would be called into the principal's office and informed I would need to improve my speech.

Of course I'm certain they wouldn't dream of doing such a thing now—it seems perfectly archaic—but back then, received pronunciation was quite the norm.

One thing was for sure: we Norlanders were going to be whipped into shape pretty damn fast whether we liked it or not.

"Come on," I said, putting my arm round Margaret. "Let's go for dinner. Things won't seem so bad on a full stomach."

All the students and lecturers ate their meals in the same room on long, scrubbed wooden tables, with Miss Whitehead and senior lecturers seated at a top table.

The maidens served us our meals. I always made a special effort to be nice to them. I'm sure I didn't deserve to be served by them for one moment.

"Thank you very much." I smiled at the young maiden as she heaped a steaming pile of beetroot and spinach alongside my meat.

Mother and the rest of the family always called me the human dustbin for my seeming ability to eat whatever was put in front of me, but aside from junket, which was the devil's work as far as I was concerned, beetroot was the only food I truly loathed. How could anyone like something so slimy?

I wolfed down the meat and spinach but left the beetroot.

Suddenly, an unmistakable voice boomed across the dining room. The infamous Miss Whitehead. "Brenda Ashford. Rule one: never leave anything on your plate. When you are in charge of children, you have to lead by example. How can you expect them to eat everything if you do not? Now eat up."

Flushing the same color as my beetroot, I forced it down.

First the window, now the beetroot. Could I not do anything right?

Miss Whitehead's public scolding always stuck in my mind, and I'm not sure that telling children off in such a way is the right thing to do, nor insisting they eat every last morsel of a food they hate. If ever I need to teach a child right from wrong, I do so in a firm and quiet voice, and that usually does the trick.

As for food? As long as a child at least tries the food on his plate before he says he doesn't like it, then that's a start. There is little point in insisting a child scrape his plate clean and instilling in him a lasting phobia of beetroot.

Nowadays people know more about food and the lifelong issues they can instigate. It's far healthier to ask children to try but not pressure them too much. Their palates will change as they get older. Provided they eat a balanced diet, why focus on force-feeding them food they don't like?

I was always strict on one issue however. If a child said he didn't want the whole meal presented to him and requested something else, he would always get the same retort: "This is not a restaurant and if you don't eat that meal, you will be going to bed hungry!" Don't give him options, otherwise he will expect a menu next! Also, small children don't know what's good for them. That is for you, the responsible adult, to decide.

Besides which, it's extraordinary how you can learn to like something— even beetroot—when you have to!

THE NEXT DAY WE BEGAN HOUSEWIFERY, taught by Miss Danvers.

She was lovely, softly spoken with a kind voice and a gentle manner— the good cop to Miss Whitehead's bad cop.

"Our first lesson, girls," she said, smiling angelically, "is to learn how to clean a toilet properly."

Every girl in the room looked horrified. This wasn't why we had come to the Norland. Where were the adorable children and the strolls in Kensington Gardens?

I could virtually hear Yvonne weighing up whether to call her mother now and get the chauffeur to come and collect her.

Instead, she stayed glued to her seat as Miss Danvers handed each of us girls a bottle of Jeyes Fluid disinfectant and a scrubbing brush and pointed us in the direction of the toilets with the command, "Don't forget to clean under the rim."

After that, we learned not to dare to complain and to do everything that was asked of us.

For three months we scrubbed toilets until they were so clean you could eat your dinner off them; polished shoes to such a high shine Miss Danvers could see her reflection in them when she came to do an inspection. Down in the chilly stone basement, we scrubbed all the Norland's Marmet coach prams until they gleamed. Pram parade was at 3:00 PM sharp every day. We had to line up our polished prams on the lawn outside in a semicircle so Miss Danvers could conduct her inspection. At these times she was the domestic equivalent of a drill sergeant. Every girl held her breath as Miss Danvers walked slowly past each pram, nodding and making notes.

The soft leather bonnet had to be well waxed with Johnson's Wax Polish, the high black sides shining, the white cushions and blankets spotless and plumped up, and the wheels without a trace of dirt. Any unfortunate girl who failed pram parade was sent back to clean it until the pram was up to Miss Danvers's exacting standards.

"Please don't let it be me today," muttered Yvonne under her breath, as Miss Danvers inspected every nook and corner of her carriage.

"You bonnet is lacking shine," she commented.

My turn. I held my breath as she cast a critical eye over my pram.

"Very good, Brenda," she said finally.

It was backbreaking and exhausting work. It's amazing no one dropped out, though I am certain it must have crossed poor Yvonne's mind. The Norland might have required girls of a genteel background, but they had better jolly well work like soldiers in His Majesty's army.

Soon I was so hungry I learned to eat every last scrap on my plate, Yvonne was making beds like an expert, and even poor Margaret was starting to sound like a southerner. I doubted her parents would even recognize her.

We fell into bed exhausted each night, our fingers almost bleeding and our backs aching. I didn't even mind the freezing wind that blasted through the open dorm windows.

Slowly it began to dawn on me: I was having the time of my life.

I was learning a trade and I loved every second. I learned how to sew, cross-stitch, how to knit children's woollies, and how to make a delicate smock dress out of the finest linen. Miss Danvers showed us how to do the most intricate needlework. Woe betide you if you didn't do it right; you would stay in that needlework room until you could show her the finished article.

What's more, I began to realize I was actually pretty good at it all.

"Very good, Brenda," said Miss Danvers one morning as she surveyed me embroidering a little pink cotton dress. "You have a definite knack for this."

I basked in the glow of her praise.

But there was one room we dreaded: the laundry.

The modern laundry is unrecognizable from those of yesteryear, or certainly the ones we worked in at the Norland.

Today's housewife enjoys a multitude of machines to make laundry work a thing of ease. She has a washer with a spin cycle, a number of rinses and temperatures—all at the touch of a button—and even a machine to dry her clothes . . . not to mention an electric iron. Oh, the luxury of an electric iron!

Back then, all we had were vast stone sinks, a mangle, a packet of Lux, and the dreaded flat iron.

As you can imagine, with a large house filled with women and children, there was an awful lot of laundry to be done and cloth nappies to wash.

Mary, Joan, Yvonne, Margaret, and I plunged our arms into the huge sinks of warm soapy water and scrubbed until our hands were numb.

The laundry room was fiercely hot, and soon all our faces were flushed red from the heat. Three big copper boilers, heated by gas flames, dominated the room; and all the sheets, pillowcases, napkins, clothes, and nappies went in there to be boil washed.

Nowadays I hear a baby needs anywhere between six and eight thousand nappy changes from birth until he or she is potty trained. Back then, we used two dozen cloths per baby to see us through, all of which needed regular boil washing and soaking in a bucket of Lux.

We scrubbed by hand what couldn't be boil washed.

Afterward the clothes had to be wrung on a giant mangle, which required the biceps of a sailor to turn. Then everything had to be hoisted up onto giant wooden maidens attached to the ceiling to dry.

This was easy work in comparison to the ironing.

We worked beside a hot stove where two or sometimes three irons were heated before use. The knack was to alternate the irons, moving them from stove to ironing table and back again in an endless cycle of heating, pressing, and reheating.

The irons were heavy, too, and one had to press down with great force to get the result Miss Danvers required. But they also required great delicacy and care, because there were no temperature controls, so it was easy to scorch fabrics. The irons had to be kept spotlessly clean with no trace of ash or dirt to soil the clean laundry.

It was hot, tiring, relentless work; and we had to complete it all wearing our lisle stockings, uniforms, and aprons.

When we weren't scrubbing, cleaning, polishing, sewing, knitting, or lining up for pram parade, we gathered in the drafty, freezing-cold lecture rooms for lessons on neatness, punctuality, speech, and moral tone.

"Moral tone" sounds very pompous and outdated, but in fact many useful things were conveyed to me in these lectures and have served me well throughout the rest of my life. Lessons on fairness, truth, and politeness are something they should perhaps teach in schools today, instead of computer skills and foreign languages!

A sound moral compass is a far stronger guiding light and will take your child much further in life than knowing how to browse the Internet.

Miss Whitehead gave some of these lectures herself.

"The future is made by the children for whose characters and training you are responsible. Your contribution and examples are valuable," was one of her favorite sayings.

The other thing that the institution believed in more than any other was telling the truth. (Telling a little white lie to avoid ruining the fun of Christmas by saying that Father Christmas doesn't really exist didn't count.)

We were taught the value of the tremendous force of absolute truthfulness.

"When your charges ask you where babies come from," Miss White-head was fond of intoning, "they do not appear under gooseberry bushes, neither are they parachuted in by an obliging stork. They come from mummy's tummy."

I made sure to maintain this rule throughout my working life and I was always honest with my charges. In fact, in every area of my life I have been most careful to never tell a lie. It's something that I feel most strongly about. Dishonesty is such a rotten thing, to my mind. Little white lies about tooth fairies don't count, I hasten to add. Why can't everyone be more careful to tell the truth? At least we would all know where we stand in life.

I hate the thought that I am not being true to what I believe. How awful to be known as someone who says one thing and does another.

We were also taught children's nursery rhymes, stories, and prayers. I love nursery rhymes, so for me this didn't even feel like work.

The lecturers observed us as we recited poems and stories in front of class. I hated this part and always wished the ground would swallow me up. To help me, I'd close my eyes, think of David, and suddenly I'd be back at Hallcroft.

I could almost smell the sweet musky scent of his head as a baby, feel his little fingers curling round mine. I missed him fiercely.

Miss Danvers also took us for another element of domestic science: what to do with little children when they are ill.

Today we have Band-Aids, Tylenol, and no end of over-the-counter medications we can reach for when little heads are hurting or knees are bleeding; but back then we had to be a little more resourceful.

The cupboards were groaning with items we had to learn how to use.

Olive oil had a multitude of uses. Rubbed into the scalp it was a cure for dandruff, or warmed and massaged into a baby's back and chest it was comforting and helped to fend off colds.

I learned that an ounce of warm water will quiet a fretful baby and cure wind.

A handy recipe for diarrhea? Take a cup of milk and two glasses of port wine, heat milk and add wine, bring to boiling point, stand till curd breaks, strain, and give a lukewarm tablespoonful to the affected child.

A bath with baking soda in it has a soothing effect on heat spots. Eucalyptus oil can be dropped in hot water and inhaled for colds, and carron oil makes an excellent dressing for burns.

There was bottle after bottle in Miss Danvers's cupboards, all with some medicinal purpose. Brandy, dill water, borax, glycerin, ginger, camphorated oil, Dr. Bow's liniment, castor oil, Gregory's Mixture, and peppermint oil. Miss Danvers elucidated in precise steps what purpose each could serve.

At this point you might be wondering where on earth all the children were. Just whose nappies were we washing and whose prams were we cleaning so diligently?

Norland *did* have resident children. Number 11 Pembridge Square was converted into several nursery rooms, christened Spring, Dawn, Bluebell, Daisy, and Forget-me-not. A quiet back garden led into Kensington Gardens.

The children who lived here were usually the offspring of civil service families posted abroad who didn't want to take their children with them for fear of illness or danger. The institute also cared for children whose mothers died in childbirth and illegitimate children. It offered a continuous child care service at least until the age of seven, when the children were sent to boarding school. Their day-to-day care was in the hands of the trainees in their third term, not first termers like me.

It was agony for a young girl who was itching to care for children. Mastering an iron was all well and good, but when would we ever get to the real thing?

But rules were rules. First term was to learn moral qualities, housewifery, and domestic science; second term was training in hospital; and third term we would finally get to train alongside the children.

I saw them outside playing or being strolled out to Kensington Gardens. Occasionally their sunny laughter drifted up to the lecture rooms from the gardens. Joan loved children as much as I did and sighed when their excited chatter carried through the walls. It was torture to know children were so close and yet not be able to care for them.

I suppose in some ways this may have been an unusual childhood for these children. They were left in the care of strangers who used them as a sort of training ground; but they always seemed so happy and well cared for that no one thought it out of the ordinary.

They were taken for walks in the park; to dance classes; on trips to the zoo, the circus, and shows; to tea with friends; and on day trips to the seaside.

Smacking was strictly forbidden by the nursery, something I whole-heartedly agree with; and I, too, adopted a no-smacking rule when I was working. Smacking doesn't teach a child a lesson; it just says that you have lost control of the situation and that violence is an acceptable response. I find a lot of people are just venting their own personal frustration and anger on a child and in fact are just doing it to make themselves feel better. This is entirely wrong and teaches anger, not discipline or respect.

In those days, punishment was being made to stand in the corner or the withdrawal of jam for tea.

To my delight, I realized that I was really learning a lot during my time at Pembridge Square, and though I never even dared dream it, I hoped my efforts were impressing Miss Whitehead.

As we approached the end of our first period of three-month training, Mary and I were summoned to Miss Whitehead's office.

Oh, crumbs. I wondered what I'd done this time. But once inside the same office where I'd had my interview, I realized Miss Whitehead was actually smiling. At me!

"Well done, girls," she said. "I have been observing you both and it has become clear that you have excelled at your training and both have leader-ship potential."

I felt Mary swell with pride next to me.

"For devotion to duty and ability I am making you head girl, Mary, and you are her second-in-command, Brenda. That is how you shall both be known henceforth. That is all. You may go back to your training now."

I left Miss Whitehead's office, feeling ten feet tall. We had done some-thing to make Miss Whitehead pleased. My joy was only matched when I was handed my black testimonial book: good, very good, or excellent in all my subjects.

I floated on air for the rest of the day. All was well in the world.

Or so I thought.

Little did we know it, but our comfortable, well-ordered world was already in peril. . . .

Nanny's Wisdom

GIVE PRAISE WHERE PRAISE IS DUE!

How wonderful it is to be praised for a job well done. I still remember the pride I felt in being made deputy head girl by Miss Whitehead for my devotion to duty and my ability. It's the little things that count; and a kind word of encouragement in a child's ear can last for a lifetime and go a long way to making a confident and secure adult. That praise, when accompanied by a kiss, a hug, or even just a pat on the back, will be felt a million times more deeply.

That said, I do hear some parents going overboard and cheering their children for things they are supposed to be doing anyway. I do think you can take it too far at times. But if your child has worked hard at her homework, demonstrated a spectacular handstand, or just drawn a lovely picture, then tell her so! Good deeds and hard work deserve *your* praise. The next time she comes to tackle a difficult task, it will feel all the more bearable. Hard work pays off—even if you are doing something you don't want to be doing (like laundry or making the bed).

ENJOY YOUR FREEDOM FROM THE DREADED LAUNDRY ROOM.

You don't have to sweat away in a hot laundry room like I had to. Nowadays there are no end of products on the market to remove stains; and you have washing machines and tumble driers that at the flick of a button can save you hours of work. I still find some of the traditional remedies are the best, though!

Try this for removing mud and grease stains from white fabric: boil the article of clothing in a large saucepan with a chopped-up lemon. The lemon and high temperature bleaches the stain, then wash as normal in a washing machine.

REPORT FROM THE HOSPITAL (3 months).

N.B.—Kindly put one of the following remarks against each qualification :—*Excellent, Very Good, Good, Fairly Good, Fair.*

Punctuality		Very Good.
Neatness { in person		Very Good.
{ in work		Very Good.
Cleanliness { in person		Very Good.
{ in work		Very Good.
Attention & Kindness to Patients...		Very Good.
Adaptability		Very Good.
Interest in her Work		Very Good.
Obedience to Instructions... ...		Very Good.
General Tone		Very Good.
General Capability		Very Good.

Signature of Matron ___Darley A. Lane.___

Hospital ___The Hospital for Sick Children___
___Great Ormond Street W.C. 1.___

Date ___August 31st 1939___

CHAPTER 4

CARING FOR SICK CHILDREN

GREAT ORMOND STREET HOSPITAL
LONDON, ENGLAND
{ 1939, AGE EIGHTEEN }

Cry, Baby Bunting,
Daddy's gone a-hunting,
Gone to fetch a rabbit skin
To wrap the baby bunting in.
Cry, Baby Bunting.

—ENGLISH LULLABY

Schedule

6:30 AM: Woke in my dormitory, washed, and changed into my Norland uniform.

7:00 AM: Had breakfast of porridge in the nurses' canteen, where only nurses were allowed. Sisters and doctors always ate in separate quarters.

8:00 AM: Reported on the ward for duty and received our orders from the ward sister.

8:15 AM: Made bottles and feeds in the milk kitchen. Each child had a different formula. This was before the days of dried formula milk. Back then, it was cow's milk with added lactose, glucose, and water. It was terribly complicated. I am no mathematician, so I always got in a frightful muddle mixing it all up.

9:30 AM: Took the children to the nappy room and changed their nappies, then washed and dressed the children.

10:00 AM: Fed the cleft palate babies their milk.

11:00 AM: Cleaned the nurseries and wards—and I mean cleaned everything, from toilets to bedpans.

11:30 AM: Took the children's temperatures. Younger children's were taken in the groin and older children's in the armpit.

11:30 AM: Wheeled the younger children out onto the balcony in their cots for fresh air.

12:00 PM: Lunch.

2:00 PM TO 3:00 PM: All children encouraged to have a rest or a sleep, while we caught up with administration.

3:00 PM TO 4:30 PM: Parents visited—always a happy time filled with laughter.

4:30 PM: Tea of jam sandwiches and milk for older children and milk for the babies. Fed cleft palate babies their milk.

5:30 PM: Cleaned wards, washed bottles, changed bedpans, cleaned sluice.

6:00 PM: Read stories to the children.

6:30 PM: Off duty.

As Hitler mobilized his troops I merrily moved on to the second phase of my training in a state of blissful ignorance as to the horrors that lay ahead.

Second term was to be spent training in a London hospital.

Emily Ward had had to work hard to get the matrons of London hospitals to accept Norlanders. The matrons, quite rightly, were less than keen to let a load of young, untrained girls loose onto their rigidly controlled wards. Emily persisted, staunch in her belief that every Norlander should gain an insight into the life and struggles of the poor and sick. She typified the spirit of Victorian philanthropy that maintained the rich had a duty to help the poor and suffering.

By 1939, thanks to the support of Sir Robert Hutchison, an eminent pediatrician, there were a number of London hospitals willing to take Norland students.

We were acutely aware of the need to be on our best behavior, particularly when Miss Whitehead sat us down in the drafty lecture room before we left.

"Although you are trained to care for healthy children, some insight into the principles of sick nursing is of great value to those in charge of nurseries," she said. "This is a timely opportunity to remind ourselves of the traditions of the Norland. As well as maintaining high ideals and Christian beliefs, we are here to serve. While at hospital you must forget yourselves. You are merely a pair of hands for service, to minister to the suffering children and make them as happy and comfortable as you can. You will learn that your lives during your career will be full of self-sacrifice, for the needs of your charges will call forth all your love, devotion, intelligence, and watchful care. Remember our motto: 'Love never faileth.'"

As I sat in the taxi en route, the real reason my body was drumming with anticipation was because finally, finally, I could get to look after my beloved babies and children. Don't get me wrong, I loved needlework and nursery rhymes, but caring for children was the reason I had joined the Norland, after all.

Pulling up outside the hospital, dressed in my freshly pressed Norland uniform and cape, I paid my fare, then stopped to take in my new home.

The magnificent red brick building soared into the sky, among a jumble of eighteenth- and nineteenth-century terraced homes.

On that day the majestic building looked like a grand old dame, with the cluster of little houses, her charges, sitting at her feet.

Goodness gracious, didn't I feel humble to be standing here.

Staring up at the imposing edifice, I felt honored.

Hadn't I already come a long way from my village? I was more determined than ever to make Mother proud.

I and another three Norlanders who were also training at the hospital were instructed to report to the matron's office.

Finally, we would be assigned some babies. After a rundown on hospital etiquette from matron we were given a tour of the wards.

The sight of all those sick children reduced me to mush. Rows and rows of cast-iron beds with sad little faces peeking out from under white starched sheets.

The children made for a pitiful sight, and something inside my soul stirred when I saw them. Some suffered from rickets, their legs so bowed they could scarcely walk; others, suffering from dyspraxia, were strapped to a bed with both legs in plaster. The children on the wards were being treated for everything from lupus to rheumatism.

Some were so ill and listless they could barely lift their heads from the pillows. Most of the poor scraps didn't even open their eyes much, but those who did wore little smiles that broke my heart.

Unwell children, unlike adults, do not feel sorry for themselves.

How could these beautiful and brave little children battling every day *not* affect me?

Walking through the wards was a humbling experience that left me breathless with admiration. Too many adults, busy in their everyday world, sever links with childhood. These children reminded me what it is to be human: to never lose touch with what is important.

Each time I am feeling anxiety in my life I think of the little children at Great Ormond Street, smiling through their sickness. They don't know the meaning of stress, just a daily fight with pain. Their battle is nothing short of courageous.

Charles Dickens summed it up well when he wrote, "A sick child is a contradiction of ideas, like a cold summer. But to quench the summer in a child's heart is, thank God! not easy."

And you couldn't quench the sense of mischief in some of the children either. . . .

Great Ormond Street, like the Norland, was a great believer in the restorative power of fresh air, and patients were wheeled out every day to get their dose.

The year before I started, the new Southwood Building, complete with balconies, had just opened. Children who were in the recovery stage were wheeled out in their wrought-iron cots onto their balcony. Can you imagine the sight of all these rows of children in their cots staring down from on high?

Apparently, neighbors complained bitterly about the noise, but the fresh air breaks were deemed too important to be sacrificed. They also gave children who hated their uninspired lunch of watery mince and tapioca the chance to sneak it outside under their sheets and hurl it off the side of the balcony. There were great shrieks of laughter when some tapioca landed with a splat on the glass roof of a balcony below.

Did I scold them? Not at all. It was hard enough for the poor little poppets being cooped up inside. What good would a dressing-down do for their recuperation? Besides, harmless mischief was a good sign. A child who has the energy for fun is a healthy child.

Senior nursing staff always scolded them but I said nothing, just gave them a little smile.

"I rather think you must be feeling better," I told one little boy after I caught him dribbling his dose of cod-liver oil through the balcony railings onto a doctor's head below.

The children's laughter was always music to my ears, and some of my happiest times came from seeing the delight on their little faces when we served up jam sandwiches for tea.

But happy times were far and few between during my three months at Great Ormond Street. At the time I felt lost in a bewildering, frightening world where etiquette and rank seemed to supersede basic human care.

Forgetting to put on your cuffs while addressing the ward sister or knocking unannounced on the matron's door seemed more important than how you spoke to a sick child.

It is really only now, at age ninety-two, that I see everything in life happens for a purpose and that in many ways, what I saw and experienced on the wards back then informed my opinions to such an extent that it changed me as a caregiver and as a person.

Back then the doctors', matrons', and ward sisters' words were the law. While they may have been world-class in their diagnosis, treatment, and medical care—not to mention exacting in their standards of cleanliness, hygiene, and ward discipline—they were a little short on basic love, affection, and touch.

From day one I was told "not to befriend" the children or give them "cuddles." It was utterly bewildering and, for a naturally tactile person like me, heartbreaking. When you see a sick little child crying, instinct tells you to cuddle him, doesn't it? In Great Ormond Street this was forbidden. I learned the hard way.

The first time the doctor, who in many ways was regarded as a god, swept through the ward, I was astonished at the reaction. It was like the parting of the Red Sea. People scattered and the ward went deadly quiet.

I was just taking a child's temperature, when I became aware of the kerfuffle on the far end of the ward.

"Brenda," hissed another junior nurse, "what are you doing?"

Bewildered, I looked at her terrified face.

"Taking this child's temperature, of course," I replied.

"Make yourself scarce," she said, frantically gathering up the sheets she was changing. "Doctor's here. Junior nursing staff are not allowed to be here when he's on the rounds."

Suddenly, I found myself being bundled unceremoniously into the milk room.

"This is ridiculous." I giggled. "Who does he thinks takes temperatures and changes sheets? The hospital fairies?"

But she didn't laugh. She looked half frozen in fear of a dressing-down.

I peeked curiously round the door as the doctor got to the little chap I'd been tending. The little lad was no more than three, and he had both legs in plaster from his feet to his hips.

The doctor picked up the clipboard, glared at the child, and then turned to the senior nurse by his side. "Temperature," he boomed.

"Normal," she replied.

"Bowel movements," he barked.

"Twice daily."

On and on they went, talking away over the little boy's head without once looking at him and addressing him directly.

To them he wasn't even a human being and therefore not worthy of being talked to directly. As I watched them, it occurred to me that they looked like they were having a business meeting, not caring for a sick child.

My blood boiled. The poor little treasure looked terrified and bewildered at the stern man in the white coat who used long words and never once deigned to look at him.

His lip trembled as they tapped his plaster cast and talked about breaking him out of it. I longed to run to him and scoop him into my arms, but I knew it would be more than my life was worth.

Finally the doctor turned on his heel and without so much as a by-your-leave or a single word to the boy stalked off down the ward.

I burst out of the milk room and ran to the boy's side. The encounter had clearly been too much for him as he dissolved into floods of tears.

"There, there, poppet," I soothed, wrapping him in my arms. "You'll be right as rain in no time. Don't mind the doctor. He's just doing his job, which is to get you better and back to your mummy."

His body relaxed instantly to my touch and big juddering sobs heaved over his little chest.

"That's it, little lamb." I smiled, stroking his forehead and planting a kiss on his head. "Better out than in—you cry as long as you want to."

Suddenly, I felt the temperature drop a couple of degrees and I looked up and found myself staring straight into the chilly face of the ward sister. One look at her face told me she was not pleased.

"There is no place for high emotion on my wards, Nurse Ashford."

"But I'm only trying to give him a cuddle and make him feel better," I said, quivering.

"That is what his parents are for," she said shrilly. "Now return to your duties this instant."

Gently I took my arms away from the little boy and smiled at him.

"Cheer up, chicken." I grinned.

I may have been smiling as I walked away from the little boy, but inside I was simmering with rage. What was wrong with these people? These were children first, patients second, not the other way round. Sick children needed love and affection all day long, not just at the hour of their parents' visit.

What was so dreadfully wrong with showing love and affection?

Well, I'd show her. She may have thought I was properly put in my place, but did I do things her way from that moment on? Not for a second. Any chance I got, or as soon as the senior nursing staff's backs were turned, I dished out love, cuddles, smiles, and hugs by the bucket load.

And do you know, it actually worked! I saw the children's eyes light up when I came on duty, and I knew that my smiles and cuddles were just as effective as the medicine prescribed by the officious doctor.

If a child's legs were madly itching under his plaster cast and driving him to distraction, I'd take a cold flannel and gently press it to his head to distract him from the itch. If she was missing mummy and sobbing, I'd sit and stroke her head and gently hum a nursery rhyme under my breath until she grew calm.

A plumped-up pillow and gently holding the hand of a listless little mite recovering from a stomach bug were miles more effective than antisickness tablets.

I learned that a nurturing, respectful touch speaks volumes to a child. By providing it to a sick child you are helping to release the feel-good hormone oxytocin in their bodies. Gently holding, stroking, and cuddling a child forges bonds of security and trust: it says you care and it boosts a child's self-esteem.

I noticed that not once did that doctor look children in the eyes, smile, or talk to them directly. Why? All it did was to tell the children that they were not worth the effort and to build their sense of frustration and despair at not being heard. Well, while the doctors were handing out their form of medicine, I was quietly dispensing my own through nurturing touch.

I'm sure my reassuring smiles were contagious because when I was on duty I heard more laughter and less sobbing.

For every injection, scan, or dose of nasty medicine prescribed, I handed out my own by rocking, patting, soothing, singing, hugging, cheek stroking, and smiling.

No one told me to behave this way and daily I knew my behavior risked a dressing-down, but it came instinctively to me.

Another thing I learned was never to force a sick child. Although gracious, the senior nursing staff could be ferocious. Each child was forced to take his medicine whether he liked it or not. I'd watch as they insisted every child chug back every last drop of it and frown disapprovingly as it dribbled back down their chins.

Other times they would insist that every last morsel of food be eaten and then gasp as the poor child vomited it back again.

Instinct told me this was wrong. Surely we should trust a child to know enough about what's good for his or her body. I never forced a sick child to eat a mouthful more than he or she wanted.

They'll eat when they're good and ready, I reasoned. Instead, I stroked their heads and administered little sips of water, or I joked with them.

"What's your favorite food?" I'd say with a smile.

"Jam roly-poly" was often the response.

"Close your eyes and imagine you're in a pudding factory," I'd say. Children have vivid imaginations and love games. Soon little eyes would be squeezed tight and I'd spend ten minutes walking them round the factory, telling them tall tales of rooms filled with lakes of custard and chocolate rowing boats.

Soon they'd be like Charlie in Willy Wonka's chocolate factory and have quite forgotten that I'd been popping in little mouthfuls of tapioca into their mouths and not gobstoppers.

A silly face would often have them in fits of giggles and make them quite forget that a second ago their mouths had been clamped shut when I'd held out a spoonful of cod-liver oil.

"Upsy-daisy, hold your nose. Swallow hard, and down she goes," was another old favorite that always seemed to help the medicine go down.

Every day my confidence as a children's nurse grew. Thank goodness it did because throughout the rest of my life I have continued to behave this way with small children, sick or otherwise.

The love-starved wards of Great Ormond Street were building my resolve to never fail a single child and be the best possible nanny I could. Children everywhere were being failed, even at the so-called highest levels, and a nanny dispensing cuddles was vitally needed.

Children needed and still need affection. It builds pathways in the brain, teaches them important lessons about love and trust, and reminds them how to behave like a civilized human being. In many ways I suppose

I have lots to be thankful for to the nursing staff of Great Ormond Street circa 1939. I knew how not to be around sick children.

Thankfully, holistic care is now taken seriously by the medical profession—and I daresay a nurse who never looked at her patient or smiled would be instantly dismissed—but it shows the restricted and narrow-minded thinking of the day that smiles were all but banished from the wards.

How fortunate we are that things have moved on: the benefits of touch through massage, acupuncture, and the countless other alternative therapies now available are actually used alongside conventional medicine. I still say there is no greater medicine than a smile.

Of course, the only downside to my hands-on care was that I had less time to do the practical side of my job. There were dozens of daily repetitive tasks that had to be carried out by the junior nursing staff, including the endless washing and making up of formula; clearing of bedpans; washing out of potties; bottle washing; soaking nappies; washing floors; changing sheets; taking temperatures; feeding babies; changing nappies; and serving and clearing up of breakfast, lunch, and tea. Instead, I forfeited my breaks and just worked straight through.

Reading a story to a sick little angel or taking the time to play trains with a boy with his leg in plaster was more important to me than getting a cup of tea and a breather. I was fortunate enough to be able to walk out of those wards at the end of my shift. Those poor little scraps in their hospital beds couldn't.

The trickiest of all my daily tasks and the one I dreaded the most was feeding the cleft palate babies.

There were four of the poor little mites, all under the age of three months and all at various stages of surgery.

Their feeding was left to the less experienced hands of one Brenda Ashford.

When I was first allocated the task, I wasn't too daunted. I had fed my brother his bottle all the time when he was just a babe in arms.

Surely it couldn't be that difficult, right? Wrong.

I spent hours trying to feed those poor little babies. I was never taught or shown how to, just left to get on with it. The milk would bubble out of their noses or come gushing out of the sides of their mouths.

All the while their little faces would grow red with frustration and hunger as they roared for food. It was so distressing and heartbreaking. At night their cries echoed in my ears.

I didn't dare tell the ward sister I felt uncomfortable doing it. I would doubtless have been sent off with a flea in my ear.

Once it was assigned to a junior nurse, but I heard her mutter to her colleague, "Let the Norlanders do it." After that I knew my place.

The memory of this has stuck in my mind over the remaining seventy-three years because it shows how little we knew.

Today, the job of caring for a newborn with a cleft palate is considered tricky and given to a specialist in the field with appropriate training, but back in 1939 it was left to girls with very little experience.

As far as I was concerned it all just compounded my sense of failure at the hospital.

Or maybe it was simply because we were living in a very intense bubble. Time off would, perhaps, have given me some perspective on the situation but, as at the Norland, there was very little of that, and the wider world didn't permeate the intense order of the hospital wards. Half a day off a week and every other Sunday seems to be the rule that governed my working life right up until I retired.

I saw things changing by the 1960s and 1970s as workers' rights came into play and people began to expect, and indeed demand, more time off; but by then my work ethic was so deeply ingrained that I continued to work the hours I always had.

When you have never had much time off, you don't miss or expect it. Hard work and long hours were expected of everyone back then, and people just got on with it without grumbling.

Perhaps we were made of stronger stock? Who knows—but we very rarely complained.

Back then, spending my life on the wards, in common with most of the doctors and nurses, seemed the absolute norm. Having a social life wasn't why I went into child care!

Perhaps I was overpossessive of my job and should have made more of an effort—perhaps I would have got a boyfriend if I had—but I loved my job, so I never hankered for a life outside.

In any case, student nurses didn't want to socialize with us "untrained"

Norlanders, so most evenings I sat in my room reading or simply fell asleep exhausted. I was so focused on my children and trying not to get into trouble that I quite forgot we were slap-bang in the middle of a seething metropolis, one that was about to undergo one of the most devastating events in its history.

I was busy at work with the babies one morning when the ward sister approached me.

"You and the rest of the Norlanders are to report to matron's office immediately," she said.

I hurried down the corridor after her and waited to be announced to the matron. Once we were all ushered inside, the matron opened her mouth to speak, and seconds later, all my worries suddenly paled into insignificance.

Matron's usually composed face was ashen. Her voice when it came was strangely stilted.

"At eleven fifteen this morning Prime Minister Neville Chamberlain speaking on BBC radio announced the news that we are at war with Germany. The hospital is being evacuated. You are to go home immediately and await further instruction from the Norland."

We sat in deafening silence before getting to our feet, thanking matron, and then returning to our rooms to pack up our belongings.

The unthinkable had happened.

As I exited the hospital, blinking in the sunlight, I took great gulps of fresh air.

For a good few minutes I stood stock-still on the pavement, my head spinning. Everything had happened so fast, I felt as if I'd been dumped there by a whirlwind.

I must have been the only person in London standing still. The streets were a teeming mass of bewildered people, all scurrying around like worker ants. It was a strange sight to behold.

Catching the tube and then the train on my own would usually have been a thing of great fear and uncertainty, but I took this journey in a total daze. Even my feet seemed to move with a life of their own.

It was gone 10:00 PM by the time I alighted at Leatherhead station in Surrey, but despite the dark, the streets here were teeming with life and activity, too.

Brick dust and mortar hung in the air from where people had started adapting old outhouses into rest centers. In my absence many people, predicting the outbreak of war, had already erected Anderson shelters in their back gardens. Trucks trundled past, loaded with green stretchers and blankets. First aid posts and air raid shelters were springing up all over the place.

Civil defense plans were already bursting into life. Everyone had been expecting it, had seen it coming. Suddenly, I felt a little foolish. With all the arrogance of youth I had been so immersed in my life that I had failed to see what was going on in the wider world.

Wearily, I let myself into the kitchen, much to the surprise of my mother and father.

"We'd have collected you if we'd known you were coming back so soon," Mother said.

All the boys were still at school on the Isle of Wight and Kathleen was in London. I sat at the table with only Mother and Father and drank cups of hot sweet tea. We didn't want to go to bed; I doubt anyone did that night.

A few days later an air raid siren was installed in the center of our community, and it was quickly agreed that a trial run was necessary.

Nothing could have prepared me for the noise. I was helping Mother peel potatoes when it sounded. My knife dropped into the sink with a clatter.

The siren's haunting wail left us speechless. I could feel its sickening drone right down in the pit of my tummy. Paralyzed with fear, I stayed rooted to the spot.

Mother put her arm round me to comfort me, but this was one fear she couldn't banish with a cuddle.

People huddled down in shelters. The world watched . . . and waited.

Nanny's Wisdom

A SMILE IS THE PERFECT ANTIDOTE.

All children adore smiles, particularly sick little children.

I always made a point of smiling at all the children on the ward. After I saw a gruff consultant or a stern matron staring down at them, I figured that a little kindness and a soft smile would be just what they needed to raise their spirits. It cost nothing but it counted for a lot.

BANISH SORE THROATS.

Over-the-counter cough medicines are expensive and in my opinion rarely work. There is no replacement for gargling with warm salt water. It really does work.

REPORT from the INSTITUTE { Educational Period of Training (3 months).

SUBJECTS.	TERM'S WORK.
Principles of Education... ⎫ ...	very good.
Practice of Education ... ⎬ ...	
Infant Welfare	good.
Child Psychology	very good.
Nature Study...	very good.
Story Telling and Children's Literature ...	very good
Handwork	good.
Nursery Songs and Games ...	very good.

Moral Qualities

Punctuality	very good.
Neatness	very good.
Personal Neatness	very good.
Tact	very good.
Interest in her Work	very good.
General Tone	very good.
General Capability	very good.

Teaching Experience ... ... 5 Weeks

Signature___ Ruth . Whickend

Principal

Date___ December 20 1939

Night, Night, Sleep Tight

HOTHFIELD PLACE
HOTHFIELD, KENT, ENGLAND
[1939, AGE EIGHTEEN]

Twinkle, twinkle, little star, how I wonder what you are!
Up above the world so high, like a diamond in the sky
When the blazing sun is gone, when he nothing shines upon,
Then you show your little light, twinkle, twinkle all the night.

—NURSERY RHYME

Schedule

7:00 AM: We woke and washed. We bathed only twice a week, fortunately, as it was freezing cold in the old servants' quarters where we had to bathe.

8:00 AM: Breakfast of porridge downstairs in what was the library.

9:00 AM: Lectures in psychology on Froebelian principles and child education.

11:00 AM: Practice of education. Taught children how to read, do basic sums, first stages of maths, and experience being in a classroom.

12:30 PM: Lunch. All students and children ate together in the library in a riot of noise.

2:00 PM: Older children went to play and babies were put in cots to sleep.

4:00 PM: More lectures.

5:30 PM: Tea of bread, butter, and jam. Milk and water were the only drinks available.

6:00 PM: If I was in charge of the baby room, I would be there, but if not, I studied and wrote up lecture notes.

8:00 PM: Rested and read in bedroom, wrote letters home. Chatted to other girls while we smocked, sewed, or knitted.

9:30 PM TO 10:00 PM: Prayers and lights out.

WITH THE SOUND OF THE SIREN still ringing in my ears, I boarded a train bound for Ashford in Kent. I had received word that I was to join the Norland to continue my third and final term of training at Hothfield Place in the village of Hothfield.

Bathed in late summer sunshine, Kent looked absolutely glorious. The skies were dappled with clouds, and the apple orchards took on a pinkish hue.

The loud shriek of the train's whistle announced my arrival.

Lugging my huge trunk onto the station platform, I tried to get my bearings.

Just then the steam cleared and a familiar figure emerged.

It was none other than tall, athletic, and highly efficient Mary Rutherford, our head girl. With her Norland cape flapping behind her as she bounded along the steamy train platform, she looked like a supernanny!

"Brenda," boomed Mary, enveloping me in an enthusiastic hug. "Marvelous to see you again, old thing."

We were joined by the rest of the gang—shy country girl Joan, exotic French aristo Yvonne, and lovely Scottish Margaret.

Norland had sent a car to collect us, and soon we were whizzing through the stunning Kent countryside.

I thought where I lived in Surrey was picturesque, but the landscape of the garden of England was simply beautiful. Hop farms and orchards, still groaning with late summer fruit, stretched out as far as the eye could see. In places, a light mist swirled over the fields, punctuated only by the tips of the roofs of curious-looking houses.

As we got closer to Hothfield the landscape changed.

Hothfield Place was located in the ancient village of the same name. Wide, flat, and boggy heath led into the village center, with a beautiful common and a thirteenth-century church at its heart.

Livestock grazed on the common, and a sense of tranquillity abounded. People round these parts lived off the fat of the land; and village life had remained unchanged for centuries.

It was a peaceful idyll. The only sounds were the gentle warbling salute of a blackbird from the eaves of a stone cottage and the far-off rumble of a tractor.

As the late afternoon shadows lengthened and the sun dipped over the church spire, I could make out blackberries glistening invitingly from the hedgerows, just begging to be picked.

Smoke curled from the chimney pots of warmly lit cottages as young boys playing football on the common packed up and headed for home, summoned by the thought of dripping-covered toast in front of a parlor fire.

"Hard to believe we're at war," murmured Joan, gazing out the window.

I nodded. Where were the German bombers and constant air raid sirens we'd all been prepared for?

That blissful six-month period came to be known as the Phony War, a slow start to hostilities that would soon enough become horrific beyond our comprehension, but back then it was all too easy to fool oneself into thinking that Neville Chamberlain's announcement had all been just a nasty dream.

I had heard that Hothfield Place was a stately home, but nothing could have prepared me for its dramatic beauty.

As the car turned a corner onto a long drive, we five girls all gasped simultaneously.

A beautiful big Adam mansion set in 350 acres of rolling parkland stood before us. The gathering dusk served only to make its facade more dramatic.

"Wow." Joan whistled.

"So beautiful," said Margaret, sighing.

"I can't believe this is to be our home, girls," I said, grinning excitedly.

By the time our car slid to a halt, it was obvious that the old house was in fact a hive of bustling activity. As well as the nursery staff and the rest of the students, the entire Bethnal Green day nursery was here, too, having been evacuated lock, stock, and barrel a couple of weeks before. We numbered forty-four children and seventy-five adults in all.

Heavy furniture was being lifted in and out of the magnificent stone-arched doorway, coach prams were lined up like soldiers on parade in the driveway, and excited little children tore round the grounds like tiny tornadoes.

Where once horse-drawn carriages would have slowed to a halt and aristocratic ladies and gentlemen graciously alighted, now little East End evacuees chased one another in a riot of noise. The babble of their excited voices merged into one big humming sound. Doleful-looking cows in neighboring fields stared curiously over the fences at the commotion.

Presiding over the lot, like an oasis of calm, was Miss Whitehead, still managing to look immaculate and unflustered in her blue uniform and scarlet-lined cape.

One little girl nearly knocked Miss Whitehead clean off her feet as she chased a little boy up the drive, her blond curls bobbing furiously.

I smiled as I remembered the games of cowboys and Indians that my brothers and I had played growing up in Hallcroft House. Children's games don't seem to change that much, wherever you're from.

Over the years I saw some of my wealthier charges with the very latest in toys, from model railways to cars, doll houses to miniprams; some of them had nurseries simply stuffed with the most beautiful must-haves, and yet I still say there is no greater game than having to use one's imagination.

I'm certain children's intelligence develops all the more if they aren't spoon-fed games and are just left to get on and play in a make-believe world.

Give children a chance to use their brains and imaginations, and they will. Put a computer console into their hands, and they won't.

Put a book there instead or plant them in an empty field or park and suddenly the world opens up and becomes a fantastical place of make-believe and adventure.

Seeing those children playing in the fresh air was a joy to behold.

"Slow down, Elsie," barked Miss Whitehead. "You'll do someone an injury."

But instead of cowering under the principal's steely gaze, the little girl grinned cheekily up at her, her blue eyes flashing with an irrepressible spirit.

She may have had the face of an angel, but her voice when she spoke was like nothing I'd heard before.

"Gor blimey, it ain't 'arf perishing 'ere, Miss White'ead. I goddi go in the cat and mouse and get me weasel and stoat, so's I 'ave," she jabbered. "If you sees that Pete Brown, tell 'im 'e better watch it an' all. Reckons I pen and ink like a bleedin' pig, 'e does — 'e can stick that right up 'is Khyber, I'm tellin' yer."

I didn't have a clue what it was she had said, but it was all rattled off like machine gun fire. *Pen and ink . . . weasel and stoat?* Elsie may as well have been speaking in Spanish.

Born and bred in the back streets of the East End, this girl had been brought up around the rich and colorful dialect that is cockney rhyming slang.

I really understood only snippets of what she said, but I liked her instinctively. She was bursting with an exuberant joy.

I winked at Elsie and she winked back.

"My brothers and I used to play It just like you are." I smiled. "I think you and I are going to get on famously. Perhaps I'll join you in that game soon."

"Alwight," she said, wiping a snotty nose on her sleeve. "Bet I beat ya."

I had a feeling she might just, too!

I laughed. "All right." I grinned. "You're on."

The Bethnal Green evacuees, or "Bethnal Greenies" as they came to be known, were like no children I'd ever met before. They were tough little children who walked with a swagger and talked in a language of their own. They may have been uprooted from their homes and separated from their families, but nothing could crush their spirits or dampen their excitement at being in Hothfield. Most of them had never left Bethnal Green before, much less been to the countryside. A few may have been to Kent with their families for the annual hop-picking harvest, where whole East End families worked by day in the fields collecting the hops, slept in barns at night, and treated it as a holiday. But for most, the fresh air, fields, and wildlife of the countryside were completely alien.

Imagine never having seen a pig, sheep, or cow in your life, then suddenly being exposed to them all? The fresh air, coupled with all the abundant nature and the enormous house, had the Bethnal Greenies in raptures.

"Are you having a lovely time?" I asked Elsie as Miss Whitehead retreated into the safety of the house.

"Not 'arf," she said. "We saw a cow being milked afore. Knows where the milk comes from?" Her blue eyes grew as wide as dinner plates. "Only from a 'ole in its bum."

I snorted with laughter.

Seconds later she was gone, sprinting toward the house and bounding up the stairs two at a time.

"I think I'm going to like it here very much," I said to Joan, linking arms with her and walking into my new home.

Joan and I paused inside the black-and-white-marble-floored hall and stopped to take in our surroundings.

"Wow." I whistled. "This hall is bigger than my whole house."

We headed up a sweeping marble staircase and onto the first floor, where we found the sense of excitement and confusion was only slightly reined in.

Norland's registrar, Miss Hewer, a usually unflappable woman in her fifties who always wore her gray hair scraped back in a rather severe bun, was looking decidedly flustered as she stood in what was once the drawing room. Priceless furniture and valuable heirlooms were stacked up in the middle, looking for all the world like an antiques bonfire.

"One knows not where to start," she muttered, staring at a sea of boxes.

All the babies were in two nurseries called Daisy and Spring; the older children were in night nurseries around the gallery that looked down on the main hall. The Bethnal Greenies were in a big nursery in what was once the billiard room. Miss Whitehead's office was in a small drawing room. The library was turned over to a communal day nursery for meals, play, and lectures. Our kitchen was an old stillroom; and a laundry was made of a brushing room. Dozens of bicycles for our use were lined up in the stables.

Hothfield wouldn't have looked out of place on *Downton Abbey*, and one half expected an earl to come striding round the corner with his Labrador at any moment!

Centuries of unchanged tradition had all been turned upside down in the space of weeks.

Best of all, the children's rooms had the most wonderful views over lush green fields. Painted in sunshine yellow, they contrasted beautifully with the light oak wooden nursery furniture.

A nursery today might contain any number of things, from musical mobiles, digital video baby monitors, and bottle warmers to nappy bins and fleece-topped baby changing tables. Back then, all they contained were plain wooden cots with cotton sheets and eiderdowns—pink for the girls, blue for the boys—and a few simple toys donated by generous locals, and plain wardrobes.

There were no cupboards and toy boxes groaning with toys, no flat screen televisions mounted on the wall, no computer consoles littering the floor.

In many ways the earlier days of nannying were far simpler; and it was a more organic lifestyle for the children, too.

We all used our imaginations and didn't have to rely on twenty-four/seven entertainment to get us through the day. A child could play with the same toy for months at a time and not get tired of it. Hard to imagine that now, that's for sure!

I'm not saying that the old days were necessarily better, just different. We had little but the necessities, and yet we still got by and never seemed to be bored.

We didn't rely on monitors—a baby's cry was usually sufficient to wake us. We had no need of nappy bins—all the dirty nappies were dumped in a bucket of warm water to soak before being scrubbed clean.

All children had their weekly bath in a huge tin tub filled with pails of water from the laundry room. The Bethnal Greenies took their lessons in the billiard room, and the younger children played in the library.

Break times were to be taken in the fields surrounding the house. You always knew when lessons were finished by the stampede of little feet through the grand hall and outside. Elsie usually led the way. Their boisterous babble could be heard drifting over the countryside as they squealed and played.

Where smart ladies and gentlemen once took a turn around the grounds and politely conversed on society matters, now all you could hear was the jubilant battle cry of "coming, ready or not."

Breakfast, lunch, and dinner were to be eaten at long trestle tables in the old dining hall. As in Norland in Pembridge Square, we dined with the children so we could lead by example. The children were far more likely to develop healthy eating patterns if they could see we finished everything on our plates.

Once I caught Elsie stealthily stuffing carrots in her pocket. I said nothing. The shame of my public dressing-down at the hands of Miss Whitehead still lingered and I wasn't about to subject her to the same misery. On the way out, though, I whispered in her ear, "We won't be doing that again, will we?"

She shook her head vigorously. "Besides," I said with a wink, "they say carrots can help you see in the pitch-dark of the blackout."

Her eyes widened at the possibilities and the mischief she could get up to with such a superpower at her disposal.

She wasn't to know this was simply government propaganda, put about to get us to eat our vegetables during wartime. It worked, though, as from that day on I caught her eagerly wolfing down all her vegetables, not stuffing them in her pockets.

This taught me that a little fun and imagination can go a lot further in getting a child to do what you want than a telling off.

At night they were read stories from the few books donated by local villagers.

Most evenings I and the rest of my set sewed, read, or wrote letters home. No one was ever awake past 10:00 PM. During the autumn months it was too cold, too dark; and we were, for the most part, simply too tired to stay up later.

We never listened to the wireless. I think Miss Whitehead may have had access to one, but certainly we didn't. As for a television? Forget it. But do you know, of all the periods of my life, this is the one that sticks in my mind most for the fun and camaraderie we had. We talked and shared in one another's lives because we didn't have the distraction of television. Such innocent pastimes and such a straightforward way of life was infinitely more rewarding and life affirming. I still believe that today. It was a simple but busy life, and my duties left little time for reflection or fear.

As we settled into the huge house I couldn't help but speculate about the previous occupants of Hothfield Place. Just where were the owners? Had they offered it to the Norland, had the house been requisitioned for our use, or had they simply left at the outbreak of war? It was so strange and baffling.

One thing was for sure, the house fairly hummed with the spirit of its ancestors. All along the walls, ancient portraits of past generations of Hothfield's resident family, the Tuftons, gazed down on us with a look of mild surprise. How shocked they would have been to see the Bethnal Greenies tearing around the grounds.

Suddenly, we became aware of Miss Whitehead's clapping her hands and summoning everyone into the library. We hurried in and took our places.

Miss Whitehead cleared her throat. "Lord Hothfield, by whose generosity we are here, is letting us have practically the whole house, which has not been used for some time. He and his family live in only a small part of it, but you must show them the utmost consideration and courtesy should your paths cross."

Heads nodded eagerly.

Ah, the mystery was solved. How generous this gentleman was to hand his magnificent house over to the institute. Mind you, I suspect he found it hard to say no to a request from Miss Whitehead.

"Our part, ladies, is to keep war from the children, to give the evacuees' parents the comfort and security of knowing their children are happy and safe, and to carry on as normally as we can. If we can enjoy a realization that what we are doing is useful, then some personal discomfort should be of minor importance. To these small folk, the war with all its suffering and anxieties must be a sealed book."

I thought of little Elsie's parents, still living and working in Bethnal Green, facing God knows what dangers. What they wouldn't do to be in this haven of tranquillity with their beloved little girl. I owed it to them to care for Elsie as if she were my own blood.

Nighttime falls quickly in the countryside and after a delicious supper of cold meat and potatoes, followed by blackberry and apple pie with thick double cream, it was time to retire to our beds.

By 8:00 PM the whole house lay under a heavy blanket of velvety dark, with just a dusting of stars. I had never known a night like it. With no streetlights and not even a solitary lamp from the village twinkling over the fields, we were engulfed in jet-black.

For the rest of the night not a living soul stirred. I lay there in the dark, nervous yet full of excitement. At last, I was finally able to care for children.

My time at Great Ormond Street had been difficult and made me realize I definitely wasn't cut out to be a children's nurse.

In my heart I knew I was a nanny, and at long last I could begin my training and work with children. I had never dreamed it would be under such strange circumstances, mind you—shut away in a big old house in the country—but I suppose what little I knew of children already made me realize one had to be adaptable. Circumstances change all the time, and I had to be ready to move with those changes if I was to keep pace and be the best nanny I could possibly be.

ON THAT FIRST DAY, after a warming breakfast of porridge, we had a walk around and bumped into Miss Edith Taylor, who ran the Bethnal Green nurseries and was in overall charge of the evacuees. She was coming back from a walk with some of them.

Her merry laugh and open features always inspired trust and confidence.

"Everyone has been so kind and we are so indebted to Miss Whitehead for bringing us here," she said. "Well-wishers have sent our little children glucose sweets and tins of biscuits. I think it's safe to say they are having the time of their lives."

Right on cue, a curious noise rang out from a neighboring field.

"*Weee . . . weeeeee . . . weeeeee.*"

The pitch grew higher and higher.

Suddenly, a squealing little pink piglet burst out of a hedgerow and galloped full tilt the length of the field, with a crowd of Bethnal Greenies in pursuit on the other side of the fence.

"Children, calm down," hollered Miss Taylor as they disappeared behind an ancient beech tree.

"Forgive them," she said, with an apologetic smile. "It's a new experience, and the fresh air has quite gone to their heads."

"Nothing to forgive," I said. "I love to see them playing so carefree."

Miss Taylor nodded her agreement.

"True, Nurse Brenda. They are well, sturdy, and happy—and that is the most we can hope for. Their little souls are being filled with the beauty of nature."

OVER THE COMING DAYS, as the Bethnal Greenies grew accustomed to their new home, I lived to see their little faces light up when they made some magical new countryside discovery.

The gentle slopes on the far side of the parkland made a perfect spot for roly-polies. You could bet little Elsie would be first to hurl herself down with a whoop, skirts tucked into her knickers.

Her joy and love of our new home was infectious.

"'Ere, Brenda," she called to me one morning. "Cook said I could 'elp collects the eggs for breakfast. I was looking in the trees, so I was. . . . They only come from an 'en's arse."

Later, at playtime, I saw her poking around in the ornamental pond in the garden with a stick, her skirts spattered with mud.

I chuckled, then thought nervously of other stories I had heard of evacuee children frying goldfish they had found to eat.

When they weren't climbing trees, wading in streams, and collecting feathers, they came in from their walks with their mouths stained bright purple from eating blackberries straight from the hedgerows.

"There's a lot of room in the countryside, ain't there?" Elsie remarked one day.

I couldn't have put it better myself.

"How about that game of It now, Elsie?" I said. "I'm dying to play."

Her eyes lit up like stars. "All right. Coming, ready or not!" she yelled.

I spent a glorious afternoon with Elsie and her chums, playing It and catch. We scarcely had a toy between us and yet the hours slipped by like minutes.

I quickly realized children have inexhaustible reserves of energy and never seem to tire. Not only that but they have a boundless capacity for fun.

Fortunately, a childhood spent chasing my brothers had left me pretty fit, which was just as well as I could see child care didn't leave one with much time to rest.

"Brenda, let's pretend to be pirates now," said Elsie, after she had caught me ducking behind a hedgerow.

She picked up a stick and quickly clambered up a nearby tree stump. "What a wonderful idea," I praised. "Let's take it in turns to be Captain Blackbeard on the tree stump ship."

Spotting a feather I picked it up.

"Here"—I grinned, tucking it in her hair—"you'll need this if you're a true pirate."

Picking up a dandelion, I squeezed the head until my fingers were stained yellow, then used the natural dye to place two yellow streaks across her face. "There. Now you look truly ferocious," I said.

She simply could not believe her eyes. By using a feather and a flower, I had made our make-believe game burst into life.

Her blue eyes sparkled at the possibilities, and I learned a valuable lesson by observing this.

As I grew in confidence throughout my career I learned that children love when an adult can understand their world and play on their level.

I think the problem for so many mothers now is that most of them have so much to deal with. It must be like keeping plates spinning for the poor modern mum.

How a woman nowadays juggles work and child care I shall never understand. I daresay finding half an hour to sit down with your children, much less unlocking their secret world, is a perplexing and exhausting struggle. My heart goes out to every mother today. I think too much is expected of them, I really do.

But if one can take the time to understand children's worlds and what motivates them, the rewards are endless. Even if you spend just ten minutes after reading a bedtime story to ask what made her laugh today, what scared her, and what made her excited, you can learn so much about what makes your child tick.

Seeing the Bethnal Greenies was an enormous learning curve for me and a lesson to treasure always.

Likewise so was dealing with their little tantrums, of which all children are more than capable of throwing.

When Elsie refused to give up command of the ship, I remembered my mother's words: *what I do for one, I have to do for all.*

"Come on now, Elsie," I said firmly. "It's time to let someone else have a go."

"No!" she shouted. "Don't wanna."

Was I nervous, scared at the scene that could erupt and leave me like a fish out of water? I was only a nanny in training, after all.

Slightly, but instinct told me that now wasn't the time to show fear—now was the time to get stern. If I didn't, I would lose her respect forever.

"Well, you have no choice I'm afraid, Elsie," I said lifting her down. "Now, up you go, John," I said with a smile, hoisting a little boy up on the tree stump.

"Spoilsport," she grumbled, kicking the stump.

"Come now, Elsie," I chided. "It's such a waste of time being beastly when you could be doing other things—like being a ferocious pirate."

There was little point losing my temper with Elsie. A girl like her would only have yelled back louder. Instinct told me reasoning and logic was the way forward.

For all her bravado I could tell she was sensitive and probably very intelligent. If I could make her see that being horrid wasn't a waste of my time but hers, I might get through to her. It worked, because two minutes later she had focused her attention on trying to make cannonballs out of conkers.

Tantrum averted. I breathed a sigh of relief. I suppose some parents today would have issued her with a short, sharp smack, but I was a Norland nanny. By training with them I rejected the use of smacking, and jolly grateful I was for that, too.

Imagine if I had left that little girl with a stinging hand mark on her leg? I would have lost her trust forever; and once lost, trust is something you can never get back.

I learned another important lesson that afternoon. Children are not like peas in a pod: no two are alike.

John, whom I had just helped up onto the tree stump, was as different from Elsie as chalk is to cheese. Maybe it was because he had been wrenched from the security of his family, but he was a quivering mass of nerves, poor little soldier.

"I don't think I know how to steer the ship," he said, his little lip wobbling. "I want to get down."

"You're doing marvelously."

"If you think so," he said nervously.

"I know so," I trilled. "Really, you are the most splendid captain," I said with a grin. "Isn't he, Elsie?"

Tantrum forgotten, she smiled and galloped off over the fields. "He'll never take me alive, me 'arties," she bellowed.

"I'll make you walk the plank, so I will," said John shyly, a lovely smile spreading over his sweet freckled face.

Soon everyone was playing again. Phew. Disaster averted. Just observing these little children playing was teaching me so much: that each child is as unique and individual as the trees that grow in the fields.

Miss Taylor, who had watched the whole episode, came up behind me, smiling. "Well done, Brenda. You're a natural with those children. They seem to really respond to you."

"Thanks." I beamed. "I think it's about understanding and respect. If I respect them, they will respect me in turn. Likewise, I think I understand a little something of what it's like to be a child. My sister, Kathleen, was a bookworm, you see, always reading in her bedroom, whereas I was like Elsie here—couldn't wait to get outside and get my hands dirty. It can't hurt to take a little extra time to understand what makes them tick. . . ." My voice trailed off. "What?" I asked. "You're looking at me funnily."

"Nothing, dear Brenda," she said, smiling and putting her hand on my arm. "I was just thinking what a really excellent nanny you're going to make."

I was walking on air as I gathered the children up and ushered them inside for tea. Well, what about that? Maybe I really was going to be good at something, too.

As I drifted off to sleep that night, with the sound of the children's laughter and images of Elsie's pirate chasing through my mind, I dared to dream. Maybe, just maybe, I might have it in me to be a very proper nanny.

OVER THE WEEKS THE CHILDREN GREW to not only love but also respect the countryside and its furry occupants. Particularly young Elsie, who befriended every horse, pig, and cow within a twenty-mile radius.

But one crisp morning Elsie and her gang saw something that I am sure, if they are still alive today, they will remember as if it were yesterday.

We were coming back from a stroll when a shrill noise screamed across the fields. Every animal and small child in the vicinity paused, nostrils quivering.

Seconds later a fox leaped from its hiding place and tore toward us, followed by a pack of slavering beagles.

The children didn't know it but they were witnessing the Ashford Valley Hunt, a local tradition.

Suddenly, the ground seemed to shake beneath our feet as over the brow of a hill a dozen or so magnificent horses galloped in our direction, their tails streaming behind them.

The master, resplendent in his scarlet jacket, had the fox in his sights and the hunt was on.

The dogs, scenting a kill, upped their pace.

The terrified fox bobbed this way and that, but he was no match for the dogs and he seemed certain to meet a grisly end in the jaws of one of those beasts.

Suddenly, little Elsie drew herself up, her face red with rage. "Flamin' cheek," she huffed. "Who they fink they are, chasing an 'armless fox? *Run!*" she hollered.

She was joined by the rest of the Bethnal Greenies.

"Leg it! Run!" they whooped and yelled, stamping their feet and bellowing like a pack of angry fishwives.

Perhaps his own personal East End cheerleading team spurred the fox on because he ducked into thick brambles and outwitted the dogs, much to the relief of Elsie and her gang.

"Aah." Behind us Miss Whitehead sighed. "The agonies of anxiety."

I'd have loved to spend more time with the Bethnal Greenies, but my attentions had to be elsewhere. Knowing how Joan and I loved the babies, Miss Whitehead had put us in charge of the baby nursery. Every student had to have a go, and presently it was our turn.

We had five babies in all, ranging from one month to eight months. When we were on night duty, we slept in the nursery in the large double bed that also served as the perfect place to change a baby's nappy during the day.

Joan and I were on duty together, and we took it in turns to do the night shift, with one sleeping and the other getting up to tend to whichever baby had woken up. Well, I say *sleeping,* but you try sleeping when five babies decide to wake at once. Invariably whoever's turn it was to stay in bed ended up getting up to help out.

We were discouraged from giving milk to babies older than three months to get them back to sleep, so Joan and I offered water. Then we seemed to spend the rest of the night pacing the nursery, each with a little baby on her shoulder, soothing them back to sleep. Pacifiers were taboo in those days: they were looked upon as the poor man's trick. I must have walked marathons round those nurseries.

But I didn't mind, as I was close to my beloved babies. You cannot imagine the noise of those nurseries. If I close my eyes, I can still hear it now. We didn't get much sleep!

When we were in charge of the baby room, we got up at 6:00 AM and got dressed and ate breakfast as quickly as possible before the babies woke.

For the rest of the day, we were constantly juggling feeds, sleep times, burping, and naps. The babies always had to have a walk in the morning. Then we combined feeds with playtime on a little mat on the nursery floor. After that, all the babies were lined up outside in their prams for their afternoon naps. While they slept, we cleaned the nurseries, changed the sheets, and prepared the bottles. Goodness, we didn't stop for a moment.

Bath time was a lot of fun. The babies weren't washed in tin tubs like the Bethnal Greenies. Back then, we had these sort of strange folding rubber baths that were erected in the nursery and filled with jugs of warm water. We didn't use soap or anything to wash them, just warm water.

Afterward they were towel dried and then liberally sprinkled with talcum powder to blot up any remaining dampness Nowadays they say it blocks the pores of the skin, but those babies seemed just fine on it. If they had a particularly sore-looking bottom we fetched up a jug of olive oil from the kitchen and rubbed that in. We didn't have nappy rash cream back then, but olive oil always did the job.

Next, we put their terry cloth nappies, fastened up with a big safety pin, on them, then gently got them dressed in little cotton or soft Viyella night-ies. We didn't use "baby grows" because they hadn't come in by then. How I loved that time of day when the babies were all lined up and kicking their pudgy legs on the double bed.

They were all sweet smelling, soft, and sleepy and looked simply ador-able side by side in their pristine white cotton nighties.

After feed times, we swaddled the ones younger than six weeks, then all babies were put down to sleep by 7:00 PM latest. One of us would stay in charge and sit in the darkened nursery and sew by the light of one small lamp in the corner.

Pacing a nursery night after night with at least one crying baby as we did, it was inevitable that exhaustion and self-doubt did at times creep in. If I couldn't settle a baby, despair would grip my heart. What was the point of being a nanny if I couldn't get a child to sleep? Eventually, the baby would drift off. Joan and I would crash back onto our shared bed, overcome with exhaustion. At least we had each other for company.

But there was one thing, thank goodness, I did seem rather good at.

I remember sitting one morning with a baby nestled in the crook of my arm. From time to time the Norland lecturers came up to observe us going about our duties, and on this occasion two of them were watching me give this baby her feed.

Presently one turned to the other and whispered in her ear. The other one nodded and then continued to stare.

Oh, crumbs. What had I done wrong?

I was supporting the baby's head, the bottle was at the right angle to get a good flow, baby had a good attachment to the bottle and was feeding happily, and I had my muslin cloth to hand to dab away any milk from round baby's mouth.

So what on earth had I done wrong? They couldn't take their eyes off me.

"Am I d-doing something wrong?" I stuttered eventually. "It's just that I notice you're looking at me a lot."

"Don't worry, Brenda." One of the ladies smiled warmly. "We were actually just saying how good you are at feeding babies, a natural, in fact. You look as if you've been doing it all your life."

Me. Brenda, a natural? A warm glow of happiness spread through me. I could scarcely wipe the silly smile off my face.

How perfectly, perfectly wonderful.

As the baby finished his milk and rounded it off with a soft burp, I chuckled to myself and gently put him over my shoulder to wind him. Then I swaddled him tightly in a blanket and tucked him up in my arms.

Watching him snuggle down and drift off to sleep, his soft little fingers splayed out, his chest softly rising and falling, I felt a rush of love so strong it took my breath away.

He, like all babies I had ever held in my arms, was heartbreakingly innocent and vulnerable.

The world might have been an uncertain place, but there was one thing I was growing more sure of by the day: babies and children were my destiny.

While my days were filled with milky burps, cuddles, fun, and laughing at the adventures of the Bethnal Greenies, my nights were a little lonelier.

When one sense is blocked out, the others quickly become more acute.

The darker the nights got as the year turned to autumn and the less we could see, the more sensitive my hearing became.

The old house was forever creaking and groaning, the ancient plumbing put under extra strain by its new occupants. Burst pipes were often followed by sudden deluges through the roof.

The hooting of owls drifted through the night and occasionally the soft cry of a little Bethnal Greenie, suddenly missing his or her mum, reached the baby nursery.

Upon hearing those pitiful little cries, my mind always returned to my own family. At night I missed Mother, Father, and David. I thought of them all sharing cocoa and listening to Father reading *Rupert Bear* and my heart ached just a little.

Christopher, Michael, and Basil had one another for comfort at school on the Isle of Wight, and Kathleen was busy with her training in London, but David was at home with Mother and Father.

How I longed to have a cuddle with them all.

But then my mind drifted to the Bethnal Greenies. They, like me, had been parted from their loved ones, and they were much younger than I. Yet somehow, they took it all in stride, and, apart from the odd cry in the night, were a resilient and cheerful bunch, not prone to feeling sorry for themselves.

Their poor parents were goodness knows where, risking their lives. The children had no idea when they would see their parents again, but did they complain? Not once. Perhaps, I realized with a wry smile, I should take my cue from these little folk and let them be the teachers. Thankfully during the day there were plenty of chubby little souls that needed my cuddles and love.

I was in my element caring for the newborn babies. They were illegitimate, born as a result of a no doubt scandalous liaison. It is impossible to overstate the stigma then attached to bearing a child out of wedlock. To find yourself unmarried and pregnant in the 1930s was a quite intolerable position in those harsher, more judgmental times.

Child adoption only became legal in 1926, so the fate for babies born out of wedlock was often uncertain. This was where the Norland stepped in. They gave a home to young mothers and their children until more permanent arrangements could be made.

In return for cooking, cleaning, and general domestic duties, young mothers could lodge at Hothfield, and we students cared for their babies and gained valuable experience. The mothers came and breast-fed their children before returning them to us for their day-to-day care.

We weren't allowed to form friendships with the mothers or even eat with them.

This may all sound strange to you, but in many ways it was a godsend for the mothers. They had a roof over their heads, regular meals, and the knowledge their babies were being cared for, all away from society's prying and judgmental eyes.

These ladies turned up at all hours with tiny babies in tow. I knew better than to ask where they had come from or what their stories were. But it didn't stop us from wondering. Were the babies the result of illicit liaisons between workhouse masters and young inmates, or perhaps a chambermaid at a London hotel and a wealthy married businessman? One thing was for sure: these women were nearly always young, pretty, and vulnerable.

Meeting them was a privilege in many ways, as it taught me a very important lesson and one I have carried with me throughout my life: do not judge or be judgmental. Those women were just girls really, scared out of their minds and in need of my love and support, not condemnation.

It was not my place to purse my lips and tut disapprovingly. It was my place to help them and do all I could to make their lives a little less frightening.

Fortunately today for young women, having a baby out of wedlock is no longer frowned on. Back then it was a huge disgrace, and these girls would have been treated harshly from the moment their bumps started to show.

The world would be a much nicer place if people just tried to understand a little more instead of sitting in judgment. Think how many fewer wars, political rows, and family disharmonies there would be if only people didn't judge. . . .

One morning I was summoned to the nursery to meet a new resident who would be under my care. The baby allocated to me was about ten days old and screaming at the top of her lungs. Her mother, Rose, a pretty, timid little thing about the same age as me, looked utterly distraught.

"M-my milk hasn't come in," she managed between sobs. "My baby, Lilly. She won't feed."

Breast-feeding had always been championed by the institute. It was drummed into us that only three things are needed to establish successful breast-feeding: a healthy mother, a good sucking baby, and a stable nervous system.

Mabel Liddiard, in her *The Mothercraft Manual*, asserted that "the mother should have good food, not too much, fresh air and healthy occupation. The only excuse for failure would be a very poor mother living on the dole."

Well, this girl, slim as she was, didn't look as if she were starving.

A good sucking baby. "Some babies are rather sleepy and require concentration."

It couldn't be that; this little one was raising Hothfield's rafters.

A stable nervous system. "The nervous mother, unsure of herself, frightened that the baby is not progressing, imagines all sorts of non-existent complications, which reacts on the baby."

I suspected this was the problem. Poor Rose looked scared stiff, and who could blame her? Poor mite. She needed confidence and cheerleading, not my condemnation. She was such a pretty little thing, with her big brown eyes and soft brown curls. I wondered, as I always did, what on earth had led her here.

One thing was for certain, I wasn't about to judge. Whoever the father was, he didn't want to know, otherwise she wouldn't have been there, but he was obviously wealthy. This baby wanted for nothing but stability. She had the best of the best—a shiny new Burlington carriage pram, no doubt purchased from that emporium of fine goods, Gamages in Holborn, and the finest soft smock dresses. But her poor mother looked like she would have traded it all in a heartbeat for some love and a kind word. She was so shy she could barely meet my eye.

I thought of my first trembling days at the institute.

"Come here," I said, smiling and laying my hand on her shoulder. I felt her relax to my touch. "Let's see if we can't get that milk to come. Your little girl is hungry."

Together we gently applied the breast massage I'd been taught at Norland in London, and when the first trickle of milk came in, her eyes shone and she gasped. "Oh thank you," she cried.

Picking up Lilly, I handed her to Rose—and the little one instantly latched on, gently suckling milk.

The screaming stopped and peace descended on the nursery.

"You're doing marvelously," I reassured her, fetching her a glass of water.

I wondered at the bond between mother and baby as I watched this most magic and bonding of rituals.

When the baby finally fell contentedly asleep, little pools of milk gathered at the corners of her mouth, cheeks rosy, I felt a warm glow of satisfaction. The mother smiled at me and I knew in an instant that life didn't feel quite so bad for her.

"I have to go and report to Miss Whitehead for my duties now but thank you, miss," she said, looking me in the eye. She handed me her sleeping babe and scurried off.

We didn't speak much after that and I didn't dare risk a telling off by inviting friendship, but an unspoken bond existed between us. She entrusted me with her baby day after day.

I often wonder what became of Rose and baby Lilly after I left Hothfield. I have no idea, but I hope she found the peace and security she and her little girl needed.

WITH EACH PASSING SEASON the bonds between us girls strengthened and the camaraderie deepened. The misery of Great Ormond Street was long forgotten and even home and my beloved baby brother didn't crowd my thoughts as they once had.

Autumn blew in, and Hothfield became a kaleidoscope of red and gold. The breeze carried the damp smell of fallen leaves.

The annual burning of winter bracken took place on the common nearby, and its rich smell revived the senses. Windblown conkers were eagerly scooped up by the Bethnal Greenies, who challenged each other to conker fights.

What the Bethnal Greenies loved most, though, was charging their way through great drifts of fallen leaves, relishing the crunching noise they made under their feet. Little wonder. The concrete streets of Bethnal Green didn't contain many leaves, much less leaf mountains.

"Look at me, Brenda," Elsie said with a whoop, as she threw them over her head. "It's raining leaves."

I laughed heartily.

For all the world she looked like a little princess in a falling-leaf snow globe as they tumbled over her blond head.

"Why don't you keep some?" I suggested. "I'm sure we can find you a scrapbook somewhere. In fact, let's hunt out all sorts of things to stick in. There're acorns, wildflowers, beautiful leaves."

She wrinkled her nose. "But won't they go moldy and yuk?"

"Not at all, darling. The wildflowers will dry if you press them right. I'll show you how later. Don't you think when you see your mummy next she would love to see all the beautiful nature you're surrounded by? She'll be so much happier, knowing you are in such a beautiful place—and if you show her the flowers, she'll be able to imagine it for herself."

At the mention of her mother, Elsie smiled, and I knew that had sunk in. "Yeah," she said, brimming over with excitement. "She ain't never seen an acorn afore. Nice one, Brenda."

What a voyage of discovery Elsie and I went on that afternoon. We made necklaces of pretty leaves and showed the other Bethnal Greenies how to paint their faces with earth. We poured water on the ground to make the worms wriggle their way to the surface and laughed as the children gasped in amazement.

Seeing their excitement that day made me realize what a good idea that was for all children; and later in my career I always went nature hunting with my charges. It costs nothing. A nanny's treasure box, filled with seasonal treats of nature—from fallen leaves in autumn to shells in summer—is a lovely way of having fun and teaching children something at the same time. I always encourage them to collect things and treasure their collections.

Treat nature as a toy box, and the rewards are endless. Even now if I see a lovely conker or a beautiful leaf, I have to stop myself from picking it up to hand to a little child.

But the lovely autumn quickly gave way to freezing cold and snow.

We awoke one morning and pulled aside the blackout curtains to see that a blanket of powder had arrived overnight, covering everything as far as the eye could see. It was magical.

Muffled squeals of delight rang out over the house when the Bethnal Greenies realized their playground had been transformed into a winter wonderland.

Wellies and mittens were hurriedly pulled on as the children charged outside between lessons. The snow was so deep it went right over the tops of their boots. Elsie and her gang let out great excited yelps as the snow melted and trickled between their toes. It would take more than soggy socks to stop these intrepid children; and soon the gardens glittered like a snowstorm as snowballs were hurled back and forth.

The winter of 1940 was the coldest one recorded for forty-five years, and the snow lasted for weeks. I can't remember anything like that winter in all my life. Milk, butter, and other supplies were brought in from the village by sled. The pipes' constantly freezing was enough to try Miss Whitehead's legendary calm to the limit. The building looked like a giant white wedding cake with huge drifts of snow piled on the roof and fringes of icicles hanging off the edge of the porch.

But even the subzero temperatures weren't enough to stop Miss Whitehead from insisting that all the babies receive their daily dose of fresh air. We couldn't wheel the prams outside in such thick snow, so instead we moved all the cots out there. Nothing, but nothing, would come between those babies and their fresh air!

What a sight! Rows of cots were lined up in the snow. In them, chubby, rosy little faces peeked out from a warm nest of blankets.

They looked so cozy nestled up that I half longed to join them, but there was far too much fun to be had at break times with the Bethnal Greenies.

"Gotcha," yelled Elsie as an expertly rolled snowball caught me right round the side of the face.

"That does it," I hollered, charging after her.

Joan, Margaret, Yvonne, Mary, and I couldn't resist joining the children. The tough little East Enders were expert at dodging this way and that, and their snowballs were delivered with stinging precision. Suffice to say, we students came off a lot worse than them!

The same slopes that had made such a perfect place for roly-polies in the late autumn sunshine now made ideal sled ground.

Many an exciting hour was spent clinging to the edge of a toboggan as Elsie and her gang launched you off down the icy slopes. With the cries of " 'Ang on, Brenda" still ringing in my ears, my nerves tingled all over as I hit a tree stump and found myself suddenly airborne.

Later, as a clear moon rose over the house and the temperatures plunged, we all trooped inside for a warming mug of cocoa.

We had so much fun and banter every day that it was easy to forget we were in the middle of a war. In all the weeks we'd been here there hadn't been so much as a whiff of Hitler's forces or the threat of imminent invasion that had driven us all to this beautiful corner of Kent.

"What a funny collection of people we are, gathered under this roof," I mused to myself one evening. Norland matrons, young students, Bethnal Green evacuees, and illegitimate children all were blissfully coexisting, all helping one another through these uncertain, troubled times. I had grown most fond of our little community and the safety and warmth it represented. In fact, I thought it couldn't get any better . . . until Christmas and all its magic arrived.

What a joyous occasion. We had a never to be forgotten festival, and each child was sent presents and photos from home.

There were tears as the children suddenly remembered their mamas and papas left behind in London. But tears were quickly replaced with gasps of delight when after a dinner of turkey with all the trimmings, kindly donated by local farmers, each child opened a well-filled Christmas stocking made by us nurses.

Then we all marched upstairs to the spacious hall, where Miss Whitehead had prepared an enormous tree. A toy babe snuggled in a manger. The lights twinkled on the tree and then . . . the most magical thing of all happened.

The door swung open and a jolly fellow in a red suit appeared.

"It's Father Christmas," screamed little Elsie.

Forty-four little jaws dropped.

Chaos broke out as Father Christmas walked in, ringing a large bell and, joy of joys, pulling a sleigh groaning with presents.

"Me . . . me . . . me," clamored the excited evacuees happily.

Wrapping paper was eagerly torn off and discarded and murmurs and whoops of delight filled the room.

I looked over at Miss Whitehead. She was standing back, watching with a tired but happy smile on her face. Only a woman such as she could have pulled all this out of the bag in the middle of wartime!

Next, we sat down to a tea of ham sandwiches and fairy cakes, followed by party games.

As I watched the evacuees and the nurses, I realized we were in a haven of security and joy. We may not have had our loved ones around us, we knew not what the future held, but we were all making the most of it. Even shy Rose was joining in the games, laughing and clapping, her pretty brown eyes shining with delight.

That night the great house was comfortably silent as every occupant fell into a deep, exhausted, and contented sleep.

That Christmas was one of the happiest times in my life and I will remember it always.

It taught me that you don't need to have a lot of money to enjoy a magical Christmas. A few well-chosen toys are better than piles of presents and, as long as everyone is prepared to join in and put their troubles to one side for a day, a wonderful time can be enjoyed by all.

So many children get so much for Christmas these days that I fear that the magic of it is quite ruined.

Put aside those endless toys, switch off the television, and play games with your children. It is those fun times they will remember, not the toys. It's the emotion of the day that carries through over the years and lives on in our hearts.

EVENTUALLY, THE FREEZING SNOWS of winter thawed and revealed a countryside beautiful almost beyond recognition. Lambs frolicked round the fields, giving endless joy to Elsie and her crew of Bethnal Greenies, wildflowers burst from the hedgerows, and a mist of blossom spread over the orchards. The woodland around the common was blanketed in bluebells.

Again I marveled at the fact that we were in the middle of a war. Rationing didn't much affect us, thanks to the abundant food supplies in the countryside and the kindness of the locals. The skies were endless and blue, without an enemy plane in sight. No one knew what the future held, so all we could do was live in the present.

And then, suddenly, I had more pressing problems than worrying about the German army. I had to take my final exam!

Mother had written to inform me she had a job with a family friend lined up for me the moment I passed; plus if I failed the exam, I might not get the funding for another term, as my bursary would run out.

And so I found myself one spring morning staring balefully at an exam paper.

"Your time starts now," said Miss Whitehead, leaving me alone.

Question 1—"What do you consider Froebel's most notable character-istics as an educator?"—became blotted and blurred.

The first teardrop was quickly joined by another.

Question 2—"Define the following methods of cooking: baking, stew-ing, roasting, and steaming,"—soon became an inky jumble.

Question 3—"Why is air the greatest necessity of animal life and how do we ensure that children get a constant supply of it night and day?"—was washed away under the deluge of tears.

Soon my eyes were a puffy mess as I broke down, my whole body jud-dering as I sobbed. My head pounded and everything ached. Even my eye-balls throbbed. I was extremely emotional—taking tests always vexed me.

Finally I cast one bleary eye at the clock. Oh, crumbs. I'd been sobbing for nearly an hour. I had just half an hour to finish the paper.

I realized this was my only chance. If I failed this, I doubted I'd ever receive another bursary. I'd be letting Norland down, letting my family down, letting myself down.

And then what? Back to my parents and an uncertain future.

I'd wasted so much precious time already. "Pull yourself together, Brenda Ashford. You can do this."

After that my pen became a blur as it whizzed over the page at break-neck speed.

By the time I put my pen down I was spent.

It was a miracle I passed: 76 out of 100 meant I was in line to receive the preliminary certificate of training from the institute. It would take another year of successful work in a private post before I could receive the full cer-tificate, but I had done it.

Along with the rest of my set, my time at Hothfield had sadly come to an end. I held back tears as I kissed good-bye my beloved Bethnal Greenies; beautiful little illegitimate baby Lilly, and her shy mother, Rose; not to mention my loyal friends.

Everyone knew this was the end of an era. Not a single person's future was secure.

"I don't know when I'll see you again," said Margaret, hugging me tight. "But thanks for your kindness. I'll never forget it."

I smiled wryly. The world was already such a changed place since Margaret was asked to take elocution lessons thirteen months previously. Now, in the grand scheme of things, the way she spoke barely mattered.

The stone porch was filled with leather trunks, bags, and girls sobbing farewells. Promises to stay in touch however or wherever we could echoed round the steps.

Even Miss Whitehead looked moved.

My funny little family was to be scattered to all parts of the country.

Sad times, but with all the arrogance of a nineteen-year-old, I didn't look back. I picked up my case, and as a newly qualified Norlander, marched to my first post with a spring in my step and a song in my heart. War . . . pah, what war? I saw no evidence of it, so how bad could it really be?

But as I traveled north by train, huge changes were already taking place. And these changes when they arrived came thick and fast and were full of terrifying surprises.

Nanny's Wisdom

LET CHILDREN BE OUR TEACHERS.

Sometimes we adults get so caught up in our obsession to impart knowledge to children that we can forget that children have a lot to teach us, too. The Bethnal Greenies at Hothfield were so brave about being parted from their loved ones. I never once saw them feeling sorry for themselves, and it made me realize how I should take my cue from them. I think we can all learn from children, if we only just stop and listen to the little people in our life. Their minds are young, uncluttered, and unbiased. They see things very simply and without prejudice—surely the perfect way to approach any situation in life.

GET YOUR DAILY CONSTITUTIONAL.

I'm not saying you should make your children take their naps outside, as we did at the Norland, but I simply cannot overstate the importance of fresh air to children, and adults, too, for that matter. Switch off the mobiles, televisions, and computer games and get them outside in the fresh air for a short walk at least once a day.

REPORT FOR TWELVE MONTHS' WORK IN A PRIVATE FAMILY.

Date of Entry into Post **May 20ᵗʰ, 1940.**

This Testimonial is not to be filled in under twelve months' work in one situation, unless by the written request of the Authorities of the Institute.

It is suggested as a guidance that one of the following remarks should be used:—*Excellent, Very Good, Good, Fairly Good, Fair.*

Number and age of Children at present date	*Two Boys.* 2 4/12 years 1 3/12 years.
In capacity as—	
(a) Head Nurse ...	
(b) Second Nurse...	*Single Handed.*
(c) Single-handed (with or without assistance)	
Care of Toilet and Nursery Requisites	Very good.
Physical Care of Children	Excellent.
Personal Neatness of Children... ...	Excellent.
Needlework	Excellent.
Management of Clothes	Excellent.
Nursery Teaching & Powers of Amusing Children	Excellent.
Happiness of Children	Excellent.
General Tone	Excellent.
Moral Training	Excellent.
Method	Excellent.
Punctuality	Excellent.
Personal Neatness	Excellent.
Temper	Excellent.
Tact	Excellent.
Adaptability	Excellent.
Sense of Responsibility	Excellent.
General Capability	Excellent.

My First Family

THE BEAUMONTS

APPLETON, SURREY, ENGLAND

[1940, AGE NINETEEN]

Girls and boys, come out to play.
The moon doth shine as bright as day.
Leave your supper and leave your sleep,
And join your playfellows in the street.
Come with a whoop and come with a call,
Come with a good will or come not at all.
Up the ladder and down the wall,
A half-penny loaf will serve us all.
You find milk, and I'll find flour,
And we'll have a pudding in half an hour.
But when the loaf is gone, what will you do?
Those who would eat must work 'tis true

—NURSERY RHYME

Schedule

6:30 AM: Boys woke. My room was next to their nursery so I rushed in and tried to give them toys so as not to wake parents.

7:00 AM: Got the boys dressed. They had to be smartly turned out in sailor suits or slacks and pullovers. I put their clothes out the night before.

7:30 AM: Cook brought breakfast—scrambled eggs and bacon or boiled egg and toast soldiers—up to day nursery. Rationing had started, but we still did well with sausages and bacon, thanks to kindness of local farmers.

7:50 AM: Grace was said at the end of every meal, including breakfast, and I always insisted the boys politely request to get down from the table, just as my parents had.

8:00 AM: Potty time; praised them when they did it well and said "better luck next time" if not so well. Washed hands.

9:00 AM: Out in garden and the boys played in the sandpit while I made beds and tidied rooms.

11:00 AM: Both boys rested or slept before lunch.

12:30 PM: Washed hands and then cook brought up lunch and I laid the nursery table.

2:00 PM: Walked to feed the ducks, pick pretty leaves and flowers, and collect eggs from the chicken coop.

4:00 PM: Simple tea in the nursery: jam sandwiches, slices of cheese, glass of milk, followed by jelly or a slice of apple. Washed their hands after tea and wiped their faces clean.

5:00 PM: Delivered both boys to the drawing room to spend time with their parents and visitors while I prepared for their bath time.

6:00 PM: Bathed both boys, then dressed them in flannel pajamas.

6:30 PM: Read them stories in bed.

7:00 PM: Prayers and lights out.

7:00 PM TO 10:00 PM: I ironed, sewed the boys' clothes, mended, and washed nappies while listening to the wireless. No time to read.

10:00 PM: Bedtime.

I FELL IN LOVE WITH twelve-week-old Benjy Beaumont the moment he fixed his big, melting chocolate-brown eyes on me.

Benjy's mother or father must have been of Eurasian origin, as he had the softest, dusky skin and a head of thick jet-black hair. There was no doubt this little chap was going to grow up to be heartbreakingly handsome.

"Well, aren't you a dear little fellow?" I said, beaming as I tickled his chin.

A big gummy smile spread over his face, and it was like the sun coming out from behind a cloud. His dimpled cheeks creased in delight as he pumped his chubby little legs and arms in frantic excitement.

What a perfectly adorable little man.

"I think you and I are going to get along just fine," I said, laughing and scooping him into my arms.

As I breathed in his sweet milky smell, the years rolled away and I found myself smiling as I remembered the first time holding my baby brother.

I feel this way each time I hold a small child for the first time. It's a magical feeling cuddling a fresh, young life with it all ahead of him. . . .

Why would anyone want to give this little angel away?

Benjy was adopted, you see, as was his new brother, two-year-old Peter. Along with his adoptive parents, Iris and Frank Beaumont, they were to be my new family.

My first charges in my first proper job! Gracious, I was nervous. A million feelings raced through me, from nerves to excitement. I was so eager to get started.

Iris and Frank Beaumont were wealthy and well-respected members of the local community of Appleton and good friends of my parents.

Frank's father was the minister of the local church, where his rousing sermons and strong morals made him a popular figure. Frank shared his father's religious ideals but had made his money in the textiles industry and obviously was not short of a bob or two.

When Iris told my mother they were planning on adopting Benjy and Peter, she instantly suggested me as the boys' new nanny.

I think Mother was keen to help Iris in any way she could. Iris and Frank had been good to my parents after Father had lost all his money, lending us bell tents and a caravan to take cheap holidays in. I was very grateful to Iris, if perhaps a touch intimidated by her.

In later life I stopped being intimidated by mothers. I saw that for the most part they were as apprehensive of me as I was of them. Once I made them realize I was only there to help and support them, in most cases, first day nerves melted away. Mrs. Beaumont was somewhat more aloof, though, and had firm ideas on how she wanted things.

She was also exquisitely beautiful with high cheekbones and a cut-glass accent to match. She had a complexion like double cream and intense cornflower-blue eyes that narrowed like a cat's when she looked at you.

Her chauffeur-driven navy-blue Rolls-Royce was a familiar sight about the village of Appleton as she nipped from the golf course to the various parish lunches she hosted.

Iris had been caring for the boys on her own these past few weeks while she waited for me to complete my studies, and seemed awfully relieved that I was finally there.

"I'm exhausted," she cried, fanning her beautiful face as she placed Peter into the crook of my other arm. "Thank goodness you're here, Brenda, or Nurse Brenda as I shall call you from now on."

I nodded eagerly.

"I should warn you," she added, "I like things to be done in the traditional way. You are to wear your uniform at all times and I expect the boys to be well turned out. Cook will bring you tea in the nursery every afternoon promptly at four, when I shall also visit. There may be a war on, but there is no need to let standards slip. Wouldn't you agree, Nurse Brenda?"

I nodded even more furiously. "Absolutely, Mrs. Beaumont. You know, they're gorgeous boys." I smiled. "You must be so proud."

"Well, yes," she muttered. "We got them from an orphanage in London."

I quickly came to see that Iris, for all her beauty, was not a particularly loving woman and was not prone to shows of affection. Nor did she ever seem entirely comfortable with the boys. Most mothers were more at ease with their children, but I think it must have been different for Iris. She had only just adopted them, after all, and was still finding her feet, so I fear hugs and kisses didn't come naturally.

But I couldn't judge her for that. She had demonstrated the ultimate act of love: she had plucked these two boys from an orphanage that still operated according to Victorian notions of discipline, and now they had a beautiful, rambling farmhouse to call home.

Their world had been transformed. Stark dormitories had been replaced by day and night nurseries, painted powder blue. The spacious sunlit rooms were stocked full of fine clothes and the best toys, including an electric Hornby model railway set, which can't have been easy to find. Supplies of toys had fallen by 75 percent since the outbreak of war so. most people improvised, making cars out of tin cans and sewing their own teddies. Not so for the Beaumont boys. In fact, the whole house oozed comfort.

As well as the chauffeur, a good-looking young man by the name of Bill, Frank and Iris employed their own cook. Not only that: cook had a fridge. She was a short, dumpy, no-nonsense woman who came in daily from the village, and she was extremely proud of her fridge. Only she was allowed access to it, and she guarded it as if it contained the crown jewels.

I suppose that's not so surprising when you consider that only 25 percent of people had a fridge in those days. As with most kitchen appliances, mass production of fridges didn't really begin until after the war. The price of such luxuries simply put them beyond the means of most families, so food was kept cold on a marble slab at the back of the larder or outdoors. Fridge adverts at the time boasted "how big is yours?" Well, the Beaumonts' was huge.

For all her bristly ferocity Cook was excellent at her job and could seemingly make a feast out of nothing. Food rationing had stepped up since the Hothfield days, when only sugar, butter, and bacon were rationed. For the last four months, more or less everything had been rationed, but thanks to vegetables in the garden and the odd rabbit or chicken given to Frank by local farmers, the boys and I were to eat like royalty.

Cook's omelets, made of Mullins' powdered egg and bulked out with stale bread crumbs, tasted as good as the real thing, and she had an excellent trick of dipping stale bread in milk and then heating it in the oven with cinnamon to make a delicious afternoon tea for the boys.

I learned a lot from Cook about stretching and making do. We never threw anything away. In fact, it was regarded as a crime to throw away even stale bread. Vegetable peelings could go on the compost; every last leftover bit of food could be used to make a tasty dish for the next day; old bones were boiled to make stock for delicious soup. We thought very, very hard before we put anything in the bin. From food to scraps of cloth, there was little that couldn't be recycled.

I had a day and night nursery to work in, which were to be totally my domain, a comfortable salary of £15 a week, and half a day off a week.

These little chaps were to want for nothing, except maybe a cuddle from their new mother.

I had to remind myself that not every parent was as tactile or loving as my mother and father, and for the hundredth time since leaving home I blessed my lucky stars for having such wonderful parents.

Besides, it didn't matter that Benjy and Peter only received a cool little kiss on the head from their new mother as she breezed out of the nursery to play golf; they had me to shower them with love and kisses now. I was determined they would have the same happy childhood I had enjoyed.

Benjy and Peter stared sadly after their mother as the door swung shut, leaving us in a cloud of Chanel No. 5.

I looked out the window as Iris's chauffeur-driven Rolls slid away from the house, then turned back to my new charges.

"Right, boys," I cried. "Who would like to go for a walk and feed the ducks?"

There may have been a war on, but we still had to get outside for our daily blast of fresh air. To stay in was considered positively degenerate.

"Quack, quack," said Peter, bouncing about on the spot. Benjy gazed adoringly up at his new big brother as if he couldn't quite believe his good fortune.

Peter's skin was as milky white as his new brother's was dark, but it gave me such a glow to see the way they looked at each other. They didn't see each other's skin color, just a fun new playmate.

Having tucked them both up in their beautiful new coach pram, we set out to walk the village streets. Perhaps I'd even have time to pop in and show off my new charges to Mother. Amberley wasn't far away.

Walking out down the drive, my palms felt suddenly clammy on the pram handles. Fear nagged. Two young lives were entirely in my hands. All the training of the previous year buzzed around my head. Did I have spare clothes and cloth nappies, a drink of water? Were the boys' clothes immaculate and their faces squeaky clean? These were the minister's grandsons, after all, and it wouldn't do for them to be seen around town with grubby faces and hands.

No, a thorough inspection revealed them to be the picture of angelic perfection, propped up in their pram in their new sailor suits.

My freshly ironed and starched Norland uniform was immaculate, my leather shoes gleamed, and my Norland cape swung merrily behind me as I marched up the drive. I was finally on my own!

I strolled into the center of the village. Hadn't Surrey changed since I'd left for Hothfield nine months previously!

Something about the sight of my smart uniform seemed to inspire respect among the villagers as shopkeepers and male passersby nodded and lifted their caps, and mothers and elderly ladies looked into my pram and smiled warmly. I was the picture of respectability and didn't I feel it.

These children were seen as part of their family, so I felt the duty fell to me to keep them looking as lovely as possible and the pram and its occupants gleaming.

I would never have fed them snacks while out and about in the pram. We never had snacks back then. In fact, I can't even remember giving a child snacks at all. If a child has sufficient breakfast, lunch, and dinner he shouldn't need a snack. If she said she was hungry, I'd say no, you won't eat lunch.

I don't really like it today when I see children being wheeled along in a pram, stuffing things in their mouths. Isn't it dangerous? Surely they could choke on their food while being bumped along. There is such a culture of children grazing on food all day long. I don't approve of this.

Children shouldn't need to eat snacks, and it teaches unhealthy eating habits. If a child comes back from a sporting activity and is ravenous, then I will give her a banana or another piece of fruit, but other than that snacks should be banned. I've never snacked and I've made it to ninety-two in good shape!

On my walk I stopped to chat to people I recognized and show off my new charges. I was as proud of them as I would be if they were my own.

With every step, every cheery greeting issued, and every smile that came my way I felt my confidence soar.

I had followed my heart, worked hard, and it had led me to this: a very proud, newly qualified nanny, pushing her smartly dressed and adorable charges through the streets. It made me realize that hard work pays off and the rewards for sticking at it are endless.

I wish more people remembered that. Hard work does pay off and wouldn't it be dull if everything we did in life we found easy? Where would the challenge be?

Such happiness I never knew existed, and I wasn't alone. There might have been a war on, but every villager seemed filled with purpose, determination, and optimism.

The village had come alive in a way I least expected. The community was thriving and people were determined to look after one another, come what may.

Our country, to quote Churchill, had found its soul.

By the time I reached my family's home I must have passed a dozen houses with their windows crisscrossed with sticky tape to stop them shattering. Every window had blackout curtains ready to be drawn at dusk and heavy sandbags on their doorsteps to put out fires.

Most back gardens had also been transformed, with everyone digging up what spare land they had for vegetable patches.

This country was ready for whatever the war was about to throw our way.

If I thought the villagers seemed happy, it wasn't a patch on my mother. She loved babies almost as much as I. When I proudly pushed Benjy and Peter's pram over the threshold of their small cottage, a babble of voices hit me.

There were children everywhere! I spotted twins, a little girl of about three with red hair, and another girl of two with huge violet eyes and poker-straight tresses.

Sitting in the middle of them all, with her knitting and a look of quiet satisfaction, was Mother.

Something was bubbling on the stove for tea, giving off the most mouthwatering smell; and a fire flickered in the hearth, a hod of coal placed beside it. The children were all happily playing with our old toys and were dressed in clothes that quite frankly had seen better days.

I thought of Benjy and Peter's well-stocked nursery. It may have had the latest toys, but it simply didn't give off the same warmth as my parents' home.

Untucking the boys from their pram, I gently placed them next to the other children to play.

I think it's so important for young children to spend time with other children. It's all well and good being around adults all day long, but only around other children can they learn the true meaning of play and how to share.

Benjy and Peter looked delighted with their new playmates and soon they were all gurgling, giggling, and happily waving at one another.

"Hello, darling," Mother exclaimed, leaping to her feet to give me a kiss. "Meet my evacuees. Aren't they all just gorgeous?"

I had to laugh. Mother had never hidden her desire to have twins, and thanks to the war, her wish had now been granted.

Father had joined the Home Guard and was terribly busy around the village with them, and all the boys, including David, were now at boarding school and had been evacuated to the Lake District. I rather suspect the evacuees were helping my mother with her empty-nest syndrome.

"They're not with us for long, sadly," she said, looking at the twins. "But this little one is Rita," she said, pointing to the serious-looking red-head who was clutching a battered old doll. "And this is Sally. Your father's grumbling that the house has been taken over, but I know he's secretly delighted."

Rita and Sally's stories were fascinating.

Little Rita was from Croydon. Back then, Croydon was home to one of the greatest airports in the world and certainly the largest in London, receiving international airfreight into the capital. This made it a major target, so Rita's evacuation had been swift.

"Poor little scrap," whispered Mother. "She's illegitimate, you know. Seems to have a new father each week. When she came here, she was to be called Rita Ratcliffe. When her mum turned up to visit from Croydon last week she tells me I now have to call her Rita Fowler."

"Me no Fowler," piped up little Rita, shaking her head defiantly. "Me Ratcliffe."

"That's all she says. I'm at my wits' end with her mother."

Seems little Rita's mum had been using the cheap railway fares the government had issued specifically so mothers could visit their evacuated children to go off for jaunts with her latest fancy man.

"She turned up last weekend and spent an hour with Rita, then vanished and was gone for days. Fed me some cock-and-bull story about getting lost, but I'm not daft, you know. I know she was getting up to fun and games."

I could see why Mother was cross. Rita's mother had turned the war to her advantage: now she had free child care and the means to get up to goodness only knows what.

I stared at little Rita, who had climbed onto my mother's knee and was now happily curled on her lap.

"She calls me her mummy now." Mother smiled, reaching out to stroke her hair.

Her smile was so tender and her manner with these little evacuees so gentle. It was plain to see she had already formed strong bonds with the girls. I felt alarm bells jangle at the back of my mind. One day, these children would have to go home. How would she cope then?

Now her eyes were shining with love as she told me Sally's story.

"She's illegitimate, too. Her mother had been working in a hotel and having it off with all sorts and didn't have a clue who the father was. Then Sally was adopted by Lady Lillian. Her ladyship is single, but I imagine, as she is titled, she pulled some strings and was able to adopt Sally."

I had heard of Lady Lillian. She was a well-known member of the aristocracy who lived nearby in a very grand house. Back then, it would have been almost impossible to adopt as a single woman, but she'd obviously used her considerable influence.

But there was one thing puzzling me.

"Why has Sally been evacuated?" I asked Mother. "She doesn't even live far from here."

"Lady Lillian has turned her house into a rest home for injured soldiers, says she can't have Sally there during the war. She's been here eight months now, but Lady Lillian must be terribly busy as she hasn't visited once."

I felt rage bubble up inside me. What was wrong with these women? Rita and Sally were beautiful, happy little girls that surely any mother would long to spend time with. Children weren't commodities to be shipped around on a whim.

Over the course of my career I met some neglectful parents—not many, thankfully, but some—and it always enraged me. Quite simply, what is the point of having children if you can't be bothered with them? Few things anger me in life like that.

On the walk back to the Beaumonts' I remembered Norland's motto, "Love never faileth." It seemed that, thanks to the war, there were more children than ever who needed love and security.

At the time of the evacuations there wasn't a great understanding of children's emotional needs and the impact that loss and separation could have. My Froebel-based Norland training gave me an insight into what it must be like to be a frightened evacuee. All these children were like frail little flowers that had been uprooted. They needed love, security, and understanding to flourish and blossom in their new homes.

My resolve to do the best I could by these children stiffened as I let myself back into the Beaumonts' spacious farmhouse.

Suddenly, I realized the time: 4:30 PM.

"Goodness gracious," I gasped. I'd been gone longer than I realized.

There was just enough time to get the children fed their tea and washed and scrubbed up, ready to be presented in the drawing room.

In those days it was quite commonplace for children of wealthier families to go to the drawing room for the hour after tea, to spend time with their mother, father, and visiting relatives before being taken back to the nursery. Often it was the only time a parent might spend with their child in the day.

This was the tradition of the times, and for many families it was set in stone. I don't think they were being unkind; it was just how their parents had done it and these routines get passed down through the generations.

Fortunately, it hadn't been like that for my parents, who simply adored spending time with my siblings and me.

I like to think that's why we all grew up to be secure, empathetic, and loving individuals. The time our parents invested in us paid off.

Over the years this attitude did soften and gradually I realized parents were starting to spend more and more time with their children; but back then, certainly among the upper classes, spending more than the required hour with your offspring simply wasn't done. That was what nannies were for, after all!

Once Peter and Benjy's faces were scrubbed clean with a warm flannel and their clothes were neat and tidy, I duly knocked on the drawing room door and presented my charges.

Iris looked like a Hollywood movie star in her stunning satin evening dress. She was sipping a martini. She smiled when she saw the boys but didn't get up. As always, I felt a little on edge around Iris. There was just something I couldn't quite put my finger on.

In contrast Frank beamed and leaped to his feet.

"Hello, boys. Your grandfather is here," he cried, ushering them in.

There in the corner, nursing a whiskey, was Iris's father, a dour Scotsman.

He nodded and issued a gruff welcome. The man positively radiated disapproval.

Then I saw something that made my heart take a nosedive.

He looked down at little Benjy and disapproval flashed in those steely eyes. I'd seen it only fleetingly, but it was enough for me to realize that he was not impressed with his new dark-skinned grandchild.

As the drawing room door swung shut behind me I stood stock-still on the landing, trembling. I wanted to run back in there and pluck up dear sweet little Benjy and take him to the warmth of the nursery. But I couldn't. I wasn't the boys' mother. I was their nanny.

At first I found that hard—caring for children, then leaving them when told to do so—but if my training had taught me anything, it was that a nanny is there simply to minister to her employer's needs and wishes. It would have been unprofessional of me to allow my feelings to interfere in my job.

Professional Norland Nurses respected the parents and did what they told us, full stop. You would never dare question their methods or presume to love their children more than they did.

There were very clear invisible lines drawn and boundaries one knew never to cross. Of course I loved those little children, and every day the bonds between us grew stronger, but I knew my place. I was there to care for those children when and where the parents dictated.

I walked out of that room and took a deep breath. It wouldn't be the first time I had to walk away from children. I would have to do it many times over the course of my career, but there is something about being young that makes one resilient and less sentimental.

Young people in all walks of life accept change a great deal easier than older people. I accepted what people told me to do and I grew accustomed to it.

I even became good at walking away. I don't say that to sound callous, but that was the way it was.

My belief in being the best and most professional nanny I could possibly be was overriding.

Of course, now that I'm older and a great deal more sentimental, I think I would have a harder time just walking away from children; but back then I did my duty.

Later, after I had read them their story and tucked them up in their beds, I spent the evening as I spent every evening—washing nappies, knitting them little woollies, or sewing. But the work that usually gave me such comfort couldn't save me from the agony of remembering the look Iris's father had given little Benjy.

Gazing at him sleeping soundly in his cot, I planted a gentle kiss on his forehead and said a prayer for his future. In fact, I prayed for the good fortunes and secure futures of all the children I knew, but especially Benjy, Peter, Rita, and Sally.

Unable to settle, I paced the nursery, then sneaked a peek out the window onto the dark, deserted streets. My thoughts were interrupted by a shout from below.

"Deal with your curtains," yelled a faceless air raid precaution warden.

Letting the curtain drop, I looked back round at the nursery.

The winter nights were drawing in, so I'd jolly well better get used to this room. I'd be spending a lot of time here. It was a little lonely but, like walking away from children, loneliness was something I quickly got used to. I was always to be found in the nursery, you see. *By myself.*

Every evening was spent in the same way; knitting, sewing, washing and scrubbing soiled nappies in great buckets of soapy water, or ironing. My job wasn't done until I had finished all my chores, and usually these could only be completed after the boys had gone to sleep. I was rarely done before 10:00 PM and I could hardly go out after that, especially not when little people would be waking me up at 6:30 the next morning.

We didn't get—or expect—much time off, not like today's modern women. I tell you this not to invite pity or to sound like a martyr; that was simply the way it was and our expectations didn't extend beyond that. Being a nanny is a fairly isolated life, at least in terms of adult company, and you don't go into it if you expect a full and busy social life. There is only so much you can fit into one half day off a week, after all.

Little wonder that so few Norlanders married. A formal survey conducted in 1935 showed that only 25 percent of nurses tied the knot.

Socializing belowstairs or with one's employers was unthinkable, and many of us found ourselves alone with our charges for the majority of the week.

There was an unstated implication in Norland during the thirties that personal fulfillment was to be found in serving your family and being the very best nurse you could possibly be. Becoming a nanny is a little like giving yourself to the Lord: you have to do it with your whole heart. And for the most part, I did.

Apart from anything else, there were simply more pressing things to worry about.

That night I snuggled down under my eiderdown and was just drifting off to sleep when I heard the siren go off.

I sat bolt upright in my bed. Had I dreamed it? No, there it was. That unmistakable drone that bore right down into the depths of my belly. As I sat in my pitch-black bedroom my brain scrambled to focus.

Come on, Brenda. The children, the children.

Leaping out of bed, I threw on my dressing gown and slippers and tore into the boys' nursery. On the landing, Frank and Iris were emerging from their room.

"The shelter, Brenda. Get down there now," urged Frank. I hardly had time to question where they were going.

Instead, I scooped little Benjy out of his cot and gently woke Peter. I was as gentle as possible, so as not to scare them, even though I was scared myself. So scared in fact my heart was pounding in my chest.

Minutes later we were fumbling our way through the dark and out into the garden.

The cold night air stung my cheeks and whipped up and under my dressing gown.

"What's happening?" mumbled Peter sleepily.

I gripped his hand tighter. "Nothing, darling. We're going to sleep in the shelter tonight. Won't that be fun?"

My heart was banging out of my chest by the time we bent down to get into the Anderson shelter at the bottom of the Beaumonts' garden. Once inside, I finally felt I could breathe.

The shelter was small, just four and a half feet wide and six and a half feet long, but there was enough room for two tiny bunks and a box of provisions. Jam, cocoa, Mullins' powdered egg in a tin, powdered milk, and jugs of water and water-purifying tablets. Frank had also left some comics there for Peter. Light came from a torch.

But we didn't touch any of the provisions. I drew the boys close to me, and we all snuggled together. A nursery rhyme would help fill the time and calm the boys until we got the all clear.

"Twinkle twinkle little star . . . how I wonder what you are," I sang gently.

Soon the boys' eyelids had grown heavy and they were drifting off.

"Up above the world so—"

Boom. The sound from up above was so ferocious that my words broke off.

Bang. Bang. The bombs were coming thick and fast now.

The noises were like nothing I'd ever heard before. First a low drone, then the scream of the bomb as it hurtled to the ground, then a sickening thud, followed by an explosion. Menacing crunches and whining sounds were heard all over Appleton.

These shelters could withstand most things except a direct hit. I squeezed my eyes shut and issued a silent prayer.

"What that, Nanny Brenda?" quivered little Peter, his eyes suddenly wide with terror.

"It's just the bang bang," I said as chirpily as I could muster. "Who wants to hear a story?"

An hour or so later the siren sounded the all clear, and I carried the boys back to their beds. I could barely sleep for the rest of the night. The reverberations of the bombs still seemed to linger.

The morning after that first attack, breakfast was a strained and exhausted affair.

Iris came into the day nursery as the boys were tucking into their porridge.

"Everyone okay?" she asked.

"We're all still standing," I replied.

"Goodo, Nurse Brenda," she replied. "Frank and I were at the post last night helping out. I'm off to see what needs doing round the village. I'll see you all at teatime."

It struck me as odd that she wouldn't prefer to stay with her sons in the shelter during a raid, but I bit my lip, as I did many times at the Beaumonts'.

If it were my parents and we were little, I know without a shadow of doubt that they would have been snuggled down there with us, making sure we were safe and free from fear, but the Beaumonts were different. Every parent, I came to realize throughout my career, is unique in his or her outlooks and attitudes toward child care.

Leaving your children in the middle of an air raid might seem perfectly normal to some but perfectly abhorrent to others. Such is the complexity of child care.

Seeing their attitudes taught me important lessons in how people react around their children, and I noted it all.

There is no one size fits all when it comes to parenting. I forced myself to detach from my emotions, stand back, and remind myself of my number one belief: I wasn't there to judge the parents, I was there to care for their children!

After breakfast we took our morning walk and I took the boys over to Mother's to check that she and her evacuees were all right.

"We're fine, darling, aren't we, girls?" she said cheerily.

"Yes, Mother," said Sally, smiling.

"She's not really your mother, you know," I said gently to Sally.

The poor little thing looked genuinely bewildered.

My heart ached. This little girl had been shunted from home to home and had now been dumped by her adoptive mother. All she wanted was someone to call mummy, a real family to belong to. Not for the first time, I was struck by the thought that these children were war casualties, too.

Sometimes days went by with no bombs, then other times we found ourselves in the shelter twice in one day, all huddled together for warmth and comfort. Occasionally Frank and Iris joined us, but more often than not they went to the post when the siren sounded.

Their frequent absence meant that the bond between me and the boys was getting stronger, and my love for Benjy and Peter grew with every hour spent underground.

But, despite all this fear and uncertainty, something extraordinary was happening inside me, too. With every bomb that was dropped on us, I found my confidence growing.

The woman that a year ago wouldn't have said boo to a goose, much less dare answer Miss Whitehead back, was now becoming stronger, turning into a woman who could dodge bombs and run through the night with her charges.

Thanks to these experiences, I came to expect the unexpected—handy when you're looking after children—and it made me that bit tougher and more resilient, too.

Every time I found myself in a situation, be it huddling underground in a shelter with my charges or running from bombs, I found my confidence grew. What doesn't kill you makes you stronger; and day by day I was becoming a stronger, surer, more adaptable nanny.

Living through conditions like this also makes you realize that what you think is bad or stressful more often than not isn't.

I don't sweat the small stuff. For the rest of my career, and even now, I'd think to myself, Well, I survived the Battle of Britain, none of my charges died—who cares if I've burned the lunch or missed a bus?

All we have in life is our health and our experiences; and fortunately mine were shaping me for the better.

As the bombing began, blessedly, to die down, things in Appleton grew calmer; that is, until the peace and quiet of the nursery was shattered one morning.

I was changing Benjy's nappy when I heard an ear-piercing scream. Whirling around I saw Peter sitting on his potty, his little face a picture of pain.

"Sweetheart," I gasped. "What on earth is wrong?"

It was then that I saw his willy was in his hand. He'd been playing around, as three-and-a-half-year-old boys do, and somehow he'd managed to get the foreskin rolled right back and it was stuck fast.

"My winkie hurts," he roared.

Oh, crumbs. The Norland taught me for every eventuality except this one. In fact, over the last year and a half I daresay there was little I hadn't encountered in my first job. Now certainly wasn't the time to lose my head.

Dashing downstairs I picked up the phone and rang the doctor's surgery.

"It's Peter," I said to the receptionist. "He's got his foreskin stuck."

Not five minutes later, the GP was bounding up the stairs, his black leather bag in hand. He took one look at Peter, who by now was quite red in the face.

"Hmm." He frowned. "We need to do something about this now. Get him on the nursery table."

Sweeping aside my knitting, I lifted Peter off the potty and onto the table. Poor little mite was howling in pain.

Seconds later the doctor had administered chloroform with a cloth over Peter's face, and Peter's little body slumped back on the table.

The doctor moved with astonishing speed. Whipping his scalpel out of his bag, he took Peter's penis in his hand and with a few deft cuts had circumcised him . . . right there on the nursery table. I couldn't believe my eyes.

Bewildered, Peter came round to find his willy wrapped in blood-soaked gauze.

I had to break the news to a bemused Iris later, when she visited the nursery for tea. She was relieved that Peter was going to be perfectly fine, of course, but she stayed no longer than usual and there was still nothing but that chilly kiss on the forehead for either of her sons.

It was me who cuddled little Peter when he cried, me who whooped with delight when I saw Benjy's first teeth break through his gums, and me who watched his first faltering steps in the garden with pride. Both boys ran to me instinctively when they hurt themselves and needed a cuddle.

I daresay they loved Frank and Iris, who, in turn, loved their adopted sons, but really the only time they spent with them was an hour or so a day. The boys' entire lives and day-to-day care was in my hands. I had grown to love them dearly, but my bond with Benjy was absolute. I suppose when you've shared a child's first milestones, you feel your life is intertwined with his.

I have often thought of those moments and shuddered at the emotion of them. Of course it hurt to walk away from him to my next job, but my devotion to duty was everything and overrode any feeling of attachment.

Benjy was a part of my life, but I didn't own him, nor was he my child. Today I consider it a privilege to have been a part of his life and to have influenced it in some small way.

I feel that way about all my former charges, in fact. Being a part of children's lives and witnessing the events that shape them and their minds and bodies as they blossom and grow are an honor, not a right. I just wish more people realized that.

I certainly got an enormous thrill out of watching Benjy blossom into a cheeky, happy little boy. His legs were nicely chubby and his cheeks had filled out like ripe plums. But as he approached his second birthday and Peter his fourth, my time with them was coming to an end.

As ever in wartime, events moved rapidly, and something was always round the corner to make you realize that your life was never really under your control.

By December 1941 all single women ages eighteen to sixty-five who weren't already contributing were to be conscripted into the war effort, whether they liked it or not. They had to take up work either in the services, nursing, factories, transport, or the Land Army. Five million women were needed to help fill the roles that the men, fighting on battlefields, had left behind.

Iris's days as a lady of leisure were up, and so was my time in her household. It was considered selfish, reckless even, for a woman to employ a nanny to do a job she could quite easily be doing herself. In any case, Iris may have been exempt from conscription, but I wasn't. War was about to open up a whole host of opportunities. Or so I thought.

I marched along to nearby Leatherhead to register.

En route all sorts of fantastical and exciting possibilities whirled around my mind.

Perhaps I could join the RAF, learn to fly a plane like those brave Spitfire pilots who'd captured my imagination ever since I saw them shoot down a German. Or get my hands dirty driving an ambulance or an army truck.

The sky was the limit. . . .

"Impossible," snapped the bespectacled clerk with whom I had just shared my ambitions.

My dreams burst like a balloon. "But why?" I asked.

"You have a skill," he said firmly. "You are a trained nursemaid. Do you know how many evacuees there are in this country?"

Not off the top of my head, but I could see where this conversation was going.

He was right: I must have been mad to think I could learn to fly a plane.

My thoughts drifted back to the Bethnal Greenies and to little Rita and Sally. I had to stay focused on why I had trained with the Norland in the first place.

What was it that Miss Whitehead had drummed into us over and over? "The future is made by the children for whose characters and training you are responsible. Your contribution and examples are valuable."

There was no point lamenting the fact that I wasn't going to drive ambulances. My contribution was more powerful and needed more than ever before: construction, not destruction. I couldn't fail my charges now. The children of this dreadful war needed stability and love.

Soon after my meeting with the conscription clerk, I received notification of my next assignment. Scanning the letter, my eye fixed on the signature of my new employer: Lady Francesca Smythe-Villiers of Granville House in the village of Little Cranford.

I gulped. Who'd have thought it? Little Brenda Ashford mixing with the aristocracy.

What was I to call her? Francesca? No, that wouldn't do. Lady Smythe-Villiers, or even your ladyship? My tummy did little flip-flops of nervous excitement.

I did so hope she was nice. Some of these ladies had some funny ways, as well I knew after hearing about Lady Lillian.

When it was time to kiss little Benjy and Peter good-bye, I found myself sadder than I could ever have imagined. But as sad as I was, there was also another emotion tingling just beneath the surface.

Excitement!

Excitement at the children I'd yet to meet and the adventures I'd yet to have. That's young people for you, I suppose, always looking to what's around the corner.

I kissed and hugged them tightly.

"Be good boys for your mummy, my darlings," I whispered.

Bill drove me to the station in the Rolls. As the car pulled off down the drive, I turned to wave a last good-bye to my charges through the back window.

Peter was waving furiously and smiling, but Benjy's little face wore a worried frown as he stared bewildered after my departing car.

I sighed heavily. So many changes already for him—how I hoped his life would settle down and he'd get the stability he so desperately needed.

But as we sped to Leatherhead train station I could never have guessed at what was coming his way next. Something unspeakably awful and tragic had been unfolding, right under my very nose.

TESTIMONIAL

Nurse Brenda leaves of her own accord to take up work in a war nursery. We are very sorry to lose her as she has always proved to be a very capable and conscientious nurse. She was kind and patient with the two boys (aged two and four years) and also took great pains in their training. In short she was very satisfactory in every way and she leaves with our genuine regret.

—IRIS BEAUMONT, JANUARY 1, 1942

Nanny's Wisdom

RESPECT YOUR CHILDREN.

Why is the saying "respect your elders" so well known but not "respect your children"? I believe that respect should go two ways; and even though they are little, children deserve our respect. Don't lie to them, treat them like fools, or tease them.

Also, and this is something I feel passionate about, I simply never call children "kids." Baby goats are kids, not children! I know it may seem silly to some, but it's something I feel most strongly. If we respect little people, then they in turn will grow up to respect others.

LEARN TO SEW.

So many people these days simply don't bother, but I can't tell you what an invaluable skill it is.

In my day people always darned and knitted. During the war everybody lived by the principle "make do or mend." Surely now, in these times of economic hardship, that principle is more relevant than ever.

Even if you just learn how to sew on a button or do a hem, it will help you so much, not to mention save you money. Learn and then teach your children, and they in turn can teach their children.

SEW A BUTTON.

At the beginning and at the end of sewing your button on your garment, don't tie off the thread with knots, which can easily come undone and create too much of a pull. Instead, add several tiny stitches into the fabric for extra security. Next, sew loosely in two loops across the holes in the button. Don't just go across the top of the fabric, go through all the layers. This creates a more secure base. Wind around the threads to create a shank—but don't make the shank too thick. To finish off, take the thread to the wrong side of the fabric and sew a few more tiny stitches to secure the end.

Yes, Your Ladyship

LORD AND LADY SMYTHE-VILLIERS, GRANVILLE HOUSE
LITTLE CRANFORD, DEVON, ENGLAND
[1942, AGE TWENTY-ONE]

Hush a bye, baby, on the treetop,
When the wind blows, the cradle will rock;
When the bow breaks, the cradle will fall,
And down will come baby, cradle and all.

— LULLABY

Schedule

7:00 AM: Woke children and got them dressed and ready for breakfast.

8:00 AM: Breakfast of bread, jam, and milk in the day nursery. Children to ask to be excused from the table when they have finished their breakfasts.

9:00 AM: Washed hands. Toilet trips. Teeth brushed and faces wiped clean.

10:00 AM: Supervised playtime. There were very few toys, so one had to ensure everyone shared.

10:30 AM: Cleaned day nursery and got children's dirty clothes ready for her ladyship's dailies to collect and wash.

11:00 AM: Gave children drink of milk. Then dressed them in boots, coats, and mittens and took them out for morning walk in the fresh air.

12:30 PM: Back to the house for lunch in the day nursery. Good manners to be observed throughout the meal.

1:30 PM TO 3:00 PM: Quiet time. Rest and sleep for younger children. Quiet play and reading for older children.

3:00 PM: Outside for games of catch and hide-and-seek. Or we picked strawberries straight from the bush and wildflowers in summer.

4:00 PM: Tea in day nursery of jam sandwiches, fruit, milk, and pudding.

4:30 PM: Visit from her ladyship.

5:00 PM: If a Friday we dragged up the tin bath and the children were bathed and washed in front of the fire (including behind their ears).

6:00 PM: Read children bedtime story by the fireside.

7:00 PM: Prayers and bedtime.

7:30 PM: Sat quietly in my room and read or darned.

10:00 PM: Retired to bed and lights out.

T*HE BOTTLE-GREEN DAIMLER WAS THE* only car waiting at the station car park, and leaning against its gleaming bonnet, with a copy of *The Times* tucked neatly under his arm, was its driver.

Mr. Worboys, his lordship's chauffeur, was dressed immaculately in a dove-gray suit and peaked cap.

"Brenda Ashford, I presume." He grinned, revealing a gap a mile wide between his crooked teeth.

He was not by any stretch of the imagination a good-looking man. His face was weather-beaten and his skin more pockmarked than a bomb-shattered London street, but everything about him invited friendship and trust.

"Come on then, Nurse Ashford," he said with a wink, opening the door for me. "Hop in. We can't keep her ladyship waiting, now can we?"

He hoisted my trunk into the boot, leaped behind the wheel, and then we were off, whizzing down the narrow country lanes. As he drove, Mr. Worboys kept up a running commentary.

"His lordship owns all the land for as far as you can see," he said, sweeping his arm theatrically over the landscape. "Twenty-five thousand acres they reckon's 'is parish."

Great swaths of farmland stretched out to the horizon. Did Lord Smythe-Villiers really own all this? What a lucky man. In the spring sunshine the landscape looked absolutely stunning. I'd never seen so much lush green pasture, such beautiful woodlands.

His lordship's property was deep in the heart of the West Country. Field after field of corn and wheat swayed gently in the breeze, and beyond that, herds of fat cows grazed contently.

In some of the fields young women, wearing fawn breeches and green jumpers, toiled away, their faces smeared with mud and sweat. As they worked they sang and laughed.

"Land girls," explained Mr. Worboys. "They weren't so welcome with the farming folk to begin with. That's centuries of farming tradition you're messing about with, letting a load of flippity young girls loose in the fields, but they've proved their worth and now they all rub along together."

I stared a mite enviously at these young women. I'd read that more than a third came from London and the industrial cities of the north of England, and now conscription had swelled their numbers to 83,000. Each land girl was paid 28 shillings a week. How wonderful it must be to be let loose in all this beauty and fresh air, away from the bomb-shattered cities.

"We're lucky, us village folk," said Mr. Worboys. "We live off the fat of the land in these parts. You won't starve, Nurse Brenda, especially not up at her ladyship's."

Soon we were driving through a picture-postcard village and Mr. Worboys was beeping his horn and waving at passersby, who stared curiously into the car at me.

"This is Little Cranford. You'll never be lonely 'ere, you know," he said with a chuckle. "Word will have already reached the furthest farm that her ladyship's Norland nanny has arrived."

If a Hollywood location agent had come looking, he couldn't have found a prettier picture of a quintessential English country village. Nothing bad could ever happen in Little Cranford, of that I was certain. White-washed thatched cottages nestled in verdant gardens, fat cream-colored geese dozed in the sun, and in the middle of it all stood a sweet little church and duck pond.

"Seventeenth century, you know," remarked Mr. Worboys proudly. "This village was founded by the Anglo-Saxons.

"And that there," he said, nodding toward the building next to the village store, "is the church hall. They have the village hop there once a month. You want to get yourself down there, Brenda, and meet some of our local lads. Farmers' boys most of 'em, bit rough round the edges but 'earts of gold. Reckons they'll love you."

With that he roared with laughter.

"His lordship owns all the cottages in this village; in fact he owns most of Little Cranford. That's Mr. Webb's place," he said, pointing to a little worker's cottage facing the church, with pink roses climbing up the side. "His lordship's valet. Her ladyship moved Mr. Webb from his old place down the road. He weren't right happy about that, I can tell you."

I was just about to ask him why she would do such a thing when he was off again.

"Susan, our district nurse, lives over there. She's friendly with the farmer's son Bill. Bill and his father, John, are the tenants of his lordship and farm his land."

"Does everyone round here work for their lord and ladyship?" I asked.

Mr. Worboys paused and smiled. "Comes to think of it, yes. A lot of the local women go up to his lordship's to cook, clean, and wash. My missus, Pat, is one of her ladyship's dailies. They keep us all occupied, that's for sure."

As we headed on the only road out of the village I noticed there seemed to be an awful lot of children playing in and around the village streets.

"We've got evacuees coming out our ears," said Mr. Worboys. "Can't blame 'em. This little corner of England has to be the safest anywhere. No one will drop an ol' bomb on your head here, Nurse Brenda."

I didn't doubt it for a moment. This sleepy little backwater was a haven of quiet. I couldn't imagine I'd be ducking flying shrapnel here, that's for sure.

"Her ladyship oversaw the evacuation, who was billeted where and with whom," he muttered.

"Oh, is she the billeting officer?" I asked.

"Nope," he said, "but she tends to oversee things."

I wondered nervously what her ladyship was like. I had met her only briefly at the family's main seat some weeks before, but the interview was too brief to get a real measure of her. I'd been so intimidated by the grand surroundings I'd just sat there in awe.

She certainly seemed to have a hand in everything that went on around these parts.

"Hard to believe his lordship owns all this," I said.

"True. Mind you, it's not like his other place, eh, Nurse Brenda." Mr. Worboys whistled. "That really is summit else, isn't it. Hundreds of rooms, hundreds.

"His lordship is lovely," he went on as we bumped down a country lane. "A nicer gentleman you'd be hard-pressed to find. I takes him to the station three times a week so as he can get his train up to the 'ouse of Commons."

"So why are they down here?" I asked.

"The big house has been requisitioned as a convalescent home for soldiers, so they were forced to move to their country seat."

And with that we came to an abrupt halt in front of one of the loveliest houses I'd ever seen. I stared at my new home in awe. Granville House, the country seat of Lord and Lady Smythe-Villiers, was a seventeenth-century manor house with a slightly wonky roof; it was set in five acres of gardens. It was so grand it really wouldn't have looked out of place on the set of *Downton Abbey*.

It was pretty as a picture. Pale mauve wisteria curled gently round the old stone porch, and swallows had made their homes in the eaves.

The golden brickwork of the house, mellowed by time, looked as much a part of the landscape as the ancient apple trees that dotted the garden.

Chickens scratched and strutted around the drive, feasting on ripe apples as they dropped from the trees.

"So beautiful," I murmured wide-eyed, as Mr. Worboys slowed the Daimler to a halt in front of a stable block, five hundred yards from the house.

The stables had been converted to house the Daimler and another car.

"Me and the missus lives up there," he said, pointing to a flat above the stable block. "If you need anything, Brenda, anything, just ask."

Mr. Worboys had given me a thorough rundown on the village, but there was still one thing about which I was none the wiser.

"What's Lady Francesca like, Mr. Worboys?" I asked.

His face darkened. "Her ladyship? Well, how can I put this . . ."

Suddenly, the door to the manor house swung open. There in the doorway was the most formidable-looking woman I'd ever set eyes on.

Lady Francesca Smythe-Villiers.

When I had first met her, she was sitting down, but now I could see she towered over me at six feet tall. Despite being well into her sixties she had an almost regal bearing and stood ramrod straight like a statue in the stone porch.

When I glanced back, Mr. Worboys had vanished into thin air. I was on my own.

Her ladyship's slate-gray eyes were piercing and seemed to stare right down into the depths of my soul. The thin lips, hook nose, and gray bun only added to the austere image.

"Nurse Ashford, are you quite well?" she said in a clipped voice.

"Good morning," I gushed. "I can't tell you how excited I am to be here."

"I'm sure," her ladyship replied in a deadpan voice.

I did what I always do when I'm nervous and in the company of someone I feel to be my intellectual superior. I start to babble. On and on I went about the journey, the weather.

"Anyway, here I am and I can't wait to get started," I blustered.

Her ladyship's eyes never left mine for a moment, and I quickly realized that hers was a face not accustomed to smiling.

"Follow me," she said eventually. "I'll introduce you to our evacuees."

The upstairs, downstairs divide might have been dying out among the aristocratic families of England, but here at Granville House, Lady Francesca Smythe-Villiers was keeping the tradition going.

"This door," she said, pointing to an old oak door at the end of a passageway, "leads to his lordship's quarters and mine. You are permitted to breakfast with us, but lunch, tea, and supper are to be taken with your charges in your quarters. You and the evacuees are not permitted in that part of the house. His lordship needs peace and quiet."

Her hard stare didn't invite any further questioning on the matter.

Our quarters turned out to be quite grand. A huge old bedroom, with the most glorious views over the surrounding countryside, had been turned into a day nursery. A coal fire burned merrily in the grate, and toys were scattered about the place. Two separate bedrooms had been allocated to the evacuees—one for the boys and one for the girls—and my small bedroom led off the same passageway.

My evacuees were perfectly lovely, charming little people, though I quickly realized, by the hushed silence that fell over the room when her ladyship strode in, that they were just as much in awe of the lady of the manor as I was.

There were five of the poor little souls, separated from their mothers and fathers. This bunch weren't from the poor East End but from other areas of bomb-hit London and weren't half as robust as the Bethnal Greenies.

"Are you having a wonderful time?" I asked the eldest boy, who seemed to have made himself unofficial leader.

I made sure to crouch down so I was at his eye level.

Throughout my entire career I have always made sure to get down to a child's level. How on earth can you communicate with a child if you are looking down on him, much less expect him to like and trust you? Children cannot get up to your level, so you have to go down to theirs, try and understand how the world looks through their eyes.

Once I was at the same height as he, I saw him relax and drop his guard.

"Yes, nurse, we are," he said with a smile.

Her ladyship hovered nearby, watching us with those steely eyes of hers.

John was the ringleader and the eldest at five; the other four ranged between two and five.

"It's great here," he told me. "There's so much to do. We've climbed trees and there's a place where you can pick strawberries and eat them straight off the bush."

"Really, how wonderful," I said. "You must show me where."

"Oh, we will," piped up a shy little girl behind John. "You know they have something called spring here in the country—they do, they have it once a year."

Her blue eyes shone with such sincerity.

It would have been so easy to laugh at the little girl's innocent remark, but I would have lost her trust forever so I kept my face as straight as a die.

"Well, that is just marvelous. I can't wait to explore."

After that, her ladyship nodded curtly, then left. The air in the nursery lightened just a little.

I stared at these sweet little souls and found myself marveling at their spirit. They had been taken from their families to live in a strange place where they knew no one. If they could find the best in the situation, then so could I.

I jolly well wouldn't let the imposing Lady Smythe-Villiers intimidate me.

The nursery was scattered with many of the popular toys of the day, little metal soldiers, not to mention a whole trove of books.

Later, in the evening, as I helped the children get undressed and into bed, I felt so sad. Each evacuee had a small case, in which they had heartbreakingly little. Each of the girls had just one vest, one pair of underpants, one bodice, one petticoat, one skirt, two pairs of stockings, a handkerchief, and a cardigan. The boys had even less: a vest, one pair of underpants, a shirt, one pullover or one jersey, one pair of trousers, two pairs of socks and a handkerchief. Apart from a comb, some soap, plimsolls, and a toothbrush, that was all their worldly possessions.

They had probably arrived bewildered and scared, and been promptly lined up in the village hall, where no doubt her ladyship would have had first pick, before deciding who was to be billeted with whom. Each billeter was paid ten shillings and sixpence for the first evacuee, and an additional eight shillings and sixpence for each extra one.

Having now met her ladyship properly, I could see how many of the local villagers would have found it hard to refuse her, particularly as it was her ladyship's houses they were living in.

Over the coming weeks I quickly came to see that her ladyship was not particularly popular in the village. My goodness, she was dictatorial. What her ladyship said, went.

There was nothing that woman didn't have a hand in. She'd moved her husband's valet from his cottage at the drop of a hat and was prone to move people around the village on a whim. No one dared stand up to her. If she turned up on your doorstep with a command to move cottages or take on another couple of evacuees, you jolly well did!

Was it all a power game to her? To know that she could uproot families at the flick of her wrist? Hard to know, but she didn't make it easy to warm to her, that's for certain.

Even her own husband, Lord Smythe-Villiers, seemed a little in awe of her. For three days a week he may have held sway over the House of Commons, but in his home it was his wife who ruled the roost.

I used to love my breakfasts with his lordship.

Every morning I took my seat at the table next to him.

"Morning, Nurse Brenda," he'd say. Well into his sixties, he had a gentle, soft voice, and seemed tiny beside his tall wife.

"Morning, your lordship," I'd reply, beaming back at him.

Lord Smythe-Villiers was as English as a cream tea. He was descended from distinguished naval captains.

Rumor had it he was also much involved in the antiaircraft defense of London. Not that I ever dared ask him about that over breakfast. Our conversation never went beyond small talk, but I loved to sit beside him in companionable silence.

Every now and again he'd pick up a dish and hand it to me. "Don't forget your Bemax, Nurse Brenda," he'd say. "It'll keep you healthy."

Bemax was a wheat germ cereal that you sprinkled onto your porridge as a health supplement.

His lordship loved Bemax. In fact, I rather think he thought liberal sprinklings of it on our morning porridge would be sufficient to win the war.

I watched in fascination as, after breakfast, Mr. Webb brought in a freshly ironed copy of *The Times*.

After his lordship finished his paper and coffee, Mr. Worboys brought the Daimler round to the front and drove his lordship to the station, where the stationmaster was waiting to usher him into a first-class carriage. It was another world.

After his lordship had left, a stream of dailies came in from the village, including Pat Worboys, the chauffeur's wife. These ladies were exempt from conscription, either because they were married or because of their age. Instead, they did no end of tasks for her ladyship, from cooking and scrubbing to washing all our clothes and linens.

Her ladyship treated these women as servants, which of course to her they were, but I always made an extra special effort to be friendly to them. I didn't want them thinking I shared her ladyship's airs and graces. We were all equal as far as I was concerned.

The wonderful side effect of having so much help was that I could spend more time with the children, and I was less tired out. How joyful to be a nanny who didn't have to spend her days and nights with her hands plunged deep into buckets of soapy suds or tackling endless mountains of ironing. I was free from the drudgery of nursery housework. It was blissful.

Little Cranford was a veritable fairyland of sunshine and fresh air. During the day we had the most glorious time. John showed me where the wild strawberries grew. As we sat and feasted on them, I'd tell stories or we'd sing songs. Sometimes we tramped through the fields for hours singing or playing It. When apples were in season, we picked them straight from the trees to give to Cook to make delicious apple pies with. Other times we paddled in the streams, picked bluebells, and collected frog spawn. The countryside was beyond beautiful and those spring days seemed endless. Away from the oppressive gaze of her ladyship we could roam free and be whoever we wanted to be.

It took me right back to the roughs and my glorious childhood with my brothers.

Our days were filled with fun, but of course I made sure to instruct my charges, too. It was vital that despite the horrors unfolding in the wider world, precisely *because* of those horrors, we maintain the virtues I had been instructed in throughout my childhood and at the Norland.

Once, I caught John eating his food with his hands.

"We don't eat with our hands here, John," I chastised. "That is what a knife and fork are for."

If I ever caught any of the children looking sloppy, they were quickly reproached. "Pull yourself together and pull up your socks," I'd insist.

We always made sure our hands were washed before we ate, no elbows on the table; you ate as much as you could of what was on your plate; never spoke with your mouth full; inquired politely whether you may be excused from the table after eating; and always made sure to say please and thank you.

I was adamant that certain basic rules be followed: never poke out your tongue, bite your nails or clean them in public; never scratch your head; and avoid all other repulsive habits including spitting, cursing, farting, belching, or using vulgar language.

Good manners had been drummed into me growing up, and so as far as I was concerned, my charges should be brought up with the same respect for etiquette. I firmly believe that if you show respect to others, they in turn will show you respect. That includes listening without interrupting to someone who is talking and looking people in the face and smiling when you meet them. It never hurts to try and remember people's names when first introduced and to use their names when talking to them. It's the little things in life that count, and kindness costs nothing. Manners are part of our national heritage and should be observed keenly. All this might make me sound like the most terrible disciplinarian, but I so believe that a child is what you make him or her.

Balance is vitally important, too. I know how difficult it is to tread that line. Even when the children had been naughty, I made sure that I didn't spend the day solely telling them off, or it would have badly crushed their confidence. I always made sure to treat John and his little friends to plenty of encouragement, praise, kisses, and cuddles, especially at bedtime. Children thrive on affection and can never have too much love. Her ladyship was most undemonstrative, so someone had to make sure their emotional needs were being met.

I wondered what her ladyship had been like with her own children. She had three of them, all grown-up and living away from home and all with terribly grand and important jobs in London. Did they ever get cuddles and kisses when they were young?

Who knew, but under my care I didn't want my evacuees to know a minute's loneliness or fear.

That's why the time of week I always relished most was bath time, always guaranteed to cheer up even the loneliest of children.

Friday night was the allocated time. The children were only bathed once a week and the hour after tea on a Friday was hotly anticipated.

Once a week may not sound much to you, but back then that was about the average. Everyone had a duty not to use much water; and the wartime ration for a bath was just three inches of water once a week.

Hot buttered crumpets were wolfed down as I fetched up pails of warm water from the kitchen.

Mrs. Worboys came in to help and together we dragged the huge tin bath in front of the coal fire.

Once the fire was stoked up and roaring and the bath foaming with soapy suds, the fun began.

"Who's up first?" I'd ask. A sea of hands shot into the air.

"Me . . . me . . . me," clamored the evacuees.

In went John first, for a good rubdown. A week's worth of mud and grime floated off as I scrubbed and sang, "This little piggy went to market," grabbing one of John's toes to wash it.

"Look, Nurse Brenda," he said, slathering foam on his chin. "I've grown a beard."

As he poked his tongue through the foam, the rest of the children were quite helpless with giggles.

One by one they were dunked in and then out, in a little cleaning conveyor belt. By the time Mrs. Worboys and I finished, there were five little children all squeaky clean and wrapped in towels.

"Hard to say who's wetter," I said, as I clambered to my feet, rubbing my soapy hands on a sopping wet apron, "us or the children."

Mrs. Worboys, flushed red with steam, laughed. "Right enough, Brenda."

Once all the children were snug in their pajamas and nighties, we huddled round the fire for warmth and I read them the adventures of Rupert the Bear, as my beloved father did all those years before.

One by one, little eyelids, sleepy and toasty warm from the fire, started to droop and close, until the floor was a mass of slumbering little bodies. The children had so much fresh air during the day that no matter how hard they tried, they could never stay up past 8:00 PM.

Together, Mrs. Worboys and I gently carried them to their beds, where the sweet land of nod was waiting.

As I tenderly tucked them in under their eiderdowns, love flooded my heart. These little people were so brave. I never heard them crying for their parents or caught them being really naughty. They just got on with things. Somewhere out there in the dark, their parents were risking their lives for our country and freedom. The children must have missed them desperately. I encouraged them to write to their parents often and tell them about all the fun they were having here at Little Cranford. In those days the phone was only for emergencies, so mail was the only option available to us.

Sadly, my charges' parents never visited—not because they didn't love them. It was just too far to travel from London, too expensive, and they didn't get enough time off.

How I prayed the homes these children had left behind would still be standing when they returned, and more important, that their families would still be intact.

During the war, 130,000 children lost a parent in active service. Goodness only knew how many orphans were being created as they slept soundly in their beds. It broke my heart just to imagine.

At the thought of orphans I remembered Benjy and Peter and made a mental note to request a call home and find out how everyone was. I hoped Peter wasn't too scarred after the stuck foreskin incident and little Benjy was feeling a little more secure after my sudden departure from Appleton.

War makes little folk resilient, and children are nothing if not adaptable. All the same, Benjy had already survived an orphanage, the threat of Nazi invasion, and the Battle of Britain and he was only two. Something made me a little more protective of him than any of my previous charges. He had a heartbreaking fragility about him that plucked at my heartstrings.

The following day, her ladyship allowed me to make one brief phone call home.

I knew I didn't have long, and my words were spilling over themselves as soon as Mother answered. I heard the worry in her voice when she picked up the receiver, but I quickly assured her that I was perfectly fine, just missing them all.

"How is everyone?" I demanded. "Sally and Rita keeping you busy? How's Father? And what news of Benjy and Peter?"

"Slow down, Brenda," said my mother, laughing. "Everyone is very well. We haven't seen Peter and Benjy around recently, mind you."

I didn't like the sound of that. The niggle of worry I had felt when I left them returned, a little stronger.

But Mother was bright and breezy, so I did my best to shrug it off and instead I told her all about my new job, ten to the dozen, before all too soon it was time to go, amid a flurry of my promises to come to visit soon and her urging me to take care.

I sighed as I heard her replace the receiver in its cradle. Hearing my mother's voice made me miss her all the more.

IT WASN'T UNTIL A FEW MONTHS after my arrival at Little Cranford that I was given leave and could travel home by train for a rare weekend off. I couldn't wait to see Mother and Father, not to mention Sally, Rita, Peter, and my beloved Benjy.

Mother welcomed me home with an enormous hug and a steaming mug of tea. Gratefully I sank down on a chair next to the fire. Traveling by public transport during the war was never easy, and one never knew entirely how long one's journey would take. I was cold, hungry, and exhausted.

As I warmed myself by the fire I was brimming over with questions.

"How are Peter and Benjy?" I asked eventually.

My mother's face fell, and suddenly an awkward silence filled the space between us.

"Mother, please just tell me," I urged.

"I heard Iris and Frank gave Benjy up for adoption."

Disbelief, then horror settled over my heart. "They did what?" I gasped.

"I'm sorry," she mumbled. "I know you were fond of Benjy."

I wasn't just fond of him. I loved that little boy dearly. A cry of anguish escaped from my lips and I put down my cup.

How dare they, how dare they do that?

I remembered his bewildered face as I'd left, and the blood in my veins turned to ice. I was filled with a hopeless rage. Why would they do such a thing? It was beyond me.

Just then Mother's face fell.

"What else? Just tell me, Mother," I urged.

"Well, they have adopted another child, so I hear, a little girl. A little white girl," she said.

I couldn't believe they had swapped Benjy for a white child!

"Where has he gone?" I raged.

"No one knows," Mother whispered.

Suddenly, I felt quite crushed by the injustice of it. My poor, poor sweet Benjy. Please don't let him be lying back on a bunk bed in the orphanage.

What was wrong with Iris and Frank? They had that little boy baptized into their family, had promised to love and raise him as their own. They were supposed to be a God-fearing family!

Was the idea of having a child of a different race really so abhorrent? They must have their reasons for doing so—they weren't bad people after all. Who knows what happened after I left and what circumstances conspired to create this situation. It was, after all, hearsay, but it did affect me so deeply.

That little boy needed love. All children just need love, pure and simple. Is that too much to ask? Loving a child, to me, is the most instinctive thing you can do. And if you live in a community, you accept who's there, and you get along with everyone, be they black or white, man or woman.

From that moment a sense of injustice settled in my heart, and even today I don't think it's ever truly left me. I felt what they did so badly, and I wasn't the only one. It broke the friendship between my mother and the Beaumonts.

Today Benjy would be seventy-three. Where is he now? I wonder. I hope he found the happiness and security he so desperately needed.

Benjy wasn't the only one suffering. Mother's evacuee, Rita, the little girl she'd cared for so fastidiously and who now called my mother mummy, had gone.

"Just like that, after two years her mother turned up one evening and said she'd come to collect Rita," said Mother.

She'd barely taken the time to write or visit. It simply made no sense at all.

"I don't know where they've gone or if I shall ever see that little girl again," my mother confided in me. "I miss her terribly."

Not half as much as Rita missed Mother, I'd be willing to bet. I wonder if she remembers her village sanctuary and the place where, for a brief while, she found a family?

Benjy, Rita, and Sally. Abandoned, ignored, and rejected. What messages were we sending to them? How would they grow up to behave?

What was the Norland motto? "Love never faileth." Well, never again, not on my watch.

Nanny's Wisdom

CHIVALRY COSTS NOTHING.

I have talked a little in this chapter of the virtue of good manners, but I also believe chivalrous men to be a dying breed.

The word *chivalry* originates from a group of French knights on horseback who embraced virtues such as courtly love, honor, and courteous behavior.

My father was the ultimate gentleman. He always opened doors for ladies, stood if a lady came into the room, gave up his seat, and walked on the outside (nearest the traffic on the pavement).

These are the old-fashioned ideas that I was brought up on; and they helped make my parents' marriage stronger, I'm sure.

When was the last time a man gave up his seat or opened a door for you? Do your bit to bring it back by insisting your sons show deference to girls.

If you do it when they're young, it will be natural to them later in life. Respect for the opposite sex is the foundation for good manners.

Impeccable manners are something I always insisted on from my charges, and I firmly believe being raised by a chivalrous man helped to instill this in me.

BAKE THE BEST APPLE PIE EVER.

We often picked apples at Little Cranford so Cook could make apple pie. Hers was good, but—and I know I am being biased here—I do believe my recipe is the best one yet. Make this and the smell of baking will have them haring for home. Serve the pie warm with cream or cheddar cheese and watch the kitchen fill up with children.

4½ cups of cooking apples
Pastry for a 9-inch two-crust pie (store-bought and
    ready rolled just as good)
½ cup sugar
¼ cup dark brown sugar
Juice of half a lemon
1 tablespoon flour
1 teaspoon nutmeg
Small teaspoon grated cinnamon
Grated zest of half an orange
Grated zest of half a lemon
6 tablespoons of raisins
2 tablespoons orange juice
2 tablespoons butter

Preheat oven to 400°F.

Peel and core apples and slice thickly. Place apples in a bowl of water with the lemon juice to keep them from browning.

Line a 9-inch pie dish with half the pastry.

Combine the sugars, lemon juice, flour, nutmeg, and cinnamon. Rub a little of this mixture into the pastry base.

Mix the grated orange and lemon zest into remaining sugar mixture.

Cover bottom of pastry with apples. Sprinkle on the raisins and some of the sugar mixture. Add another layer of apples, then more of the sugar mixture. Repeat until pie dish is full.

Sprinkle with orange juice.

Dot with butter.

Place pastry top over the pie, pressing the edges together.

Cut slits in top.

Bake for 35 to 40 minutes, until pastry is golden and crisp and apple mixture bubbling.

$\mathcal{S}$TOLEN $\mathcal{K}$ISSES

LORD AND LADY SMYTHE-VILLIERS, GRANVILLE HOUSE
LITTLE CRANFORD, DEVON, ENGLAND
[1942, AGE TWENTY-ONE]

Diddle, diddle, dumpling, my son John,
Went to bed with his trousers on;
One shoe off, and one shoe on,
Diddle, diddle, dumpling, my son John.

— NURSERY RHYME

Schedule

7:00 AM: Woke children and got them dressed and ready for breakfast.

8:00 AM: Breakfast of bread, jam, and milk in the day nursery. Children to ask to be excused from the table when they have finished their breakfasts.

9:00 AM: Washed hands. Toilet trips. Teeth brushed and faces wiped clean.

10:00 AM: Supervised playtime. There were very few toys, so one had to ensure everyone shared.

10:30 AM: Cleaned day nursery and got children's dirty clothes ready for her ladyship's dailies to collect and wash.

11:00 AM: Gave children drink of milk. Then dressed them in boots, coats, and mittens and took them out for morning walk in the fresh air.

12:30 PM: Back to the house for lunch in the day nursery. Good manners to be observed throughout the meal.

1:30 PM TO 3:00 PM: Quiet time. Rest and sleep for younger children. Quiet play and reading for older children.

3:00 PM: Outside for games of catch and hide-and-seek. Picked apples and blackberries for Cook.

4:00 PM: Tea in day nursery of jam sandwiches, fruit, milk, and pudding.

4:30 PM: Visit from her ladyship.

5:00 PM: If a Friday we dragged up the tin bath and the children were bathed and washed in front of the fire (including behind their ears).

6:00 PM: Read children bedtime story by the fireside.

7:00 PM: Prayers and bedtime.

7:30 PM: If Henry was free, we met. Otherwise I sat quietly in my room and read.

10:00 PM: Retired to bed and lights out.

BY THE TIME I ARRIVED back in Little Cranford my shock had eased a little and I found myself looking forward to seeing John and the rest of the evacuees again and putting into practice my stiffened resolve to love and protect every child on my watch.

How I'd missed my little poppets and the glorious countryside I'd grown to adore. After a wonderful spring and summer in Little Cranford, autumn was brewing and I could smell it in the air.

There is nothing so precious as autumn sunshine, and I could not wait to take my charges out in its beautiful golden, mellow light. To point out the dazzling show of red and gold from the chestnuts, oaks, and maples, falling leaves swirling in the autumn breeze.

My mouth watered at the thought of all those wild hawthorns just waiting to be picked from the bushes, ripe apples, and plump blackberries, so delicious under a cloud of cream.

I smiled as I imagined John charging through a pile of crunchy leaves in his wellies, and countless little cold hands that could be warmed by the nursery fire when we got home after one of our walks. Yes, there was much to look forward to.

The sadness that had settled over my heart since I'd heard the news of Benjy was still there, but I owed it to my evacuees not to live in the past. Children don't live in the past, after all. They are always looking onward, upward, and to the future. A furious row with another child over a toy can be quite forgotten the next day. This attitude is what I adore most about children. It's also how they remain so wonderfully accepting and harbor no traces of bitterness. We should follow their lead in this. If one lives in the past, one can never properly move forward and truly enjoy all that life has to offer.

Mr. Worboys had come to pick me up as before, and was waiting at the station with his trademark grin.

Over these past few months I'd found myself growing fond of his lordship's chauffeur. He was a real gent and a countryman through and through. He was as loyal as the day was long to his lordship, and loyalty is a much-underrated characteristic in my book.

"Hello, Nurse Brenda," he said warmly as I got in the car. "There's a few little people who've missed you, I can tell you. Her ladyship's been busy, too," he added mysteriously.

Oh dear. What had she been up to now? On the drive back to Granville House I gazed out the window and found myself marveling once again at the peace and solitude of the countryside during this time of war. This green and pleasant corner of England was in marked contrast to its bustling cities, which teemed with accents from all corners of the world. By now the war had well and truly gone global.

British soldiers, sailors, and airmen found themselves posted to any far-flung corner of the world. My brother Michael was now serving with the RAF in India, after training in Canada. Christopher, David, and Basil and the rest of the boys from their boarding school had been evacuated to Coniston in the Lake District and, from what I could tell, were having the time of their lives.

Evacuation had done nothing to dampen Basil's sense of mischief at boarding school. Indeed, he had gained a new partner in crime. He had befriended Robin Day, later to become the legendary broadcaster Sir Robin Day.

Concerned that they weren't getting their full rations of Spam, the pair managed to get into the store cupboard and enjoyed many a Spam-based midnight feast. Perhaps a childhood spent with Basil gave Sir Robin the backbone to tackle Margaret Thatcher.

Meanwhile, as our boys went overseas, so our shores were filling up with all manner of nationalities. In London up to fifty different uniforms could be spotted, as soldiers of every creed, color, and nationality pounded the streets and filled the dance halls.

Young Americans who fought in the war endeared themselves to their numerous fans by giving away silk stockings and cigarettes.

Not that there was a whiff of a foreign accent in Little Cranford or any men bearing gifts of silk stockings—just farmers and their sons.

Little did I know it then but as the leaves turned golden on the trees and the fruits ripened ready for harvest, the winds of change were blowing my way, too. A man was about to make an appearance in my life.

Back at Granville House I warmly hugged each of my evacuees.

"I've missed you all, my darlings," I said, crouching down to their level.

Just then I noticed a face I didn't know peering at me. A new evacuee had arrived in my absence.

"Hello, sweetheart," I said, with a big smile. "What's your name?"

The serious-looking girl gazed at me with big solemn eyes and said nothing. Poor mite; she was probably shy.

Just then her ladyship swept into the nursery.

"This is Gretel," she said. "She's a refugee. She will be staying with us for a while. Gretel doesn't speak much English."

So this was what Lady Smythe-Villiers had been up to. I was heartened to see her ladyship's meddling was at least in a good cause.

Gretel and her parents were Jews who had escaped from Germany. She was just one of the estimated ten thousand Jewish children who fled Germany at the outbreak of World War Two to avoid Nazi persecution.

I never could discover any more about them, their story, and how it was they came to be in Little Cranford, but the village was alive with gossip about our refugees.

Over the coming weeks I tried to reach out to Gretel, but she was painfully shy and scared witless.

Soon after she arrived there was a fierce storm. Rain drummed against the windows and lightning split open the skies.

I found Gretel huddled in her bedroom, hugging her knees and sobbing softly to herself.

"Oh, my darling," I cried when I found her. "Come here. Don't be scared. Thunder is only the clouds knocking together."

But she shrank back from my touch, terror and misery flashing in her blue eyes.

Those pale eyes said it all and a million emotions seemed to race through them: pain, bewilderment, fear.

Just what horrors had this little girl seen? How unspeakably awful that this little girl, no older than five, had been forced to flee her home and her friends and all that was familiar in her life and hide out here. She was the human face of this war, the reason we were all fighting and sacrificing so much to save our country from tyranny.

Just then there was a low rumble of thunder and a howl of anguish escaped from Gretel's lips.

"Mama. I want Mama."

"Mama and Papa will come soon," I soothed.

Her ladyship had billeted her parents with some of the locals in the village. I knew it was no business of mine, but it struck me as so odd. Could there really be no room there for her? Her father was an educated man—a professor so I heard—and her ladyship seemed to treat him with a great deal of respect. Maybe they thought it best she be around other children, but Gretel obviously didn't, and she cried day and night for her parents. When they did visit it just upset her further, especially when they left.

"Me go with papa," she would cry.

"You must stay here, Gretel," he would say softly, untangling himself from her embrace.

Gretel's papa seemed a kindly enough man, but like her ladyship he was terribly proper. He must have witnessed unimaginable sights himself, of course, but he seemed adept at keeping his feelings locked inside. I daresay he and his wife were grateful for a safe haven and didn't want to rock the boat, but I did so feel for that little girl.

For hours after their visits she sat in the corner, hugging her teddy, quite alone in her misery. It was little wonder she felt abandoned in this strange country, where lords and ladies lived in one part of the house and children in the other.

Little Gretel had no interest in playing with John and the rest of the evacuees and always hung back, even at mealtimes. Even Friday night bath time, always a time of high excitement among the rest of the giggly gang, didn't raise so much as a flicker of a smile on that sad little face.

How I hated seeing her suffering and fragility.

I racked my brains. There had to be a way to win this little girl over and gain her trust. I had to let her know I was on her side. Just getting down to her level wasn't enough, nor was singing her nursery rhymes or telling her the stories of my youth. The language barrier meant she simply didn't understand them.

"What is the key here?" I puzzled night after night. I was failing my charge, and to me that was simply unthinkable.

What language could I communicate to her in? One day the answer came to me. I suddenly remembered a lovely old nursery rhyme that always made me giggle.

Hey diddle diddle, the cat and the fiddle,
The cow jumped over the moon.
The little dog laughed to see such sport,
And the dish ran away with the spoon.

Fun! That was what was missing from her life.

So the next day, during our morning walk, I instigated a new game.

"Let's all pretend to make animal noises," I announced.

John started first with a marvelous impression of a duck. His quacking soon had everyone in stitches. Then it was my turn.

"I am a lion," I said. I tipped my head back and roared. "Let's all roar."

Soon the fields around Little Cranford were echoing with the sound of roaring lions.

I looked at Gretel.

A funny little sound escaped her lips. A laugh!

I roared again. There it was again. A throaty little giggle that lifted my sprits.

She never fully came out of her shell, but from that day on I think she knew she could trust me. I learned an important lesson from Gretel. Just as important as love, children need fun in their life.

There is all the time in the world to be serious and studious, as they get older, have to find employment, pay bills, and get bogged down in the responsibilities of being an adult, so surely little folk deserve a childhood that's full of fun? It's the single most valuable lesson in my eyes. I have always encouraged children to have a giggle wherever and whenever they can.

Having fun encourages happiness, well-being, and confidence and fosters a wonderful sense of self-esteem. Most of the well-adjusted adults I know today had a childhood ringing with fun.

A mischievous belly laugh and a child's eyes that sparkle with fun light up my heart like nothing else on earth.

Besides having fun my time in the countryside taught me a great many important lessons, not all of them to do with child care.

Country folk respect the land. When you live off it, you have to nurture it and learn to follow its natural ebb and flow. Chickens weren't eaten that much during the war, as their eggs were too important. Likewise the land needed to be treated like an untapped gold mine.

The countryside around Little Cranford was mostly farming land already, but any scraps that hadn't been given over to food production now were. During the war the number of acres of British soil under cultivation rose from twelve million in 1939 to just under eighteen million by the end of the war.

At the beginning of the war, 70 percent of our food was imported; by 1943 that figure was reversed.

Land all over the country had been dug up to provide food.

The Ministry of Food issued posters and they were plastered over the village notice boards: "It's not clever to get more than your fair share."

Here in Little Cranford the villagers operated their own unofficial food swap system. A farmer might swap the landlord of the local pub a rabbit for five eggs, or eggs for some bread. Villagers would eat anything in a pie, mostly rabbit but even squirrel and roadkill.

People rubbed along together nicely in the countryside, and no one starved. In fact, thanks to the fresh air and profusion of local vegetables, I felt better than I ever had.

We all seemed to be obsessed with staying healthy. My evacuees got free orange juice and cod-liver oil, which I administered daily; and his lordship would never sit at the House of Commons without a stomach full of porridge and Bemax.

Suddenly, everyone knew how to cook and stretch and substitute. I still say I have never seen people healthier than in wartime. We didn't overeat and we watched what we put into our mouths. Emergency measures had brought about the very reform that prewar nutritionists had campaigned for. We hardly ate sweets or chocolate or drank alcohol; and we never touched processed food, apart from powdered eggs and milk.

Food production was war work, vital to keep the nation going, yet despite the huge efforts of our farmers on the land, lots of people thought they had it easy and had somehow ducked out of doing their duty.

People judged them without knowing the full picture, always a dangerous combination. It still happens today sadly. People form snap judgments or opinions based on what they've heard or read. Nine times out of ten we never know the full story.

Thanks to the legions of opinion-biased newspapers, Web sites, and media outlets, our views are seldom our own and rarely fully informed. I urge people to always try to see both sides of an argument; that way they may just arrive at a different conclusion.

One lady whom I befriended in the village knew this attitude better than most.

Susan, the village district nurse, was courting a local farmer by the name of Bill. Bill and his father, John, were the tenant farmers of his lord and ladyship. Susan was a lovely woman, real salt of the earth and fiercely proud of her man. I admired her loyalty immensely.

For the most part my evacuees were fit and healthy, but Susan came by once a month to check on them and I warmed to her instantly. She was hardworking, and her faith in the Lord and love for Bill were everything to her. I was most impressed with her medical knowledge and care for people.

One day Susan had a suggestion for me.

"Do you think you can make it out next week?" she asked, when she stopped off on her rounds one morning.

"I could try," I said.

"Good." She gave me a grin. "The village hop is on."

With that she pedaled off and I found myself smiling. The village hop. I was sure it wouldn't be half as grand as the London dance halls, but it was no less thrilling a prospect to me. I loved dancing, lived for it in fact. When I was growing up, Mother took me for dance classes at a function room behind the local pub. It was the highlight of my week. Sadly, we had to stop when Father lost his business.

"I'm sorry, darling," she told me and my brothers and sister. "We simply can't afford it."

I was most aggrieved. "The others don't love it as much as me," I cried.

My protests fell on deaf ears. Mother was the fairest woman I ever knew.

"What I do for one, I have to do for all," she replied, indicating that the matter was now closed. Of course, I was most put-out back then, but that little lesson served me well in life. One has to be fair in all one's dealings.

This lesson lodged in my mind and I have stuck to it religiously throughout my career. One must be fair and consistent, especially when it comes to children, who are always the first to point out an injustice or to sense an irregularity!

Never, ever, be seen to favor one child over another or change the rules halfway along. Otherwise you are brewing up a whole heap of trouble. My mother had six children and loved us all and treated us all equally. If people today did the same with their children, the world would be a fairer and happier place—of that I'm certain.

Still, I did so love to dance, and the thought of dancing at the village hop filled me with excitement.

I don't think I'd had a night out since this blessed war began three years ago. How could I? I'd been too busy looking after my charges. But now that I had so much help from her ladyship's staff, there was much less for me to do of an evening. Yes, a night at the village hop would be most agreeable.

So it was arranged that I would be accompanied to the hop by a local farmhand named Tom.

I'd taken care with my appearance that night, changing out of my Norland uniform and putting on a lovely cotton floral dress. I swapped my flat shoes for a pair with a slight heel and combed my hair out, but that was the extent of my beautification. I was twenty-one and I don't think makeup had ever touched my face.

Many women in those days improvised, as makeup was scarce. Some used beetroot juice as rouge; and in the absence of foundation camomile was mixed with cold cream.

I wouldn't have known what to do with a tube of lipstick even if you'd been able to find me one.

"Best make do with what Mother Nature provided," I said to myself, fluffing up my hair in the mirror.

A small knock at the back door indicated that my date for the evening was here.

Tom was a man of few words, which was just as well as he wasn't the sharpest knife in the tool kit, but he was very sweet, not to mention jolly handsome. He had lovely thick curly hair, dreamy dark eyes you could get lost in, and strong muscular forearms, browned by a summer of harvesting hay in the fields.

Nervously he took off his cap.

"Can I accompany you to the hop, Brenda?" he said, in his thick country accent.

"Yes, please," I said, a little more eagerly than I'd planned.

He held out a hand the size of a small tractor and grinned shyly.

"You wash up real fine, Brenda," he said, his eyes shining with sincerity.

I wasn't sure if this was a compliment, but as we walked to the village I realized Tom didn't have a mean bone in his body. We didn't manage much in the way of conversation, though, so it was a relief to reach the hop.

They may have been jitterbugging up a storm elsewhere, but in these parts it was a little more innocent. Trestle tables with a small selection of sandwiches lined the edges of the village hall, and a makeshift bar was set up in the corner.

A gramophone playing dance music by Henry Hall, Jack Payne, and Bert Ambrose crackled in the corner.

"Can I get you a drink, Brenda?" asked Tom shyly.

Apart from a sip of Mother's sherry at Christmas I'd never really drunk alcohol before. I'd far rather have had a lemonade, but I didn't want to appear unsophisticated. But what to ask for? Beer was a man's drink and wine wasn't really available. Gin and tonic always struck me as a glamorous drink. Iris always used to sip a G & T in the evening.

"I'll have a gin and tonic, please," I replied.

Seconds later Tom was pressing a paper cup containing a little clear, warm liquid into my hand. It was all gin and no tonic. Ice wasn't available either, not that I would have known it needed lots of it to make it drinkable.

I took a big sip and grimaced. The liquid trickled down my throat and a second later I felt like my gullet was on fire.

Goodness gracious.

"Oh, I say," I spluttered.

"Strong, isn't it," said Tom, laughing.

As the fiery sensation in my throat died down, I felt a lovely warm glow in my tummy and soon it had spread right down to the tips of my toes.

"It's rather nice, this," I said, taking another gulp.

"Well . . ." said Tom awkwardly. Suddenly, I realized I was looking at his back retreating across the empty dance floor.

Tom had scuttled off to join all the other farmhands. The room had segregated: all the local women and land girls were standing on one side of the hall and all the men huddled on the other.

I suppressed a giggle. The women far outnumbered the men and for all the world it looked like a human cattle call, with the women eyeing up what hapless, terrified-looking males were left.

No matter, I thought, taking another swig of my drink.

It was really rather good stuff, this gin. Made me feel terribly happy and glowy.

By the time I finished my drink, I was roaring drunk. Even my face was tingling. I giggled as I tried and failed to place a fingertip on the end of my nose. Suddenly, a newfound confidence gripped me.

I had come here to dance and dance I jolly well would.

"S' where's Tom," I slurred to myself.

I started to cross the dance floor, but the tiresome thing kept moving. Weaving my way, I narrowly avoided a collision with a trestle table before planting myself in front of Tom.

"Dance, please," I ordered a stunned-looking Tom.

"You heard the lady," said the man he was chatting to, grinning.

Tom did as ordered, and before long we were spinning round the room together, his strong arms preventing me from falling flat on my face on the floor of the village hall.

Suddenly, a hand gripped Tom's shoulder and I whirled round in surprise.

"Excuse me?" said the man Tom had been chatting to before.

"Henry is the name," he announced confidently as he cut in, his hands encircling my waist. "Now be a good thing and step aside, Tom."

Tom was left standing, his mouth flapping open and shut like a stranded goldfish, as Henry whisked me into his arms.

"You don't want to waste your time with him when you could be dancing with a real man," he whispered to me, and winked.

Well, of all the cheeky . . .

Henry danced with great gusto, his tall body leading the way. All through the song he kept up a stream of constant chatter. I'd barely finished answering one of his questions when he was asking me another. Goodness, he was so interested in my life.

Henry was by no means as good-looking as Tom. He was very ordinary, in fact, with pale eyes unlike the chocolate-brown ones I preferred, but he certainly had a smooth tongue.

"You're a real lady," he whispered in my ear. "I'd never have left you in the corner."

Before long Tom had recovered from the indignity of being left standing and cut back in.

"Excuse me," he muttered grimly, firmly removing Henry's arm from mine.

Back and forth, back and forth I went all night like a Ping-Pong ball, between Tom's and Henry's arms. What a night. I had never felt so in demand.

It could have been the gin or the amorous advances of my competitive farmhands, but by the end of the evening my head was spinning and I had stars in my eyes.

"The last waltz belongs to me," said Henry, issuing me with a dazzling smile.

Succumbing to his slightly forceful charm I allowed my exhausted head to rest on his shoulder and swayed dreamily in his arms.

I'd gone to the hop with Tom, but it was Henry I left with.

As we tottered along the country lanes, the fresh night air sobering me up, I realized my hand was clamped firmly in Henry's.

It may have been a frosty autumn night, so cold and clear our breath hung in the air like smoke, but inside I was toasty warm. The aftereffects of the gin or was something more magical weaving its spell on me?

Soon we reached Granville House and on the porch we turned to face each other.

"I knew you'd come home with me," Henry said softly, a touch arrogantly.

"Oh yes?" I laughed. "And what made you so sure of that?"

"Because Tom and I had a bet on who would see you home, and I never lose a bet, Brenda Ashford."

"Good night, Henry," I said, smiling.

It was pitch-black outside, but as I turned to close the door I saw his satisfied grin. He looked like the cat that got the cream.

As I flopped into bed, my head was spinning from the events of the evening. Poor Tom. He was such a lovely chap and I hadn't meant to abandon him, but there was just something about Henry. Sure, he was cocky, but I found his arrogance endearing in a strange way. He'd also been the perfect gentleman. He delivered me home safe and sound and hadn't even tried to kiss me, though if he'd tried I probably would have found it hard to say no.

The next morning, over breakfast with his lordship, I grinned like the Cheshire cat. Even my Bemax didn't taste quite as bad. And when I took my charges out for their morning walk, I felt as if I were floating on air. Was this what it felt like to be in love? It was probably too soon to say, but one thing was for sure: Henry had left a big impression on me.

I felt like I'd gained entry to an exclusive club. Romance had finally come into my life and now I had men actually fighting over me. What fun!

Mr. Worboys was outside the stable block, polishing his lordship's Daimler, and chuckled when he saw me.

"I daresay someone had a good time at the hop last night," he said.

"I wouldn't like to say, Mr. Worboys," I said, but I couldn't hide the smile on my face.

That euphoric feeling lasted all day. Even her ladyship coming into the nursery to inspect the children didn't disperse my cloud of joy.

Henry had promised to take me out again and he made good on his promise. He turned up the very next day, clutching a bunch of wildflowers he'd picked.

I was playing with the children by the stable block when he arrived. I could tell by the way he strutted up the path like he owned the place and casually placed one foot up on the upturned bucket Mr. Worboys had been using to wash the Daimler with earlier that he'd lost none of his confident swagger.

Dressed in his casual farming gear and smelling faintly of manure did little to diminish his appeal in my eyes.

I felt my heart start to race a little.

"You look lovely in your uniform, Brenda," he said with a smile, looking me up and down.

I blushed furiously as the children stopped the game they were playing and looked at the more interesting new one being played out before them.

"How do you fancy being taken out for tea by me on your next half day off?" he asked. "They do a mean cream tea in the next village."

It wasn't much of a first date by today's standards, I'll wager, but to an impressionable twenty-one-year-old back in 1942, it was better than an invitation to the Ritz.

"Oh, I'd love to," I gushed.

"Good, I'll pick you up around three, then. Be ready."

And then he was gone. All the evacuees stared curiously after this cocky young man as he bounded down the drive, humming to himself.

"You've got a funny look on your face, Nurse Brenda," John said finally.

"Have I?" I murmured.

I counted down the days, hours, and minutes to our date, and on the day agonized over what to wear.

Mrs. Worboys found me on the afternoon, wailing to myself in the bedroom.

"Whatever is wrong, Brenda, dear?" she asked.

"It's my date with Henry. He's taking me for tea in the next village, but I have nothing to wear," I cried in despair. "Nothing."

I didn't own any of the silk stockings that some of the lucky girls in the cities were given by GIs, nor makeup or jewelry.

Her face flickered with concern.

"A date with Henry the farmhand?" She frowned. "You will be careful, won't you?"

But I wasn't listening. I was too busy trying to put on my only pair of nylon stockings without laddering them. By the time I was ready in a pretty red dress, I felt quite the catch.

Henry whistled when he came to collect me. "Brenda, you look beautiful," he said.

Then we were off, whizzing through the countryside on the local bus.

When you're having so much fun, an hour can feel like a minute.

It was nothing fancy. Just a scone, jam, and a cup of tea, but by the end my head was whirling and my mind was racing. Henry had such a way with words and made me feel like the most interesting person alive.

He had big ambitions for his father's farm and wanted to make something of himself.

"I'd love my own family you know, Brenda," he said, holding my hand over the table. "I'd like to fill that farmhouse with children."

His eyes shone with sincerity as he stared right at me.

It was all too much, just too much. Unspeakable joy flooded through me. Little Cranford was the best place to be in the whole world right now. I felt my heart would burst with happiness.

We hopped on the bus and held hands all the way home to Little Cranford.

Outside Granville House we paused.

"Well . . ." I said, shifting nervously.

"Well . . ." Henry smiled, his eyes twinkling mischievously. "Sorry it

wasn't dinner. When the war's over I'll take you out to a proper fancy restaurant."

Suddenly, he edged closer and I felt a hot flush snake up my chest.

"How does the old proverb go? Enough is as good as a feast," I blustered. "I . . ."

But then I found I couldn't speak. Henry's lips were on mine, his hands
tenderly clutching my face.

Oh my . . .

I kept my eyes squeezed shut the whole while, for fear that if I opened
them I might somehow break this magic spell. Henry tasted of cherry jam
and smelled of autumn leaves. Never was a kiss so sweet.

As we separated, I was aware of lots of little faces watching me from
the upstairs nursery window. Noses were pressed excitedly to the glass. I
smiled to myself. Little folk love it when they spot adults getting up to
what they consider "naughty business." Then another thought occurred to
me. Had her ladyship seen us? And if so, what, I wondered, would she make
of it? A little uneasy feeling nagged, but I pushed it to one side. What business was it of hers whom I was seeing?

Henry and I parted with more promises to meet up soon, and I floated
inside and up to my room in a delicious haze. So this was what love felt like?
This was what all the fuss was about? It was a revelation.

By coincidence my walk with the children the next morning took us by
way of Henry's father's farm, and there was Henry, working in the fields.

I stood and watched admiringly as he stacked hay bales onto the back
of a tractor and trailer. They must have weighed a ton, but he tossed them
about as if they were as light as baby lambs.

His face broke out like a sunbeam when he saw me.

"Think you can sneak out later?" he asked, leaning over the wooden
fence that separated us.

I felt the energy pulse between us and I couldn't help but giggle.

Her ladyship might not approve, but I'd had it with her interfering
ways; and for the first time since I'd clung to the side of a fire escape at
boarding school, my sense of adventure kicked in.

Now was my shot at romance! Why should the girls back in Appleton
have all the fun? Suddenly, I yearned for a life outside the nursery.

Before I had a chance to change my mind, I opened my mouth.

"Yes," I whispered impetuously. "But where?"

There was nowhere to go. I could hardly sneak him in the house under her ladyship's nose, that would never do, but we couldn't stay outside either. The nights were drawing in and it was perishing cold and dark in the fields after sundown.

"We'll think of something," he said, removing a stray hair from above my eye.

As his hand brushed my face I felt a tingle run the length of my spine.

"Till later then," he said, grinning.

On the way home I puzzled over my new dilemma. I wanted to see Henry again desperately, but how? The countryside in wartime England wasn't exactly set up for romantic liaisons, and I really didn't fancy puckering up in a soggy ditch.

I was still deep in thought by the time we returned to Granville House. Mr. Worboys gave me a cheery wave when he saw me.

"What's up with you, Nurse Brenda?" he asked. "You look as if you have the cares of the world on your shoulders."

I hesitated.

"I've met someone," I said. "His name is—"

"Henry," he interrupted. "I knows that."

You couldn't really keep anything secret in the countryside.

"Problem is, Mr. Worboys, we've nowhere to meet." I sighed. "I couldn't bear the thought of only seeing him on my half day off. Besides, by the time we've got anywhere it's time to come home again."

Mr. Worboys stared at me and scratched his head. He paused, as if he were about to say something he shouldn't.

"Well then, Nurse Brenda," he said eventually. "Her ladyship'll string me up if she hears this, so keep it under your hat like, but it is unlucky that you young folk have nowhere to meet.

"Tonight I'll leave his lordship's Daimler unlocked and you can meet in there. Our secret, all right?"

And with that, his lovely craggy face broke out into an enormous grin.

I could have kissed him there and then. "Oh, thank you," I said. "Thank you, thank you."

"It's all right, Nurse Brenda." He chuckled. "I can see as how you're keen on him."

Later, when my charges were safely tucked up in their beds, there was a small knock on the back door. I scurried downstairs.

Henry was waiting, with a twinkle in his eye.

"His lordship's car," I hissed. "Follow me."

Click. The door was unlocked, just as promised.

Once inside, I suddenly felt a bit scared and I realized my heart was pounding. The car smelled of leather and grown-ups. This was his lordship's car. What if her ladyship were to throw open the garage door? She'd be in a fearful rage if she knew we were in here.

"Relax," said Henry confidently, making himself comfy on the backseat. "She'll never come in here."

The leather seat creaked as he drew me close and we started to kiss in the dark. My legs began to tremble. Suddenly, I felt terribly out of my depth. I hoped Henry wouldn't get the wrong impression from our tryst in his lordship's motor. I was a virgin and I intended to stay that way for the time being.

A live-for-the-moment attitude might have seized the rest of Britain—with people having illicit affairs left, right, and center—but I had no intention of giving my virginity up on the backseat of a Daimler.

I didn't know exactly how women got pregnant, but I knew the consequences of it. This may sound highly unlikely in 2013, but it really is impossible to overstate how stunningly innocent and naive I was in 1942. I'd been taught no sex education at school; my mother had never told me anything; and I was surrounded by children as innocent and naive as I. Sex was indeed something of a mystery to me, but I feared the implications of it no end.

To have a baby out of wedlock would have caused a major scandal.

Fortunately, Henry was the perfect gentleman and didn't try anything. But we kissed that evening, oh how we kissed. It felt like hours. We smooched for so long I thought my lips might drop off. He kissed me with such tenderness I could have stayed in his arms all night. Nowhere felt more comfortable, safe, or warm.

"I'm falling in love with you, Brenda Ashford," he breathed in my ear.

Love and longing stirred deep inside me. I felt like a heroine in a Hollywood film.

"I . . . I . . ."

Just then a shrill whistle pierced the night air outside the garage doors.

"Mr. Worboys," I gasped, springing out of Henry's arms. "He said he'd whistle at half past ten."

Feeling like Cinderella, I kissed Henry one last time and leaped out of the car.

The next morning I could barely wipe the smile off my face. My poor lips felt bruised but my heart was alive. My joy must have been infectious as the children were as giddy as spring lambs. We played catch and ball games and even Gretel seemed to come out of her shell and joined in.

While I played childish games in the sunshine, I was blissfully unaware that my handsome farmhand was playing his own darker and more danger-ous game. But ignorance, as they say, is bliss, and over the next six months the love between Henry and I deepened.

He played me like a fiddle and I fell for him hook, line, and sinker.

I wasn't the only one taken in. Mr. Worboys, bless him, left the car unlocked for us most nights and I used every spare second to meet Henry down in the fields or on my half Sundays off. There was no Baptist church around for miles, so I didn't even have to feel guilty about spending that time with my suitor.

When you are in love life seems to come alive in a wonderful way, colors seem brighter, smells more vivid, the landscape more beautiful. The year 1942 would go down in history: the year I fell in love for the first time.

Henry respected me as well as loved me, I could tell. He never put a scrap of pressure on me in the back of the Daimler and he even invited me to his farm for Sunday afternoon tea with his parents.

Sunday afternoon tea was a big deal for farming folk. They'd got their best china out and even laid the table with a clean white tablecloth. Plates groaned with homemade drop scones and thick slabs of bread with beef dripping. Tea was freshly brewed and poured from an enormous brown pot. The kitchen was flooded with warmth, light, and the smell of baking.

Conversation mainly centered around the farm and when this "old" war would come to an end.

But I didn't care. Henry and I exchanged secret smiles over the scones. He was including me in his family, which could only mean one thing.

My goodness, I was nervous. So scared in fact I'm sure my teacup rat-tled every time I picked it up. My tummy was churning, too, so I could barely eat a nibble of my cake. His parents were lovely people though, and when we left we made promises to meet again soon.

In turn, on my next weekend off, I took Henry home.

My parents had moved by now from Bookham to north of the Thames to St. Albans in Hertfordshire.

Mother was in a frenzy of excitement.

"Brenda's bringing home a gentleman to meet the family." She'd smiled when I told her.

But when Henry met her and Father, a funny thing happened.

They never said as much, as they are far too polite, but I could tell they didn't like him. Just subtle little things that Henry would never have picked up on, but something told me they didn't warm to him.

When Henry talked confidently of his ambitions for the future, Father's smile never quite reached his eyes and Mother was polite, too polite.

I ignored their cool reserve though; they would warm to him eventually. Henry was the best thing since sliced bread as far as I was concerned.

Back in Little Cranford, news of our romance had spread on the bush telegraph.

I was just folding the children's clothes away in their chest of drawers one morning when Mrs. Worboys came in. I could tell by the way her mouth was twitching that she had something to say.

"I've been speaking to her ladyship, Brenda," she began.

My heart sank.

"S-she, that is to say, we," she stuttered. "We're worried about you. You *are* being, well, careful aren't you? Her ladyship doesn't really approve of your relationship."

I bristled. How dare she? She wasn't to know that Henry and I hadn't consummated our relationship and I was as pure as the driven snow, but in any case, what business of hers was it who I was seeing or what I was doing? I wasn't her servant.

"You both must think me very naive," I snapped. "Of course I am careful."

"I'm sure, Brenda," she soothed. "It's just that you know nothing of life."

She was right, but I wasn't about to tell her that when it came to sex and birth control, I did indeed know nothing. As I said, we didn't learn about the birds and the bees at school and Mother taught me virtually nothing. The only time I remember her broaching the subject of sex was when she sat me down to tell me that she used to douche with hot water as a contraceptive. The pill wouldn't be available for nearly another twenty years, so back then, that was all that was really available to her.

But even during this conversation, I still didn't really manage to understand anything about what really went on. I had a vague sense that babies came about as the result of some sort of physical intimacy, and I knew that such a thing was permissible only within marriage—I had, after all, met plenty of illegitimate babies and their poor mothers. But I was extremely innocent. I supposed her ladyship had guessed as much.

After that the tension in the nursery grew.

I made a point of being as professional as they come, I was a Norland nurse, after all; but when she came into the room, the air between us was icy and the conversation stilted. I suppose she must have resented her lack of control over me. I wasn't one of her minions she could order about at will.

But despite the oppressive influence of her ladyship, this was an exciting time. I adored my charges, I was in love, and Britain was an exciting place to be.

In May 1943 I took stock of my life. I had been in Little Cranford for fourteen months now and I was starting to get itchy feet. I loved my charges and Henry dearly, but life under the scrutiny of her ladyship was exhausting. I didn't want to end up like poor old Mr. Webb, a whipping boy for an elderly aristocrat who couldn't let the ways of the old world go.

The evacuees were settled and happy now. My work here was done. There were children who needed me more elsewhere and adventures just waiting to be had.

I confided in Henry on my next half day off.

"You must go," he urged. "We will be together when this war has ended." He smiled and pulled me into his arms.

As I nestled into his jumper I felt a pang of regret. He was so caring, so thoughtful. Was I doing the right thing?

"Besides," he added, "you can come back and visit, can't you."

He was right. It wasn't the end of us. Just me and her ladyship.

Once I'd made the decision, I felt euphoric. I told her ladyship at the earliest opportunity in her quarters.

"I very much appreciate the opportunity, but it is time for me to move on," I said as politely as I could. "I've heard a day nursery near my parents' house needs help, so I shall be joining them."

Her slate-gray eyes narrowed as she stared at me long and hard without moving a muscle.

Outside I could hear the dailies scurrying about, polishing the floors and bagging up the laundry. They lived in fear of a dressing-down from her and doubtless would be moving as fast as they could in case she opened the door.

Well, you can't intimidate me now. I'm not your servant.

"As you will, Nurse Ashford," she said finally.

Walking out of her room I felt like a weight had been lifted from my shoulders.

I was free.

It was sad saying good-bye to my charges and dear old Mr. Worboys, but as ever I resolved to look forward not back.

"Place won't be the same without you," Mr. Worboys said with a smile as he drove me to the station one last time. "No more assignations in the back of the Daimler. Right boring it'll be," he grumbled. "The little 'un's will miss you, too."

"Thank you," I said, planting a gentle kiss on his cheek. "I'll never forget your kindness."

Back at home I missed Henry desperately and, as I had a little break before starting at my next job, I returned by train shortly after to see him.

We had arranged that I would stay with Susan in her spare room, but Henry would collect me from the station.

I simply could not wait to see him. We could hold hands in the street and not feel like we were having to sneak about behind her ladyship's back.

Alighting from the train I nervously played with my hair as I waited for Henry's old farm truck to come rattling round the corner.

I smiled as I imagined the sweet kiss he would give me and his cocksure smile. Perhaps we could even go to the village hop again if it were on.

I pulled my coat around me and checked my watch. Strange. He was supposed to be here twenty minutes ago. He must have been caught up with some business on the farm. No matter. I'd walk to Susan's. The fresh air would do me good.

By the time I reached her cottage, my cheeks must have been glowing as red as an apple.

"Let me in, then," I puffed, as Susan opened the door. "It's perishing out here and I've had to walk from the station. Henry must have been delayed."

As soon as I saw her face, I knew something was wrong. She was wearing that same angst-ridden expression Mother had the day she told me little Benjy had been given away for adoption.

Oh no. Please not more bad news.

"Sit down, Brenda," she said softly, pulling up a chair by the fire.

Without taking off my coat I sat down heavily and pulled it round me as if for protection.

"Is he all right?" I blurted. "Has he been called up? Has something happened?"

"He's fine, Brenda," she said. "It's nothing like that."

Poor Susan. Her gentle, soft face was stricken. Whatever the news was, she didn't want to be the one to break it.

"It's just that, well, there's no easy way to say this. He's been cheating on you."

I froze.

"What do you mean?" I gasped.

"He's been seeing a girl two villages along," she said sadly. "I'm so sorry, Brenda. I know how you felt for him."

"W-what—the whole eight months?" I squeaked.

She nodded, as if she wanted the floor to open up and swallow her.

I felt as if I were drowning.

"No," I cried. "But he can't have been."

The betrayal hit me like a punch in the chest. I thought it couldn't get worse but then . . .

"Apparently this girl found out about you and when she heard he'd been to visit your parents, she threatened to sue him for breach of promise. It's the talk of the village."

I felt like I was going to throw up. He was promised to someone else all along. All the while we were courting, he was stringing us both along.

What a silly, silly fool I'd been.

I thought of this other girl. I had no idea he was engaged to someone else, someone who probably didn't even live that far from Little Cranford. Poor girl. She had been saving herself for heartless Henry, just like me.

Her threat to sue him for breach of promise sheds a little light on the repressed times we were living in. In the cities people may have been indulging in all sorts of wild behavior, but here in the country, saving oneself for the right man meant everything.

Henry's promise to marry this lady could be considered a legally binding contract; and he obviously took her threat to sue him seriously, given that he returned to her when she made it. Perhaps she had already given up her virginity to him and, horrified to find out about me, was concerned with the damage to her reputation and loss of status.

Changing social mores have all but led to the collapse of this kind of action, but back then in Little Cranford, breach of promise was taken seriously. Henry had been playing a dangerous game.

I slumped back in my chair, utterly defeated.

For the first time in months I saw what everyone else had seen. Mrs. Worboys, her ladyship, my own parents. They all saw through him. They knew his cocky attitude was a front for his breathtaking deceit.

He was nothing but a scoundrel.

"Oh I'm such a fool," I wept. "I was prepared to give it all up for him."

Susan placed her arms around me and stroked my hair. "No, you're not," she insisted. "You loved him, he betrayed you, and he fooled us all, Brenda."

But her kind words did nothing to ease my agony. I was heartbroken.

"I thought he was the cat's whiskers," I sobbed.

My first brush with romance had been a disaster.

As I sat in Susan's kitchen, wallowing in misery, the chairman of the Norland was sending out a newsletter to celebrate the institute's fiftieth anniversary.

"In a world wholly different from that in which Mrs. Walter Ward was inspired to found the institute, we can celebrate its fiftieth anniversary confident that it, at least, is the same," wrote Hester Laird Wilson.

But the world around me was no longer the same. Far from it; my heart had been broken, a little piece of my soul bruised forever.

Lying in Susan's spare bed that night I stared into the dark and wondered what would become of me. If not a farmer's wife, then what? It seemed that the nursery was my calling, after all. I felt so cruelly let down by love that I didn't see how I could ever risk it again.

Little did I know it, but the peace and quiet of the nursery as I knew it was to be shattered forever. Coming my way was a riot of noise, dirt, disease, illegitimate babies, adultery, deserters, and scandal all set against a backdrop of some of the most lethal warfare the country had ever seen.

Oh yes. Life was about to get interesting.

TESTIMONIAL

Nurse Brenda Ashford has been here since March 9, 1942. She has been nurse in charge of a small residential war nursery in our house consisting of evacuated children and one refugee child, ages about two years to five years. The numbers have varied from two to five children and for about the last six months, five children. Some help given. She is essentially a well brought up girl from a good home who desires to do what is true and right and to work conscientiously. She has had very good experience here. She is active, industrious, and capable. She takes an interest in the children's health and is watchful to notice if they are not well. She is helpful and obliging and does not mind what she does. She much likes children, especially I think, the tiny ones. She leaves entirely of her own wish, as she wants to work in a day nursery near her own home. Nurse Brenda has got on very well indeed with household staff and has been pleasant with them.

—LADY SMYTHE-VILLIERS

Nanny's Wisdom

Little Gretel was a child for the most part alone in her misery, until I found a way to unlock her private world by having fun. All children adore fun, even the painfully shy, lonely, and reserved ones. You don't need to have money to enjoy life. So many parents nowadays equate fun with spending a fortune. They don't need to take their children on all-inclusive vacations or to the cinema/bowling alley/shopping mall in order for them to enjoy themselves. Of course it's great, if you can afford that; but if not, a child will have just as much fun doing any of the following: damming streams, having piggyback races, searching for bugs, racing snails, playing hide-and-seek in a wood, making a mud pie, skimming stones, climbing a tree, hunting for frog spawn, picking fruit straight from a bush, playing conkers, running through leaves, burying an adult in the snow or sand, jumping in muddy puddles, rolling down a hill, searching for monsters, playing soccer in a field, collecting leaves and flowers, paddling in streams with a net, or dancing in the rain. Best of all? They are all absolutely free. Father took us to a smart Italian restaurant called Frascati once a year as a treat and I always enjoyed it, but to be honest, I enjoyed it much more when we all played make-believe games in the fresh air.

THE WAY TO A MAN'S HEART . . .

I have never had much luck with the opposite sex, but they say the way to a man's heart is through his stomach. From my experience, all men love puddings, the stickier and sweeter the better. Try this recipe for spotted dick. Serve steaming hot and smothered in warm custard and watch him melt. Serves four to six people.

¼ cup butter
2¼ cups all-purpose flour
3 teaspoons baking powder
5 ounces shredded suet
7 tablespoons caster sugar
¾ cup dried currants
Finely grated zest and juice of 2 lemons
⅓ cup milk
⅓ cup heavy cream
Custard or clotted cream, to serve

Soften half the butter and use to grease a 1¼-quart pudding basin.

Combine the flour, baking powder, suet, sugar, and currants in a large bowl. Mix well. Melt the remaining butter and stir into the flour mixture.

Stir in the lemon zest and juice.

In a separate bowl, combine the milk and cream. Slowly stir enough into the flour mixture to bring it to a dropping consistency.

Pour the dough into the pudding basin. Cover with a double layer of wax paper, tied in place with string. Place the basin in a steamer basket set over boiling water. Cover and steam for about 1 to 1½ hours until cooked.

CERTIFICATE PAGE.

This is to Certify *that Nurse*

Brenda Ashford

has given satisfaction throughout her

training and in a private post.

Nurse Brenda

now holds the Certificate of the Norland

Institute and becomes a Norland Nurse.

Signed Ruth Whitehead

Principal

Date May 30 1941

WAR NURSERY

REDBOURN DAY NURSERY
REDBOURN, HERTFORDSHIRE, ENGLAND
[1943, AGE TWENTY-TWO]

There was an old woman who lived in a shoe,
She had so many children she didn't know what to do.

—NURSERY RHYME

Schedule

7:45 AM: Arrived at the nursery; lit the fires and opened the blackout curtains.

8:00 AM: Nursery opened and children started to arrive.

8:30 AM: Once all children arrived, all were bathed and changed into nursery overalls.

8:45 AM: Breakfast of full-fat milk, bread, jam, and orange juice.

9:30 AM: Administered dose of cod-liver oil to all children and combed their hair for lice.

10:00 AM: Gave sick children medicine or applied creams for skin conditions.

10:30 AM: Playtime outside for nursery school children and walks out in prams for babies.

11:00 AM: Oversaw boil washing of nappies and dirty clothes and helped where needed with preparation of bottles.

11:30 AM: Walked round the nursery and ensured everyone playing happily.

12:00 PM: Administration duties, ordered food, and managed rations.

12:30 PM: Lunch for all.

1:30 PM: Nap time for younger children and quiet reading for older children.

2:30 PM: More administration.

3:30 PM: Visit from Nurse Trudgett to discuss sick children and funding.

4:00 PM: Issue means-tested invoices and paid nursery bills.

4:30 PM: Teatime.

5:00 PM: Story time.

5:30 PM: Changed children into going home clothes and oversaw home time. Talked to parents and answered questions.

6:00 PM: Nursery officially closed (although there were frequently latecomers). Helped staff to scrub down nursery and tidy up.

6:30 PM: Drew blackout curtains and got bus home.

It was 7:45 on a Monday morning at the Redbourn Day Nursery in Hertfordshire and all was quiet. The sickly sweet smell of cod-liver oil hung in the air, and as I shrugged off my coat it caught me right in the back of my throat.

Working quickly, I bustled round the room, drawing the blackout curtains and throwing open the windows. A stream of spring sunshine flooded in and gratefully I gulped the fresh air. Closing my eyes, I savored the sound of silence. I loved this time of the morning. The nursery was all mine and I could gather my wits about me and brace myself for the onslaught.

There was just time for my daily inspection. Rows and rows of children's pegs lined the wall. Each little peg had a boat or a gollywog emblem. I strode along, making sure that each also had the requisite little white cotton overall that I'd hand stitched, a towel, and a flannel.

Then, humming and smoothing down my Norland uniform, I threw open the door to the kitchen and lit the flame under the huge coal-serviced copper. As it began to groan and creak into life I heard the clanking of bottles outside. I smiled. Martin Webb, the local milkman, had arrived in his old blue Morris van.

Martin and his two boys, Ray and Geoff, were part of the fabric of this community. The Webbs had been serving fresh milk from a seventeen-gallon churn for more than a hundred years, first on a handcart, then by horse and cart, and now by van. The business had been handed down from generation to generation. The Webbs came from hardworking country stock and were typical of the village characters that Redbourn seemed to breed.

Situated between St. Albans and Dunstable, the village used to be a stopping point for horses drawing Royal Mail coaches en route to and from London. It was a sleepy little place where everyone knew everyone else. Even though I'd only been working here for four months, I was already feeling at home in the close-knit community.

The job couldn't have come at a better time for me. I needed a new focus, and the distraction of so many children to lavish my love on was most welcome. There was still a sharp stab of pain in my stomach every time I thought of Henry's betrayal, but I forced myself not to wallow in things. And mostly I simply didn't have time. My day started early, since it took me forty minutes on the bus to get here from where I now lived with Mother, Father, and our remaining evacuee, Sally. And once here, I immersed myself in the tasks at hand.

That life still centered around the common, where chickens and geese roamed. The village cricket team gathered there to while away lazy summer afternoons with the soft thud of leather on willow. Saturdays saw local boys and evacuees pitting their skills against one another in boisterous games of football. Come winter, these same boys would be helpless with laughter as they slid along the icy paths that cut across the open space, often landing in a scrummage of flailing arms and legs.

The common was lined with rows of pretty terraced cottages; and the high street, which was the hub of the community, ran off from one side. The narrow road was lined with businesses that had been in the same families for generations, among them a grocer's, a butcher's, a baker's, and a tailor's. It was just a stone's throw from the nursery, and I could easily wander over to top up provisions. The high street was always full of hustle and bustle and I loved chatting to the village characters.

The smell of the silver-haired baker's freshly baked cottage loaves and sugary doughnuts drifted up the street, competing with the sound of the fruiterer, John, shouting out the quality of his wares.

"Come and getcha lovely pears. Nice an sorft an' juicy," he'd bellow.

His lungs were so powerful, I was sure villagers from neighboring communities could hear him.

Redbourn even had its own resident cobbler's shop, run by a smiley, dumpy man by the name of Arthur. Arthur was as deaf as a doorpost. What he lacked in auditory ability he made up for with superb craftsmanship, and everyone in the village took everything from leather shoes to footballs and horse harnesses to him to restitch.

In the middle of the high street was Bill the blacksmith's forge. His warm workshop seemed to shelter many a man hiding out from the wife, and the sinewy old blacksmith was always ready to trade gossip.

There were pubs, of course. When I walked past the Jolly Gardeners and the Cricketers, they seemed to house many an old boy, permanently nursing a pint of ale with a cigarette clamped between nicotine-stained teeth. Not that I went into these establishments myself. There was never time, and I couldn't bear the smell of beer, either.

Centuries of unchanged tradition had been observed and celebrated by the townspeople, from May Day through to Michaelmas.

The friendliest was always the milkman, though.

"Morning, Brenda," said Martin now, beaming. "Lots of lovely milk and butter for the children today."

He unloaded vast pats of glistening unsalted butter and jugs of full-fat unpasteurized milk, collected just hours earlier straight from Fish Street Farm a few fields away. It wasn't until a few years after the war that legislation was passed to ensure that all milk was pasteurized. Back then, the milk was as fresh as it comes; and it was the milkman's job to collect it, bottle it, deliver it, and wash up the bottles afterward. The milk tasted just heavenly and it had a head of cream on it four inches thick. The poor people of the village used to buy skimmed milk for a penny a pint.

"That'll keep 'em nice and 'ealthy," Martin said with a grin. I was sure he threw in extra for the children, as there always seemed to be so much.

"Wish my evacuee boy would eat better," he said, shaking his head and mopping his brow. "He seems to survive off bread spread with brown sauce. I don't reckon he's ever eaten with a knife and fork before."

Martin and his wife, Lily, had two evacuees billeted with them at their farm, Walter and Billy. Walter was from the East End and Martin was forever telling me how utterly bemused the boy was in his new surroundings. "I don't think he's even seen the moon afore, you know," he whispered one morning. "He seems terrified of it."

I could have stayed trading stories with this lovable old milkman all morning, but there were jobs to be done. Glancing at my watch I realized it was 8:00 AM.

Outside, the babble of voices grew steadily louder . . . and louder . . . until it seemed to reach a fever pitch of noise.

The morning stampede had begun.

Suddenly, the door burst open and a stream of little folk and their mothers, brothers, sisters, or grandparents—whoever happened to be dropping them off—came pouring through in a great tidal wave of human life.

"'Ello, Brenda love, 'ows yerself?" called out one evacuee's mother as she pushed her little son Johnnie through the door. "I fink 'e's got nits again."

Little Johnnie stood scratching his head with filthy fingernails as a steady stream of snot trickled from his nose.

"Go on, yer li'l bleeder," she said, shoving Johnnie through the door. "Ta ra all."

I groaned inwardly. Not again. We'd only just got rid of the last infestation. There wouldn't be a child in the nursery that didn't have them by lunchtime.

A village local, an elderly man in his eighties, dropped off his grandson. The mother was already hard at work on the early shift, assembling war machines at a nearby factory.

"His mother'll collect," he said, giving me a grin. "Just doing my bit."

One by one they streamed in. Bleary-eyed mothers clutching bewildered babies and grubby-faced toddlers, exhausted staff, volunteers, and excitable children.

It was a riot of snot-filled, nit-laden noise and chaos.

We would be flat out for the next ten hours until the nursery closed at 6:00 PM. Breaks would have to be taken whenever and wherever they could. It was all hands to the pump in this place.

I had never in all my life worked anywhere like this day nursery.

Every morning most of the children had to be bathed, dressed in their nursery overalls, and fed breakfast or at least milk—and that was before the day had even begun.

While bathing one child, it would inevitably be necessary to rescue a would-be escapee or fend off another child's curious exploration of someone's face. Some little tyke, still slippery from the soap bubbles, would make a desperate, nude dash for the door.

I'm like the little old lady who lived in a shoe, I'd think, giggling helplessly to myself.

At times it was simply too chaotic and I despaired of the workload. How would we ever make it through to teatime? I'd wonder. But somehow we always did. It was exhausting, though, and my head was always spinning by the time it hit the pillow. But as the weeks whizzed past I realized I didn't care. I was loving every smelly, chaotic second!

It might have come a year or two too late but finally the government had recognized the need for war nurseries to be formed up and down the country.

"If anything good has come of this war, it is the fact that at last the need and the value of day nurseries has been forced upon the nation. A woman cannot be expected to pull her weight in a factory if she is worrying about her children all day," said Lady Reading, chairman of the National Society of Day Nurseries.

She was right: nursery nurses were invaluable as they enabled mothers to be released for war work. Now purpose-built nurseries like ours here in Redbourn were popping up all over the country. They were the forerunners of the ones that are everywhere today, but back then, nurseries were relatively unheard of.

With the agreement of the Ministry of Labor, the wartime day nurseries were funded by the Ministry of Health, which supplied the capital and some of the maintenance costs. Local authorities set up the nurseries and contributed to their running costs through their Maternity and Child Welfare Committees. Ours was brand-new and had been built on the village common, sandwiched between the scout hut and the boys' school.

We had about thirty children divided between the baby room and another larger room for three- to five-year-olds.

The children were a mixture of evacuees and locals. Their mums were all out hard at work, either in Luton at the Vauxhall factory making armaments, Brock's Fireworks factory in Hemel Hempstead, which now made star shells that exploded in the air to illuminate the ground and reveal the position of the enemy, or the Sphinx factory in Dunstable, making parts for Spitfires. An old silk factory in Redbourn was also a big employer of local women. It had long since stopped producing silk and had been closed for years, but now a London tea firm had moved in to escape the blitz and was keeping the locals busy packing tea and coffee.

For mums who had stayed at home to look after their children or perhaps had jobs in service, this must have come as an almighty shock; but despite the long hours they worked I only ever saw happy, cheery faces at the nursery doors. Perhaps they relished the opportunity to have a break from their children and to earn a bit of extra money.

To look after these thirty children there was me in the baby room, a frosty matron by the name of Mrs. Bunce; two lovely, smiley young junior nursemaids in their teens named Beryl and Betty; a nursery school teacher in her thirties called Joy, who ran the three- to five-year-old nursery room; and the cook, an evacuee called Mrs. Ratcliffe.

We also had an elderly lady volunteer from the village who came in and helped out, a kindly soul named Pat, with long silver hair to her waist and a face as wrinkled as a walnut.

We were a mixed bunch—some with years of training under our belts and some with none—but despite this we all rubbed along together marvelously. The more experienced staff helped out the younger untrained girls and we all got along famously, with one exception.

Sometimes when two ladies meet, the dislike can be instantaneous. And so it was with me and the disapproving Mrs. Bunce.

Mrs. Bunce had trained at a rival college to Norland, St. Christopher's, and I rather suspect she took against me because Norland was perceived to be the superior and better known institute. It didn't matter what I did, from bathing the children to washing nappies, she knew a better way.

"I think you'll find, Brenda . . ." became Mrs. Bunce's catchphrase. After dealing with her ladyship at Little Cranford I could handle a village know-it-all, but still, the rivalry between us was bubbling just beneath the surface at all times.

That morning, as the nursery began to throb with life and Betty, Beryl, and the rest of the staff bowled in with a cheery greeting, I realized someone was missing. The officious Mrs. Bunce. She was usually here by 7:30 AM prompt. By 10:00, I started to get an uneasy feeling.

"Anyone seen Mrs. Bunce?" called Joy, poking her head in the baby room. "The weekly food order's got to be made and a fella from the council's coming for some invoices."

"Not a trace of her," I said. "Most mysterious."

Finally, at 10:30, a man from the council came by. I happened to be at the door when he arrived.

"I'm afraid Mrs. Bunce isn't coming back," he said. "No reason. We're appointing you as deputy matron, Brenda, until we can find a replacement. You can start now. Your salary will be fifteen pounds a week."

"B-but I don't want . . ." I stuttered. My voice trailed off as the door slammed behind him and he beat a hasty retreat across the common.

Just like that I found myself promoted.

Oh, crumbs. I hadn't signed up for this responsibility. Running a nursery of this size was like nothing I'd ever done before.

"Congratulations, Nurse Brenda," said the cook, walking up behind me. "You must be chuffed to bits."

But I wasn't chuffed to bits. I was horrified. All I wanted to do was look after my babies, but now I had to run the place.

Whatever happened to the mysterious Mrs. Bunce, I shall never know, but back then there simply wasn't time to dwell on her disappearance. It was sink or swim!

"Pull yourself together, Brenda," I scolded myself. "How hard can it be?"

Over the coming months I began to see *exactly* how hard running a nursery was during a war. A typical day went something like this:

Oversee the bathing and dressing of thirty children.
Prepare and feed breakfast.
Administer cod-liver oil in a storm of protest.
Comb thirty heads for nits.
Check children for lice.
Apply cream for impetigo.
Prepare prams for babies' walks, toddlers' playtime.
Boil wash woollies, nappies, cot sheets, and clothes.
Fill bottles, prepare lunch, serve lunch, clear up.
Get children down for naps, break up fights, clean up.
Order weekly food, manage rations, issue means-tested invoices
    and nursery bills.
Mending, shopping, administration.
Teatime.
Story time.
Play time.
Watch out for doodlebug rockets flying overhead.
Change thirty children into day clothes, oversee home time.
Scrub nursery from top to bottom.
Draw blackout curtains and lock up.

Phew. No wonder the day went by in the blink of an eye. Once I'd been made deputy matron, the months flew by as well. With every passing week I waited for a new matron to turn up and relieve me of my duties, but strangely no one ever showed up. After about six months I began to realize that no one would. I was now the new matron of Redbourn Day Nursery, whether I liked it or not.

It makes me so cross when I think how child care workers' roles in the war are often overlooked. One hears so little of our daily efforts.

Hundreds of thousands of mothers could go to work, safe in the knowledge that their little ones were being cared for. We women workers—land girls in the fields, ladies in factories, or the women driving ambulances or trucks—worked our socks off. Blood, toil, tears, and sweat were given by every single woman from every single class and background.

But while the war raged on around the world a smaller but no less explosive little battle was being played out in the nursery.

Ever since the evacuees, who were mainly from the docks of the East End, had arrived at the village scout hut fresh off the train from St. Pancras, they had made a big impact on the village. Those who didn't come from the docks lived on the Peabody Estates in Shoreditch or Stepney. These people knew a thing or two about community, and after a few scraps to begin with, blended in seamlessly with the locals and enriched village life enormously.

All the evacuee boys had colorful nicknames like Leftie, Swannie, and Spanner. Maybe the village boys with nicknames of their own such as Podge, Fisty, Stallion, and Mr. Patch—so-named because he missed a patch when potato picking—recognized fellow characters in their midst because they were welcomed with open arms, albeit with plenty of teasing.

Football united them, and Podge and his mates pitted their skills against Spanner and his team in huge matches on the common, sometimes as many as thirty a side.

The back slang the evacuees spoke bamboozled the local lads. By putting the letter from the back of a word at the front and adding an *a* they created a whole new language that they used when they didn't want the natives to understand them. The local lads gave as good as they got though and ribbed them mercilessly when they caught them hunting for eggs in the trees.

There was widespread disbelief at how little the evacuees knew of country life. Martin the milkman was stunned when he heard tell of one little boy instructing his younger brothers and sisters not to touch a drink called milk for it could kill them. Fortunately, Martin's excellent milk won

them all round and must have done them some good, as this boy's younger
brother went on to play football for England.

Despite their cheek the evacuee boys were very respectful of their
elders and always tipped their caps to the police, the vicar, and the doctor,
as well as to me.

But there was one person I couldn't warm to, no matter how hard I
tried.

Gladys Trump was the mother of four-year-old Jimmy, an evacuee from
the poorest slum district of the East End. Single mother Gladys was fiercely
protective of Jimmy and her eleven other older children, so protective in
fact that she had insisted on being evacuated with "'er boys." She'd packed
in her cleaning job and got on the evacuee train with them.

To her credit, Gladys had got herself a job in a nearby factory and was
really making a go of it in Redbourn. Though I respected her in many ways,
I also found her infuriating beyond belief. Not since Mrs. Bunce and I had
locked horns had I been engaged in such a battle of wills.

Gladys was an imposing woman even though she was no more than five
feet two inches. She had beady dark eyes that glared through a cloud of cigarette smoke, which wafted up from the fag permanently welded between
her thin lips. Gladys had had a hard life and it showed on her face. She must
have been pretty once, but now her face was weather-beaten and pinched,
ravaged by a lifetime of raising twelve children on her own.

As I saw her push open the nursery door that morning my heart sank.
She spotted me and straightaway I saw her thick jaw tighten and start to
twitch.

Uh-oh. I was in for a tongue-lashing, and I knew precisely what it would
be about. The first time Jimmy and Gladys turned up, I had mentioned that
he, like all the other children, would be bathed every day. She had reacted
as if I were suggesting he be boiled alive.

Pushing her face so close to mine, I could smell the rotten odor of
stale nicotine and last night's ale, Gladys let rip. "Oi," she hissed. "Make
sure my Jimmy don't 'ave a bleedin' bath today, all right. 'E'll catch 'is death
a cold."

Drawing myself up to my full height, I said as politely as I could muster,
"Jimmy needs a bath, Mrs. Trump. All the children here are bathed in the
morning."

Her eyes glittered dangerously as she leaned back and crossed her arms. They were so big they were like legs of mutton.

"I'm tellin' yer, he ain't 'aving no bath, or yer'll 'ave me to deal wiv."

With that she cackled loudly, revealing a row of rotten brown stumps for teeth.

As she stomped off, I took a deep breath through my nose and exhaled slowly out my mouth.

After dealing with Mrs. Whitehead and Lady Villiers I wasn't about to be scared off by the likes of Gladys Trump. Taking Jimmy's hand, I marched him through the nursery to where Joy was standing. She was just finishing off bathing a few other children in the vast white stone sink.

"Joy. Help me undress Jimmy, will you? He needs a bath."

Poor little Jimmy. He didn't protest, in fact he looked rather pleased to be relieved of the weird assortment of garments he was wearing. His damp little trousers were held together with a safety pin and his flimsy top was ripped and filthy.

I gasped when I saw his body. He was pitifully thin, and his scrawny little torso was covered in angry-looking pus-filled blisters.

"Little treasure," I said, trying to soothe him.

I didn't like the look of that one bit. It looked like impetigo, a highly infectious bacterial skin condition. I made a note to call Nurse Sybil Trudgett, the district nurse in these parts who came to the nursery regularly to check over the children.

Poor Jimmy was filthy dirty. I don't mean the sort of dirt that floats away in water. His skin was almost dyed brown by ground-in dirt, and he smelled, oh, how he smelled.

Ignoring the acrid smell of urine, Joy and I gently washed him. We'd never get him totally clean, but we could get the worst of it off. In later life I heard of some billeters dunking evacuees from the slum districts in sheep dip and shaving their heads to rid them of dirt and lice. Well, I wouldn't stand for that here. I wouldn't fail little Jimmy. These children needed to be respected; they were the future generations of citizens who would rebuild the world after this awful war was over, Jimmy included.

Wrapping his shivering, scrawny little body up in a towel, I helped Joy dry him off and change him into his clean nursery overalls.

Bless him. His little blue eyes shone with gratitude. His face, now that it wasn't caked in dirt, looked so young and innocent.

"Fanks," he said, with a sniff. A ferocious woman might have been raising him, but he was a little sweetheart.

"Now for your medicine," I said, smiling.

His nose wrinkled up in disgust.

"Don't worry." I laughed. "It's only cod-liver oil. All the children have to have a tablespoonful each morning. It'll keep you nice and healthy."

Jimmy joined the line of other little children waiting for their daily dose.

I tried not to laugh as each child reacted the same way, with faces grimacing and noses screwed up in disgust as the fishy oil trickled down their throats. Seconds later drops would dribble back out down their chins and down the front of their overalls. No amount of boiling in the old copper would ever get the fish oil stains out of those now.

I could hardly blame them. Kathleen and I used to dread having to take it as children. In fact, poor Kathleen, being a sickly baby, was slathered in a mixture of cod-liver oil and malt, then wrapped in cotton wool. I'll never forget the smell. Still, as the old proverb by British clergyman Robert Burton goes, "What can't be cured must be endured." For everything else, there was cod-liver oil. David still takes his daily dose today!

Next it was Jimmy's turn.

He eyed the spoon suspiciously, like it was an unexploded bomb.

"I don't wanna," he cried.

"Come on," I said brightly. "Upsy-daisy, hold your nose. Swallow hard, and down she goes."

Spluttering, he gulped hard and shuddered.

"Bleedin' 'orrible," he muttered.

"Language, Jimmy," I said.

He hung his head, and then looked at me with big solemn eyes. "Sorry, Nurse."

With that he went to join the rest of the children, who were having their hair combed for nits.

Since little Johnnie had brought nits back, they'd gone round the nursery like wildfire. In the days before modern lotions and potions, we just had to comb each child's hair daily. It was a long and laborious task, and no sooner was one child nit free than another would be reinfected. We fought a losing battle with them.

Just then a high-pitched scream echoed through the nursery, followed a second later by a wild-eyed Pat racing through the room.

"What on earth?" I gasped. I thought the roof had come off.

"My hair," screamed Pat. "My hair. They're everywhere."

The poor woman clawed at her waist-length silver hair with her bony hands.

"I've got nits everywhere. I can feel them crawling on my scalp," she shrieked.

She was beside herself. The sight of this elderly lady screaming like a banshee had the children in fits of giggles.

"Beryl and Betty," I snapped, "take Pat outside and comb her hair through, will you."

"Now, now, children," I said, clapping my hands and attempting to restore order. "Outside to play at once, please."

Returning to my small office, I sank into my chair and let my head rest on the desk for a second. Between Gladys Trump, the children, and the nits, I was wrung out, and the day had barely begun.

The upside to all this work was that I really was too busy and tired to dwell on my heartache over horrid Henry. I hadn't heard much from Little Cranford since I left. Susan kept me updated a bit, though, and apparently Henry and his fiancée weren't very happy. Little wonder. Threatening to sue your intended for breach of promise is hardly the best start to married life!

That evening, when every child had been collected, there was just one little one sitting on his own in a chair at reception.

Jimmy.

"His mum's late again," said Joy. "Factories close at half past five, but I reckon she tootles off to the pub."

"You get off. You have a bus to catch," I said.

Turning to Jimmy, I sighed. What was I going to do about this woman? She knew the rules: all children to be collected by six. We all had buses to catch and homes to go to.

When she finally arrived, we glared at each other, and she left with Jimmy without saying a word.

All night Gladys played on my mind. There was no doubt she loved her son, but to me she was morally degenerate. What kind of woman allowed her child to get so dirty he smelled of urine and contracted skin infections?

The next morning I opened the door and who was standing there, casting a dark shadow over the doorway? Gladys Trump herself.

Cold, calculated fury flashed over her face, and her clenched knuckles were turning white.

"'Ow dare ya," she hollered. "It's a bleedin' disgrace."

Her face grew redder as her voice got louder. Little flecks of spittle flew from her mouth onto my face.

"Whodya fink you are? He ain't never had a barf in his life. He don't need a barf now. Keep yer 'ands offa 'im."

"I won't make any apologies for bathing your son, Mrs. Trump," I said, trying to keep my cool.

"Well, I've put a stop to yer little game so I 'ave."

With that she shrieked with laughter and stomped off to the munitions factory.

I shook my head as I watched her bowl her way across the common, scratching her head and scattering chickens as she walked.

Utterly infuriating.

"Of all the . . ." I muttered.

"Er, Brenda," piped up Joy. "You'd better come and have a look at this."

I turned around to see Joy hopelessly tugging at Jimmy's raggedy little shirt.

"She's only sewn his clothes onto him."

She had, too. Jimmy's shirt, vest, and trousers were all sewn together with rough, clumsy stitches.

What on earth?

If this woman wanted a fight, a fight she would have.

"Unpick them, please, and then he can have his bath."

And so the battle between Gladys Trump and me raged on, with both sides refusing to back down.

We bathed him, she sewed him into his clothes. I warned her not to be late, she carried on turning up at whatever time suited her.

I just could not for the life of me understand why this woman didn't want her son to be bathed or cared for. At this point I was beyond caring. I had enough on my plate. I was so busy with the day-to-day running of the nursery and spent most of my time ordering supplies, managing rations, and overseeing things—tasks that didn't come naturally to me, I might add. I didn't have time for a silly game of one-upmanship with a fishwife of a woman.

Sadly, Jimmy wasn't the only one. A lot of the evacuee children were almost as filthy. They'd come in on a Monday morning after a weekend with their mothers, their poor bottoms red raw and covered in nappy rash and sores.

I'd well and truly had it with these women. As far as I was concerned they were thoroughly irresponsible.

I thought I'd seen it all when I saw Jimmy's roughly sewn together clothes, but I was soon in for another shock. The Norland might have taught me a good many things—including how to cross-stitch; steam a pudding; and, above all, how to keep little people scrupulously well cared for—but it hadn't really opened my eyes to the ways of the world.

Over the common from the nursery there lived a lady, whose name I shan't divulge to protect her identity, who was happily married to a local man. They had two children together and when war broke out the husband was called up and sent overseas to serve in Belgium.

In his absence an evacuee family, including the mother and various aunts and uncles, moved in next door. The family of twenty-two all managed to squeeze into a tiny little cottage; how they managed I shall never know. But the oldest of them was himself a young man called up to join the troops abroad. He had done so for a short while but had soon discovered the army was not to his liking and promptly deserted. In the four years since the war started he had deserted that many times. Even numerous spells in an army prison had done nothing to curb his fleet-footed ways.

When this man wasn't deserting, he took up with his neighbor's wife. This lady and the deserter had gone on to have *five* children together.

The affair and the illegitimate children were the talk of the village. What her poor husband would make of it all when he returned to find that in his absence his wife had acquired another family was anyone's guess.

In the meantime her youngest children were under the care of the Redbourn Day Nursery. When her littlest tot needed breast-feeding we simply took him over the common to be fed by his mother, who would nip home from the factory, and then bring him back to the nursery.

One morning it was my turn to take the baby for his 10:00 AM feed. Collecting him from the baby room, I gently swaddled him in a warm blanket and made my way across the common.

"Let's see if mummy's already home, shall we?" I said, planting a little kiss on his head.

"Anyone in?" I called, creaking open the front door.

No answer.

Picking my way over the children's toys scattered through the hallway, I made my way gingerly up the narrow, creaky cottage stairs.

As I climbed I became aware of a strange noise, a sort of frantic scuffling.

At the bedroom door I paused and knocked. "Baby's here for his feed," I called.

The door swung open and missus was sitting up in bed, naked, with a thin sheet drawn over her. She looked awkward and tense.

"Hand him over, then," she muttered.

Suddenly, my eyes were drawn to the floor.

There, poking out from under the wrought-iron bedstead, was a pair of legs. The legs were in a pair of army fatigue trousers and heavy laced brown boots.

Oh, very subtle.

So this was the child's father, the deserter, cowering under the bed.

She saw my eyes flicker down to the floor and she glared at me. An uneasy silence hung in the air. I handed the child over, not a word was said, and I got out of there as fast as I could.

As I walked across the common back to the nursery, I shook my head in wonder. I didn't know how these women did it.

She wasn't the only one, by any means. Adultery was rife. I'd heard lots of talk of people having affairs, and illegitimate children were popping up all over the place. The brief encounter became a common experience as servicemen and -women and civilians sought comfort where they could find it. I suppose every day you were alive in such conditions was a gift, and it made people behave in ways they would never normally.

I looked on at this behavior in curious dismay. Now I'd seen it firsthand. I knew it was not one's place to look down or judge people—and we were living in extraordinary times, after all—but was it so hard to remain faithful? I thought of Mother and Father, still devoted to each other after years of marriage. They would never dream of cheating on each other.

That night, still perturbed by the sight of the deserter under the bed, I was in no mood to be trifled with.

Come half past six, who was sitting there at reception, still waiting for his mother to collect him? Yes, you've guessed it: Jimmy.

Right! I had warned that woman time and again not to be late; in fact I'd even gone so far as to tell her I'd leave him outside if she weren't punctual. Well, she'd pushed me too far this time. I'd call her bluff, so I would.

Gently buckling Jimmy into his buggy, I wheeled him out to the front of the nursery and pulled the door closed behind us. I left him there and took up a hiding place next to the porch where I couldn't be seen but could keep an eye on Jimmy.

"I'm right here, sweetheart," I whispered.

I daresay Jimmy was used to strange comings and goings, as he didn't even bat an eyelid, just swung his little legs from the buggy and played with his toy car.

I settled in to wait.

Presently, the figure of Gladys came swerving round the corner and gently swayed up to the nursery. She was humming a little tune to herself, probably still flushed from the warmth of the pub, but when she saw Jimmy, she stopped dead in her tracks.

My heart pounded as I waited for the explosion.

Wait for it.

"Jimeeeee!" she screeched in a voice so high-pitched it was almost off the human radar.

There it was.

The fag dropped from her lips as a terrifying scowl crossed her face. Her eyes bulged as she let rip with a stream of obscenities. My goodness, the language. She was still softly cursing to herself as she wheeled Jimmy up the road.

The next morning I braced myself. A night's sleep had done little to temper her rage.

Jabbing me with a nicotine-stained finger, she let me know exactly what she thought of me.

"It's a bleedin' disgrace. Whodaya fink you are?"

On and on she went.

"I warned you I would do it if you were late and what's more I shall do it again," I said as calmly as I could with an irate East End mother bellowing in my face.

Do you know, after that I never saw Gladys Trump again. From that day forward she sent one of her older children to collect Jimmy. It was a blessed relief. No matter that they always pinched whatever was hanging from the washing line when they collected him, at least I didn't have to contend with her again.

A few days later we had a visit from one of my favorite Redbourn village characters. Nurse and midwife Sybil Trudgett, aka Trudge, was a familiar sight pedaling through the village streets on a bike that must have weighed the same as an army tank. She wasn't the slimmest of ladies, which was probably just as well, as she needed her stout frame to propel that beast of a bike up and down the common.

Nurse Trudgett had probably delivered every baby born within a ten-mile radius. She must have been well into her fifties, and where she got her tenacity and cheerful resilience from I'll never know, given that she seemed to spend every hour God sent on her rounds. It went some way to explaining why she'd never had her own children.

One could tell she was coming by the way the evacuee boys on the common stopped whatever they were doing to raise their caps and stand clear. She was just the sort of efficient woman who commanded instant respect.

Since taking over the running of things I'd got to know Nurse Trudgett well. The nursery was means-tested and the mothers paid what they could afford. The only person who could possibly advise me on whether to charge them one penny or seven shillings was her. She knew everyone and everyone knew her. A woman like her was as vital to the lifeblood of the village as heating and water are to a home.

She had an affinity with Redbourn that flowed through her body, from the gray hair on her head right down to the tips of her hobnailed boots.

Now, seeing her large figure hove into view, I popped the kettle on. Nurse Trudgett liked her tea strong.

"How are we all today?" she called out as she bustled in.

"Lovely to see you," I said. "Couple of impetigo, a tonsillitis, chicken pox, and a suspected German measles case for you."

"Marvelous," she said, with a grin. "Keeping me busy as ever, I see."

After I'd shown her Jimmy's impetigo and she'd prescribed a perfectly horrid mauve cream to spread over his boils, we settled down to chat over tea. I confided in her my despair over Gladys Trump.

Nurse Trudgett listened patiently as I ranted over the state of Jimmy. She nodded when I told her he was sewn into his clothes, and just the merest flicker of a smile played on her face when I told her about hiding behind the porch.

"Well, you and her have been having fun and games," she said finally, folding her hands neatly on her lap.

"What else am I to do?" I cried, throwing my hands up in despair. "The woman is impossible."

She smiled and instantly her weather-beaten face softened.

"I understand, Brenda. Really I do. But, you know, you mustn't be so hard on women like Gladys."

"But Jimmy's filthy and she's always late . . ." I insisted.

"That may be," said Nurse Trudgett, her voice growing a little firmer. "But what you have to understand is that she has raised twelve children more or less single-handedly in a tiny two-bedroom flat in the Peabody Estate in Stepney. Those buildings are notorious. They are infested with bugs and in all honesty should probably have been bulldozed years ago.

"You cannot imagine the poverty. Picture the scene, Brenda," she urged. "Thirteen of them in a dirty tenement flat. There are no facilities in those places. The only lavatory is at the end of each balcony, next to a single tap. There are small children everywhere, sometimes naked from the waist down to save on washing."

I felt my attitude toward Gladys soften. I remembered that when she arrived in Redbourn I had a grudging respect for her tenacity. She had after all kept her family together under the most miserable of circumstances.

"She loves those children fiercely, with an intensity that you and I who are not mothers could never understand. They are her life! Why do you think she's here? She's doing the best she can," insisted Nurse Trudgett, aware she was finally getting through to me.

"But a bath," I protested weakly.

"The only bath they have is filled with coal," she said. "Besides, Gladys doesn't wash her children because she genuinely believes they will catch their death of cold. That belief is ingrained in her. That's why she was furious when she realized you had bathed Jimmy."

"I . . ." my voice trailed off lamely.

"She hasn't enjoyed the privileged upbringing that you and I have, Brenda. Not everyone is lucky enough to be born into comfortable houses with money in the bank."

I thought of rambling Hallcroft, my childhood home, with its many bedrooms, hot running water, rosebushes, and huge garden backing onto wide-open fields.

I smiled as I thought of how Father used to bring back brown paper bags groaning with sweets on a Saturday afternoon, of the way he mowed the lawn to look like railway tracks and spent hours playing trains with us, or his little trick of arranging the fruit on our plates to look like smiley faces. He and Mother had lavished us with love and time and built us the most idyllic home in which to spend our childhood. Then I tried to imagine the squalid, filthy, overcrowded flat of Jimmy's childhood. The gulf between my start in life and Jimmy's could not have been wider.

Shame and humility washed over me. How could I have been so impossibly judgmental? I'd grown up and then trained in a different world from these East End folk, a rarefied and privileged existence where etiquette, wealth, and standing ruled. I hadn't extended my view of life beyond the wrought-iron railings and quiet gentility of Pembridge Square.

Imagine wealthy Iris Beaumont coping in the slums without her chauffeur-driven Rolls-Royce? A woman who adopted two children, then instantly distanced herself from them by hiring a nanny to raise them. For all Gladys's faults, her raucous behavior, and her foul mouth, she loved the bones off her children. She would sooner carve off her own leg than dream of giving one of them away.

"You know, Brenda, the more I see of life, the less I am surprised by it," said Nurse Trudgett, sighing. "Each generation has its own ways of raising children and to them it is right. Old country folk round here used to wrap their children in waxed brown paper at the start of winter to keep them warm. And every year a Romany Gypsy family comes through these parts in a horse-drawn caravan. They stop to help with the fruit picking and they are respected and welcomed in the village. They are good people.

"I remember going out once to attend to a birth. The mother was a beautiful Gypsy lady with hair to her knees. The birth was peaceful and full of love. After I'd delivered the baby, she was put in a little cardboard box to sleep under the bed. Some people might frown upon that but not me. I daresay that baby was more loved and cherished than most."

Suddenly, I thought of the Norland's insistence on lining up the babies' cots outside in the snow during the coldest winter in forty-five years, so they could take their naps. That might also be counted a little bizarre, but the intention was just as sincere as that of the Gypsies, the country folk, and the East End mums.

I may have joined Redbourn Day Nursery naive in the ways of the world and a little narrow in my outlook, but thanks to the kindness and understanding of this lovely lady, I left it with a broader perspective and, I hope, a little more understanding.

Later in life I was thrilled to hear that Nurse Trudgett had been awarded the MBE in 1954 for her work in the community, and rightly so. This woman delivered 2,500 babies over her career and kept a community healthy and happy. Nurse Trudgett's compassion opened my eyes. I never did see Gladys again after our last showdown, but I like to think my new-found insight would have made me softer toward her. She had an enormous effect on me indirectly. I was certainly more compassionate toward other people as a consequence of having met her.

With all the excitement and noise generated by the older children it would be all too easy to forget the babies I spent most of my time looking after, but there was one little girl whose story particularly touched my heart.

Juliet was just a little tot of no more than two when her mother dropped her off at the nursery. She was the prettiest little thing, with soft blond curls and a smile like a sunbeam. Whenever she saw me, she threw open her arms, bounced up and down in excitement, and flashed me an adorable smile. How could I resist such a lovely invitation to a cuddle? The paper-work could wait. I always made time for a hug with Juliet.

Tragically, her eight-year-old brother had been sent to live in an institution and probably sterilized on account of the fact that he had Down's syndrome. Nowadays the medical world knows far more about the treatment and care of people with Down's syndrome and you would never dream of institutionalizing and sterilizing a child with Down's, but back in the 1940s it was a more ignorant age.

It was probably a hangover from the eugenics ideology of the nineteenth century that people with "less-desirable traits" should be prevented from having children by placing them in gender-separate institutions. Horrifyingly, some of the first victims of Hitler's euthanasia program were children with Down's syndrome, not that we knew that back then in 1943.

Juliet's parents, first cousins, were bereft at having to give up their beloved son.

"I just couldn't cope," the mother confided in me, one morning soon after Juliet started.

"He was so strong and he would hit me," she whispered. "One day he barricaded himself in his bedroom by pushing the wardrobe against the door."

She never said as much, but I knew she and the father were praying little Juliet didn't have the syndrome. That poor woman looked haunted and she doted on her little girl.

"I do so hope Juliet will be all right," was as much as she would say.

"Don't you worry," I said with a smile. "She will be fine."

After that I always made an extra special effort to spend a bit of time with Juliet and lavish her with cuddles. She was the most affectionate child I'd ever cared for, and her face lit up when I walked into a room.

"She's got a soft spot for you, I reckon," Joy said, chuckling, when she saw us.

I was in the baby room one day when I heard a funny noise. I looked down and saw Juliet, sitting on the floor of the nursery where she usually played happily with her toys. Instead of babbling to herself, she was sitting ramrod straight, her back was rigid and she was shaking.

"Darling," I said, bending down to pick her up, "are you all right?"

The episode, if you can call it that, passed in no time. She seemed fine after that, and I thought no more of it until a month or so later the same thing happened again. Only this time it was far worse. Her poor little body was in spasms and her face went bright red as she shook. I tried to uncurl her fists, but they were clenched shut.

"Juliet, can you hear me?" I cried. Finally she collapsed exhausted into my arms.

Terrified, I called Nurse Trudgett and she cycled over immediately. She examined Juliet and then promptly called out the doctor. The doctor made a thorough examination of Juliet, who was by now fully recovered and beaming at the stern man with the stethoscope like he was Santa Claus.

The diagnosis was swift.

"Looking at her facial characteristics, skin tone, family history, and behavior, I would say she has Down's syndrome," he said, frowning.

My heart sank. What would her poor mother say? Fortunately, I wasn't there when the diagnosis was passed on; I don't think I could have borne witness to her heartbreak.

I often wonder what happened to that sunny, adorable, lovable little girl after she eventually left the nursery. Of all the children I have ever cared for, she was one with the most love to give, which just makes her possible fate all the more tragic.

Characters like Jimmy, Gladys Trump, and Juliet continued to make my life in Redbourn a constant source of wonder. The place consumed my every waking thought; it was like working inside a bubble. After I'd got the bus home, Mother put my dinner on the table and it was as much as I could do to wearily raise the fork to my lips. All too soon I would be heading to bed. My life revolved around the nursery, quiet evenings at home, and Sunday morning worship—with no social life to speak of.

I was just twenty-two and in a position of huge responsibility for one so young. Consequently, I allowed the job to take over. Being conscientious I so wanted to be professional and not let the reputation of the Norland down.

My life within the four walls of the nursery ruled out any chance of finding a boyfriend. I was simply too busy, or too ill, to socialize. Hardly surprisingly, during my time at Redbourn I contracted everything the children caught. That nursery was a breeding ground of germs and my poor immune system took a battering. I even gave German measles to my brother Christopher while he was on leave before going abroad.

Outside on the village streets, however, people were beginning to relax a little as the fear of German invasion subsided.

On June 6, 1944, thirteen months after I began working at the nursery, the Allied invasion of Normandy took place.

Bulletins rang out from wireless sets all over the village. "Here is a special bulletin. D-day has come. . . . Early this morning the Allies began the assault on the northwestern face of Hitler's European fortress."

But despite its success, the dangers were far from over.

A week after D-day, on June 13, 1944, the first V-1 pilotless rocket crossed the English coast; and during the following month thousands were launched on war-weary England. The *V* stood for *Vergeltung*, or retaliation.

On September 8, four years after the Battle of Britain, the longer range

V-2s began to fall out of the autumn sky. It was too late for the Germans to win the war, but once again we found ourselves in the line of attack.

There were ten thousand casualties in the first week of the V-1s, or doodlebugs as they came to be known, but it was the V-2s, which gave no warning, that were really sinister. Unseen and unheard they plummeted to earth delivering one ton of high explosive at a speed of 3,500 feet per second.

As our troops advanced throughout Europe, the Germans retaliated by raining down these hateful missiles.

These unmanned invaders from the skies truly were the ultimate weapons of terror warfare. I was outside in the playground the first time I encountered one of them. I became aware of a strange droning noise overhead just as it abruptly stopped. A V-2 rocket!

I felt sick with fright.

I'd been warned that when the engine cuts out, that's when the bomb is ready to begin its descent. Where it landed was anybody's guess.

I stood stock-still in the playground, ice-cold panic pumping through my veins.

"Everyone inside now," I bellowed.

The staff, sensing the urgency in my voice, gathered Jimmy, Juliet, and the rest of the boys and girls together and ushered them back inside, where we quickly sheltered them under the tables. The children thought it a marvelous game of course, but we adults were all scared witless.

We stared at one another, our faces white as flour.

I was tense as a coiled spring, waiting for an almighty explosion. It never came, but the fear of waiting and the silence as we waited for the bomb to land, was unbearable.

This happened a few more times as these hateful machines of war passed over our heads. Fortunately none ever exploded in Redbourn, but the anxiety aged us no end. That was the only thing that I remember being really scared of throughout the war.

Ironically, as these rockets left people paralyzed with terror, our thoughts were already turning to peace. Thanks to D-day it was widely believed we were winning the war; and most knew these rockets were Hitler's futile last-ditch maneuver in retaliation for the Allies' advance throughout Europe. At the same time, the blackout gave way to a half-hearted dim-out and we wearily took down the blackout curtains.

Soon after the rockets began, another strange noise filled the skies over Redbourn. The village was alive with news of the day the horizon turned black. I hadn't witnessed it but many of the villagers had become aware of a strange droning sound, different from the hated rockets. Staring out their windows they were flabbergasted to see hundreds of British RAF planes towing gliders fly overhead.

One by one, villagers trickled out of their cottages until soon the common was filled with silent onlookers, craning their necks skyward, an uneasy feeling growing in the pits of their stomachs.

"It was obviously an invasion force," one local told me, "but for where?"

"The skies were black with planes," muttered another.

We didn't know the exact scale of it at the time, but some truly horrendous battles were being fought by our boys in Europe. The last year of World War Two was our country's darkest hour. Tens of thousands of sons, husbands, and brothers lost their lives. Precious few survivors of these battles walk among us now.

One person clearly affected by this was Martin the milkman.

His eldest boy, Ray, twenty-one, had joined up and was serving with the 1st Airborne Division. Martin tried to maintain his sunny disposition when he delivered the milk, but his face was pinched with worry, and his poor wife's face, God bless her, took on a haunted look.

Somehow, in some way, we all felt responsible for Ray. The Webbs were so popular in the village and young Ray was "one of ours."

A couple of weeks after the skies had turned black, I heard a furor out on the common. I glanced out the window and who should I see striding along the road but Ray himself! It was a moment of sheer joy for the village. People rushed out of their homes to applaud him. Ray was one of the lucky ones and it's a miracle he survived.

I watched with a lump in my throat. With his dark hair, chiseled features, and Errol Flynn mustache, he was so handsome. He got a hero's welcome, particularly from the young ladies of the village, who positively swooned in his presence.

The village was buzzing after Ray's return; and we all prayed as we had never done before for a swift end to this war. Two months later, barbed wire started disappearing from Britain's beaches, and Father and the rest of the Home Guard were stood down from duty.

Finally, the following May, 1945, came the moment we had all been waiting for, VE-day—victory in Europe. A huge cheer erupted from the boys'
school next door and bulletins all over the village rang out with the trium-
phant news.

The following letter was sent to schools up and down the country and
pinned on notice boards in the village.

8th June, 1946

*To-day as we celebrate victory, I send this personal message to you and all
other boys and girls at school. For you have shared in the hardships and
dangers of a total war and you have shared no less in the triumph of the
Allied Nations.*

*I know you will always feel proud to belong to a country which was
capable of such supreme effort; proud, too, of parents and elder brothers and
sisters who by their courage, endurance, and enterprise brought victory.
May those qualities be yours as you grow up and join in the common effort
to establish among the nations of the world unity and peace.*

George R.I.

London went mad with joy, people screamed and shouted, perfect
strangers embraced. Revelers danced the conga, a popular new import
from Latin America, the Lambeth walk, and the hokey-cokey.

Churchill appeared on the floodlit balcony at Buckingham Palace with
the king and queen, while the princesses were allowed to party with the
celebrating crowds below. On every street a sea of red, white, and blue flags
and bunting fluttered triumphantly.

In Redbourn, Union Jacks were hung at every window, and people finally
looked less careworn and more relaxed. Even the deserter must eventually have crawled out from under his mistress's bed! Martin Webb and the
villagers organized a huge afternoon of races, games, and tea on the common. John, Ron, and Podge celebrated alongside Spanner and the rest of
his gang with egg-and-spoon and sack races, followed by tea with lashings
of jam.

I spent my VE-day more quietly. I went home to be with my family.
I had survived incendiary bombs, flying shrapnel, doodlebugs, betrayal, a

broken heart, German measles, and ferocious East End mums. The war was over. I was shattered.

As for my siblings, Michael was demobbed from where he was stationed with the air force in India and the rest of the boys came home from their school in the Lake District. Kathleen was working as a midwife in Woking and thanks to the war was a virtual stranger to me. I was looking forward to getting to know them all again.

The all clear had sounded for good, the strains of "We'll meet again" were to be heard everywhere, and the age of postwar austerity had begun. What now for the village and the nursery?

Twelve evacuee families loved village life so much they decided to stay on. They were embraced by the local community and became a welcome part of it, settling down and raising their families in Redbourn. Even today an old boys and girls reunion is held with ex-evacuees occupying a table known affectionately as "cockney corner."

Not so for Jimmy and his mother, who decided to return to the East End.

When it came time for Jimmy to leave, he flung his arms around me.

"Fank you, Nurse Brenda. I'll never forget ya."

My heart soared.

"Nor I you, my little treasure."

He may have been filthy, thin, and pale when he arrived, but I like to think he left me rosy cheeked, happy, well fed, and clean—the perfect child. Who knew what the future held for little Jimmy?

Unrelenting poverty in a tiny two-bedroom tenement flat? Even if his home was still standing, it was set in a bomb-ravaged wasteland. Still, knowing Jimmy, he'd be all over those bomb sites, quickly becoming ruler of his strange new playground.

Over at my parents' house, life was all change, too. Soon after the war ended I came home from the nursery one day to find my mother utterly distraught.

"Lady Lillian is insisting that Sally return to live with her," she cried.

"But how can she?" I protested. "Sally has lived with us for years."

Call us naive, but as Sally had been with us for six years with scarcely a visit from her ladyship, we assumed she would be with us forever. She was one of the family now, a happy, healthy seven-year-old. We had even enrolled her in a local Catholic school as per Lady Lillian's wishes.

"She can and she is," sobbed Mother. "What's more, I'm not allowed to visit. Her ladyship has consulted a doctor who thinks it best Sally make a clean break of it and not have contact with us, as it will confuse her."

As I hugged her I realized my mother was bereft.

"I loved that little girl as a daughter," she whispered.

Saying good-bye was a painful and bewildering experience for all involved. Sally blamed herself. "When I saw her putting on makeup on a visit once, I told her my mummy doesn't wear makeup. She was angry. Is this my fault?" Sally's lip was quivering as she spoke.

"Of course not, darling," gushed Mother. "She's your mummy and she wants you home."

Mother folded little Sally into a last hug and wept her good-byes.

We never saw that little girl again.

As Mother returned to the house, I felt so scared. What would she do now without her little Sally to care for? What would women all over the country do now their roles had changed? Return to a life of domesticity? "Where Do We Go from Here?" was the title of a *Vogue* article on the future of women after the war. So many had found liberation and acceptance by wearing a man's uniform during the war that giving it all up would be a bitter pill to swallow.

In 1945 divorce rates were double what they were in 1938. Women had tasted freedom and they didn't want to return to the kitchen. (Amazingly, though, I heard the lady who had all the illegitimate children with the deserter was forgiven by her husband when he returned. Not only that but he even helped to raise all the children as his own. What a forgiving fellow! He was regarded as a saint by the village.)

Whatever women wanted, the remaining years of the forties and the fifties represented a backward step for their emancipation. There was desperation to see society return to normal, and women going back to their old domesticated role was part of this.

Things were all change for me, too. Wartime nurseries declined due to the withdrawal of Ministry of Health funding and so Redbourn Day Nursery was put into the care of the local authority. This spelled bad news. The children were leaving in droves, full-time care not being needed anymore, and the staff were losing their enthusiasm. Who could blame them? We all felt like we were just going through the motions.

I so wanted to leave, but to do what? Britain was a much-changed place.

The British nanny was dying out, a symbol of a disappearing way of life. One by one, private colleges to train nannies were closing. In 1945 the National Nursery Examination Board was founded and laid down national standards of qualification. NNEB courses were introduced into new colleges of further education. The new state-run colleges threw open the profession to girls whose families could not afford private training.

More and more families began to employ cheaper au pairs and untrained help. Postwar austerity was already biting, and social changes meant that employing a nanny in a uniform wasn't seen as prestigious in the way it once was. In three years' time the NHS would be formed and mass antenatal care organized for the first time.

Meanwhile, the Norland's headquarters at Pembridge Square had been sold off. The lecture rooms and workrooms—where we had toiled, ironed, sewed, knitted, and polished our prams—now lay empty. Miss Whitehead had resigned in 1941. No more children's laughter echoed round the grand old house.

The Norland, like so many other businesses, was engrossed in financial survival. Economy became the order of the day.

In March 1946 I could stand it no longer and handed in my notice. The nursery had lost its soul and I my enthusiasm for it, but I owed it a huge debt of gratitude. What a journey of discovery I had been on. The East Enders and this little community had opened my eyes to the world. Thanks to them, the bombs, and betrayal, I had changed. I was no longer a naive young girl but a strong woman. I could look forward with my head held high and say I'd done my duty. I'd done my little bit to help secure the safety and freedom of our children.

The world was changing, but could I change with it? Was I still needed and wanted? Could I keep the pram wheels rolling? Now that the bombs had stopped raining down, were there any children in need of protection, love, stability, or just a lap to sit in for a cuddle?

For me the route was obvious. My faith had always been strong in my life, even when I'd been a directionless child. It seemed natural that I would be drawn back to religion in some way.

Feeling lost, I was only too pleased to take up an offer that had come my way.

Mary was an old friend of mine whom I had met through the church, and, hearing I was at a loose end, she invited me to join her on a religious conference in Hildenborough, Kent.

Religious camps, or rallies as they were known, were springing up all over Britain. They were extremely popular in the postwar years and offered direction to thousands of youth. For young men and women who had seen their homes bombed, their loved ones killed, and who had survived countless brushes with death, these conferences offered hope and peace in uncertain times.

And so it was that I found myself traveling to Kent with Mary. On the way she told me whom we'd be meeting there.

"My brother Branse is going with his friend Bill," she chattered excitedly. "You'll like Bill—he's lovely. Very bright—he's studying theology at Cambridge University."

Apparently Bill and Branse were great friends and had both flown Spitfires in the RAF during the war.

"Terribly brave, both of them," Mary went on.

I wasn't disappointed when I met them.

"Hello," said the soft-spoken, blond young man, shaking my hand earnestly. "I'm Bill."

"Hello," I murmured, savoring the warmth of his hand in mine.

Oh my. Bill was quite lovely—delicious, in fact.

He radiated a goodness and a gentle sincerity I'd never come across before.

For the rest of the day we barely drew breath, chatting till the sun went down. I talked about my work as a nanny and he told me about his studies at Cambridge University. I'm quite sure he was far more intelligent than I, but he was so interested in everything I had to say, and kind, gentle, and considerate.

One evening I watched him out of the corner of my eye during a prayer meeting. His eyes were closed and a look of utter peace washed over his face as he silently mouthed the prayers.

I marveled at the strength of his faith and bathed in the gentle aura of serene reverence that surrounded him. He was nothing like cocky, boasting Henry. This was a man at peace with himself and the world.

This was a man I could truly fall for.

TESTIMONIAL

Miss Ashford was appointed as nursery nurse at Redbourn Day Nursery in May 1943. In September 1944 she was promoted to position of assistant matron. She has proved herself to be most capable in every way, conscientious, loyal, and faithful in dealing with parents and staff and her work is of the highest standard. I would add that she has been in complete control of the nursery.

—COUNTY HALL REPRESENTATIVE, COUNTY HALL

Nanny's Wisdom

STICK AT IT.

The war went on for a very long time and, I'll admit, there were times I despaired at it ever ending. They were exceedingly tough years for so many, but I, like every other citizen, stuck at it. Life is different now, but today's world throws up its own complex issues. So many people face huge financial problems or can't find a job; and when they do, they fear holding on to it—not to mention the horrors of so much crime, poverty, and needless death on our streets. In life we all need to keep our faith that things will turn out okay. If something awful happens, then I suggest people do what I always did when I was bombed or I had my heart broken: pick yourself up, dust yourself down, and start over again. We humans are an awful lot tougher than we give ourselves credit for. Keep going and keep smiling. . . .

HAVE TREASURE CHEST FUN.

You don't need expensive toys to keep children entertained. Simply keep a box of odds and ends. You can keep anything in it for children to play with, from old pinecones and seashells to crayons, stickers, balls of wool, postcards, stamps, dice, or plastic cutlery.

Every time you go on holiday or to somewhere new, find something to bring home—be it a shell from the beach or a pretty leaf—and add it to your treasure chest. It will always remind you of those times.

[LEFT] Here I am with my siblings, Kathleen (left) and Michael (right). There was never a dull moment, nor was I ever short of a playmate or two.

[BELOW] Hallcroft, the house my father built in 1929. Here we enjoyed an idyllic childhood. The garden and surrounding fields were a perfect playground.

[ABOVE] My precious leather-bound Norland Testimonial Handbook, given to me on my first day of training, March 23, 1939, aged eighteen.

[LEFT] The Norland "charge" dress worn for special occasions.

[LEFT]
The drafty lecture
hall. Note the
ever-open window.
*(Courtesy of Norland
College)*

[CENTER]
The dreaded
laundry. We spent
many hours
toiling here.
*(Courtesy of Norland
College)*

[BELOW]
Nurses on pram
parade, ready for
the afternoon
inspection.
*(Courtesy of Norland
College)*

The Norland Institute and Nurseries Ltd., Nurses and Nursery Children

Me in October 1959 with Mrs. Judith Beecroft and her two charming children, Jonathan and Sarah. They were always impeccably turned out and very well mannered. A credit to mother and nanny.

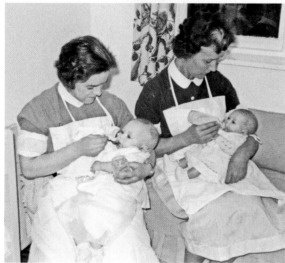

[ABOVE] Cherishing another newborn baby during my trouble-shooting years. No matter how many babies I held, nothing beat the enormous thrill of holding a fresh new life in my arms. The look on my face says it all.

[CENTER] Helping Kathleen, the midwife, with her charges.

[BELOW] A fully fledged nurse with my young charges.

In my seventies and still going strong. My hair may have faded to gray and my face crinkled with laughter lines, but my devotion to child care was stronger than ever.

SIXTH TESTIMONIAL

January 14.1952.

Nurse Brenda Ashford has been since October 1947 in entire charge of my three children now aged 4, 7½ & 11½ years. She came to me three weeks prior to the birth of the youngest child whom she took over from the maternity nurse at the age of 2½ weeks.

Her care of the baby during infancy was beyond all praise, particularly as she accepted charge of the baby at an extremely early age & after a somewhat difficult start. Subsequently her management of all three children has been admirable.

Her care & maintenance of the children's clothes, nurseries & nursery equipment excellent. She is a very good needlewoman & knitter & makes many of the children's ties & clothes.

Pages from my testimonial book. It was always nice to receive praise and recognition for my work, but being with the children was enough reward.

Nurse Brenda is extremely kind & helpful with all the household, & has become a much valued member of our family. During our absences both in this country & abroad we have left her with complete confidence in charge not only of the children but also of a large house with its indoor & outdoor staff.

Principal
1. April 1952

In May 1952 Nurse Brenda Ashford was given the Badge, the "award of highest merit for not less than five years' faithful work, three being under one employer".

Joan
Principal
& Director.

A reunion of some of the babies I have looked after in recent years.

$\mathcal{S}$AINTS AND $\mathcal{S}$INNERS

THE SACKS RESIDENCE

KENT, ENGLAND

[1946, AGE TWENTY-FIVE]

Ride a cock-horse to Banbury Cross,
To see a fine lady upon a white horse;
Rings on her fingers and bells on her toes,
And she shall have music wherever she goes.

—NURSERY RHYME

Schedule

6:00 AM: Woke half an hour before children and prepared for the day by getting twins' bottles ready and myself washed and dressed.

6:30 AM: Woke one twin and fed bottle, then when finished and burped, woke other twin for his feed. Changed twins' nappies and put them back in cots.

7:00 AM: Supervised waking of two older children, ages two and four. Washed and got them both dressed.

7:30 AM: Breakfast in the day nursery prepared by mother. Placed twins in Moses baskets in day nursery or on mat for kickabout while older boys ate breakfast. After breakfast, supervised toilet and potty trips for older boys.

8:30 AM: Swaddled twins and put down for nap, then played or read to older boys.

9:00 AM: Man of the house arrived in day nursery and collected older boy, ready to take out for the day. Cleaned nursery, made beds, did laundry, while two-year-old brother played.

10:00 AM: Started to wake twins for bottle-feed.

10:30 AM: Fed twins, changed diapers, and placed them outside in their pram for sleep in fresh air.

11:00 AM: Put two-year-old down for nap before lunch. Prepared twins' bottles for the next twenty-four hours, more washing and ironing.

12:30 PM: Lunch.

2:00 PM: Woke and fed twins. Changed diapers and prepared to take twins and two-year-old out for walk.

2:30 PM: Walked in fresh air to local park, twins slightly propped up in pram and dressed warmly. Encouraged two-year-old to walk and feed ducks before walking slowly home, talking about all we saw en route.

3:00 PM: Mother visited nursery and played with all children, while I tidied nursery and scrubbed dirty diapers.

4:00 PM: Twins napped. Older brother returned home and ate simple tea in nursery with younger brother. Both boys ask to be excused from table.

5:00 PM: Woke twins from nap before Father arrived to play with all children in day nursery. Started preparing for baths, laying out pajamas and twins' sleep nighties.

6:00 PM: Older boys played in day nursery. Left one twin in Moses basket while bathing the other. Dressed in nightie and cloth diaper, returned him to Moses basket, then bathed the other twin. Bathed the two older boys and helped them into pajamas and cleaned teeth. Told them made-up story after I got them into bed.

7:00 PM: Mother read older boys second story in bed while I fed twins bedtime bottles. All asleep by 7:30 PM.

7:30 PM TO 10:00 PM: Chores in the nursery, including sewing, darning, knitting, washing, ironing, and laying out children's clothes for next day.

10:00 PM: Woke twins and took them through to parents' room for evening feed. Collected them when finished and put in cot next to my bed.

11:00 PM: My bedtime.

IT WAS A MOST INTRIGUING request and one I knew I couldn't possibly ignore. "I really am in the most urgent need of help for my wife," said the gentleman's voice on the other end of the phone.

"Meet me at Fortnum and Mason and I shall explain more over tea. I will be wearing a bowler hat and carrying a cane. Good day to you, Nurse."

The Norland had arranged my first interview for private work since the wretched war ended nearly a year ago.

After handing in my notice at Redbourn Day Nursery, I was most eager to get back into a private household. The time I spent looking after evacuees and local children was the most eye-opening and rewarding time of my career, but since the end of the war the nursery had lost its soul and I my enthusiasm for it. I dearly wanted to get into a private household and work one-on-one with a family who needed my help.

Now it was March 1946 and postwar Britain was a much-changed place. Economy and survival were the order of the day, as women and soldiers struggled to find their place in the world. But to what world had many of them returned? The answer was uncertain.

There was a major shortage of jobs and housing, but people were being looked after in a way never seen or heard of before. The new Labor government had brought in the National Insurance Act, which marked the beginning of the welfare state. All working adults paid into the National Insurance and the money was used to fund free health care, old-age pensions, and an allowance for those forced to take a break from employment.

Mothers received a single lump-sum payment on the birth of each child, and if they had been paying NI, received an allowance for eighteen weeks. Thanks to the work that I and thousands like me had done in war nurseries, the government began to take a more collective view of child care and state involvement in families and child rearing.

The Family Allowance Act also became law in 1946, at the same time the School Milk Act came into force, ensuring that all schoolchildren would receive a third of a pint of milk each day. Women and children were being better cared for. These measures led to a new feeling of determination! We *could* and *would* recover.

Despite this, the scars of Hitler's terrifying attacks had left behind a sobering legacy.

Once glorious buildings had crumbled to dust; blown-out houses lay empty and devoid of life; closed streets and roofless houses could be seen all over the land. Pavements in the cities were pockmarked with bomb craters, and keep out signs on bomb sites acted like magnets to some naughty children seeking out thrills.

But there was also optimism among the rubble. We had survived. We owed it to those who sacrificed their lives for our freedom to restore our great cities.

Part of winning this war meant acceptance of the sacrifices and a willingness to rebuild our country from the ashes up. And so it was that I took a red double-decker bus up London's smart Piccadilly in Mayfair to meet this rather desperate gentleman and answer his call for help.

I, too, must look forward, not back. With state-run colleges opening everywhere to train nursery nurses, employing a private nanny in a uniform was not seen as prestigious as it once was. No, I should feel most grateful for a position in a house, however difficult it may be.

A liveried doorman graciously swung open the door to Fortnum & Mason for me.

War may have altered England but some traditions would never die out.

Hitler had dumped eighteen thousand tons of explosives on London, but Fortnum & Mason at 181 Piccadilly had survived. Afternoon tea here was an iconic British ritual; and I was pleased to see the place was thronged with customers, nibbling dainty sandwiches and sipping tea.

Did Hitler really believe he could replace our beloved cucumber sandwich with stollen and bratwurst?

Once inside, a welcoming rush of warmth hit me.

Smartly dressed waitresses rushed about the place, carrying tea trays piled high with bone china teapots and plates of little cucumber sandwiches with the crusts cut off.

It reminded me of a special day when Mother and I had gone for tea at Lyons Corner House all those years before as a treat for being accepted by the Norland. Two weeks after I'd been informed by letter that I'd been accepted, she had taken me to the grand teahouse and treated me to an ice cream sundae. What a wonderful afternoon that had been.

How different a person I was now from back then! But then, war had altered us all, no doubt.

I caught sight of a lone gentleman whose cane rested against the white linen tablecloth.

He was dressed smartly in a double-breasted dark suit, and he looked like a well-to-do banker or merchant.

As soon as he saw me, he smiled, took off his bowler hat, and rose to his feet. "Miss Ashford?" he inquired.

"Mr. Sacks?" I smiled.

"Yes, indeed." He smiled warmly, pulling back my chair for me. "I can't tell you how grateful I am to see you."

Soon I found my plate piled high with sandwiches, and a delicate little cup full of the most delicious-smelling tea was pressed into my hands.

I took a sip and eyed the cakes that our waitress had brought to the table. Little sponges and scones that looked as light as gossamer sat tantalizingly atop a white doily.

We'd never had anything as refined as that at the day nursery. I smiled as I pictured little Jimmy's face if someone had set down a plate of such delicacies in front of him.

I daresay it would have been demolished in the blink of an eye. Rationing was still in full swing despite the end of the war; indeed bread was more tightly rationed now in 1946 than it was during the war as the economy attempted to recover.

It could still be bought however, if you had the money to pay for it, which judging by his smart appearance and the leather briefcase by his chair Mr. Sacks obviously did.

Remembering I was a professional, I tore my gaze away from the mouthwatering afternoon tea and looked Mr. Sacks in the eye. "Do tell me about your situation and then I can see whether I can be of assistance." I smiled.

"My wife, Carolyn, has four children, two boys aged two and a half and four and a half, and baby twins, one boy and one girl, born just a few weeks ago."

"Gracious." I smiled. "You do have a houseful."

"Quite honestly, I don't know how she's coping," he said. "She is exhausted."

Suddenly, I realized he, too, had dark circles under his eyes.

"Oh, you poor thing," I gushed.

He sighed dramatically as he took a bite out of his cucumber sandwich and chewed thoughtfully.

"On top of which poor Carolyn's father is gravely ill and on his death-bed, so we need to move in with him."

His voice dropped to a whisper and he glanced left and right.

I leaned in closer.

"We rather suspect his carer is manipulating him. He has altered his will and left everything to her," he muttered. "So the move is of the utmost urgency, as I'm sure you can appreciate."

My eyes grew as wide as saucers. "Oh, absolutely I understand," I said, nodding my head vigorously.

That poor, desperate couple. Baby twins, two children, a house move, a dying relative, and a fraudster to contend with! If ever a family were in dire need of help, it was surely them!

I had already decided to take the job before he even offered it to me. "We'll need you right away, Nurse Ashford. You will take the job, won't you?"

No sooner had I nodded my head than he stood up and put on his bowler hat with a flourish and beamed brightly. "Marvelous. The salary will be fifteen pounds a week and you can report to my wife tomorrow."

With that he strode from Fortnum & Mason, hailed a cab, and vanished into London's bustling Piccadilly.

I sat back in my chair, my head still spinning from the speed of my new appointment. It was only later as I packed my suitcase and uniform ready for my new job that I realized he hadn't paid for our tea! Little did I know it then but I was about to become embroiled in a most peculiar world.

On the way to my new job I made a mental note to tell my new friend Bill of this startling event to see what he would make of it. At the mere thought of dear sweet Bill, I felt a warm glow spread through me. Bill was quite, quite lovely and the reason that I'd been wearing a smile like summer these past few months.

With his blond hair, big brown eyes, and earnest countenance he was quite lovely and very much up my street.

Nothing had happened between us—we were just friends—but I rather hoped that perhaps something might develop.

He was studying theology at Cambridge University and was fearfully bright. Surviving countless brushes with the German Luftwaffe had left Bill with a deep and profound faith, and we'd spent many an hour discussing it when we'd met.

Best of all he had invited me to visit him at university in Cambridge. I couldn't wait, and on my first weekend off from my new job I intended to take him up on his offer.

On arrival at my new employers' I forced all thoughts of romance from my head as I knocked on the door of a very ordinary semi in Pinner, Greater London.

Mr. Sacks, immaculately turned out in a pin-striped suit, answered the door with a charming smile.

"Aah, the cavalry has arrived. Welcome, Nurse Brenda. Come in, come in, do."

I had already resolved on the way here not to make mention of the small matter of an unpaid tea bill and put it down to a bad memory on his part.

He led me up a small corridor and into the sitting room. "This is my wife, Carolyn," he said.

There, huddled on the sofa, was the most pitiful sight I'd seen since little Jimmy had been brought into the day nursery.

Carolyn was tall, pale, thin, and looked utterly worn-out. Clutched to each breast was a red and wriggly little baby, who looked incandescent with rage and hunger.

My heart went out to this poor exhausted woman.

"I can't seem to feed them," she sobbed over their angry cries.

Straightaway I realized what the problem was.

I'd seen it during my training at Hothfield with the young girl and her illegitimate baby. Her milk hadn't come in.

The more an exhausted mother frets and worries, the less likely her milk is to come in, the hungrier the baby gets, and the more worried mother becomes. A vicious circle if ever I saw one.

It was my job to ease her load.

"Come here," I soothed. "Will you allow me to hold one?" I smiled.

With dull eyes she handed me one of her babies.

Violet and Peter were beautiful little babies with dark curly hair, but I could see Carolyn was too tired to appreciate the little miracles she had produced.

"Glad you ladies are sorted then," piped up Mr. Sacks from the corner of the room. "I'll be off then." Bang, the door shut after him.

I turned back to his poor scrap of a wife. I'd never seen anyone so thin after giving birth.

"Tell you what," I said softly, "how's about I make you a milky drink?"

Propping her up on freshly plumped cushions, I sorted out her two older boys with some toys, then went to the kitchen and fixed her a nice cup of hot milk and a sandwich.

When she had eaten and was more comfortable and rested, I showed her how to do breast massage.

"Don't worry," I said, smiling reassuringly. "We'll get your babies feeding in no time."

Sure enough, with plenty of rest, fresh air, and regular food, within days the color had come back into her cheeks, her breasts were engorged with milk, and the babies were feeding happily.

She and I took it in turns to hold Violet and Peter, so that she didn't need to feed them both at the same time.

I also showed her the correct way to position the babies and how to ensure they latched on properly and got a good flow of mother's milk.

We also sorted out a regular feeding and sleeping pattern that I kept note of and made sure we stuck to. I kept her older boys entertained, too, so that she and her twins got regular naps.

Violet and Peter began to thrive, her older boys looked less surly, and Carolyn looked so grateful. Peace was restored.

"Thank you so much, Nurse Brenda," she said with a smile one night over the boys' teatime. "You're a miracle worker."

"I don't know about that." I chuckled. "It's simple really. All babies thrive on routine."

I hadn't been there long when the big move to grandpa's house in Kent was announced.

"We can't possibly move with the babies," fretted Carolyn, her lip wobbling. "How will I pack and get everything sorted with them?"

"Don't worry," I soothed. "I'll take the babies off for the day. I know someone who would simply love to meet them."

Leaving the Sackses and the older boys among a mountain of packing boxes, I headed to Mother and Father's house in St. Albans.

Mother was still bereft after losing her beloved little Sally when Lady Lillian had suddenly decided to reclaim her after all those years. I knew that seeing these gorgeous little bundles would cheer her up no end.

When Mother answered the door, I could see she'd been baking, as she was wiping her hands on a white apron and the faintest trace of flour shone on her soft downy face.

Her eyes went from me to the twins, propped up in their big coach pram under a snowy white blanket. I had to admit, with their soft dark curls and Cupid's bow mouths they did look simply adorable.

Her hands flew to her mouth. "Oh, Brenda," she gasped. "Aren't they beautiful. Come in, come in—you'll catch your death of cold. I've just baked some jam tarts."

As she bustled into the warm kitchen and put on the kettle, I marveled at Mother's ability to make every house a home.

Within ten minutes I was cradling a hot cup of tea and Mother was cradling one twin in each arm.

With two babies nestling in the crook of each arm she radiated happiness. "I've got a marvelous idea," she said. "Why don't we take them to a photographer and have some photos taken?"

Her eyes shone with so much excitement I had to laugh. "How can I say no?"

Mother proudly pushed the twins along the street in their pram, showing them off to friends and neighbors on the way.

"Brenda's new charges," she explained.

Bless her. She would so have loved to have had twins.

The war in some senses had been good for Mother—she had evacuees coming out of her ears and plenty of little folk to care for. But now, with the war over, the evacuees returned to their parents, Father working hard in London, and my brothers either at school or work, I suspect she may have been a little lonely.

My older sister Kathleen was working long hours as a midwife, even though she visited when she could, like me.

Kathleen and eventually I were to be kept extremely busy, as 1946 marked the start of the baby boom. Prewar relationships were resumed and birthrates went through the roof.

For Mother, like so many other women returning to a life of domesticity after the war, readjusting was a struggle.

We had a whale of a time that afternoon, dressing the babies up in pretty bonnets and having their photos taken, followed by tea and a stroll in the park. By the time Mother and I returned home I could see she was brimming over with stories to tell Father.

"Thank you, Brenda." She smiled as Mr. Sacks's car arrived to take us to our new residence. "That was a tonic."

Seeing Mother was a tonic to me, too, and on the drive home I felt fully restored.

I was twenty-five by now, but after the war and running Redbourn Day Nursery, I felt years older. Yet despite all that I had seen and experienced, I didn't feel too old to still need my mother's love and to bathe in the warmth of her company. She made having a family seem the most natural and easy thing in the world.

Having children and a family to call my own hadn't happened to me yet, and I'll admit, there was a part of me that longed to know the love a mother feels cradling her baby. I lived in hope that my time would come and I could have the honor of making my mother a grandmother.

As we pulled up outside Carolyn's father's house, I could see our new home was somewhat grander than our previous semi. The large detached home was set in its own grounds and was surrounded by beautiful blue rhododendron bushes. A garage annex contained a little studio flat above it, too.

Inside, the boys chased each other happily through the packing boxes that were strewn over the large hallway as Carolyn busily unpacked.

"Hush, boys," she called. "You'll wake Grandpa."

"Grandpa is bedbound," she explained. "He has a new male carer. Charlie got rid of the last one, so you won't have much to do with him."

Grandpa had good taste, as the sideboards were groaning with lovely ornaments. A mahogany display cabinet glittered with silver and an exquisite duck egg blue china tea set. Beautiful oil paintings hung from a picture rail. I sighed. I should never have the money to buy such things. Little matter. Money wasn't the most important thing. Which reminded me.

"Mr. Sacks," I called brightly, as he walked past carrying a box of china to the garage. "It's my day off and I don't seem to have been paid yet."

He paused and a muscle twitched under his eye.

"Yes, yes, course, Nurse Ashford," he blustered. "Terribly sorry, I just forgot. I'll get it tomorrow when I go to London."

I frowned. This wasn't the first time Mr. Sacks was struck a bad case of amnesia. The sight of a bill seemed to have an unusual effect on his memory. I'd lost count of the number of times he'd forgotten to pay me my £15 a week.

In fact, pinning down the elusive Mr. Sacks was proving most difficult. His hours were so sporadic. Sometimes he was here all day; at other times he was gone for hours, not returning until late at night.

I never presumed to ask him what he did for a job—one simply didn't with one's employers—but whatever he did required a certain degree of ducking and diving.

Still, it was most irksome to have to chase him for my pay, but I put it to the back of my mind. Tomorrow was my day off. I was visiting Bill in Cambridge, and I was fizzing over with excitement. Carolyn was coping quite nicely now with the twins and was far more settled, so I felt comfortable taking a much-needed day off from my duties.

Bill met me at the station in Cambridge and he was every bit as gentle, kind, and sincere as I remembered.

"Let me show you round this beautiful place," he said with a smile.

I could barely take my eyes off his face. He wasn't brilliantly good-looking, but he radiated a goodness that was quite spellbinding.

We wandered round. I was totally absorbed in the sights and smells, the dreamy River Cam and its punts, the awe-inspiring King's College Chapel.

I was overawed by a place steeped in such history, learning, and beauty.

Bill fitted in perfectly. His soft brown eyes shone and he spoke with such passion and conviction as he talked of his studies and what Jesus meant to him.

He encouraged me to talk about my faith and listened, really listened, to what I had to say.

He was nothing like cocky, arrogant Henry. In fact, he suited me down to the ground.

His faith was as solid as the foundations of these grand colleges. His love for the Lord shone from him like an inner radiance.

"He is always there guiding us, Brenda," he whispered. "You just have to listen and open your heart. You should come and pray with me soon."

Staring into those shy and dreamy eyes, I'd have gone to the ends of the earth if he'd asked me. "I'd like that." I smiled, flushing pink.

When we parted, I longed for him to kiss me, but he simply smiled and shook my hand gently as we made promises to meet again.

On the train home I tingled all over and stroked my hand where he had brushed it. I wanted to hold on to the memory of his touch for as long as possible.

I enjoyed his company. Really enjoyed it. Who knew what the future held?

When I returned home later that evening with a smile still playing on my lips, a number of things had occurred in my absence.

We had a new resident. Sitting in the front room with his feet up on the coffee table like he owned the place was a most shifty-looking young man.

"This is Bob," said Carolyn, smiling nervously. "He's a friend of my husband. He will be staying with us for a while. He's started a business selling toys and he shall be living and working in the studio above the garage."

Bob was small and twitchy like a rat, with narrow eyes that bobbed this way and that. I didn't like the way he was staring at me. The velvet collar of his jacket was turned up, and he wore a cocked fedora.

What a most peculiar creature.

"Pleased to meet you, Bob," I said stiffly. "What an interesting line of work. What sort of toys will you be making?"

"Not sure yet." He sniffed. "Play ones, I expect."

"Right," I replied, puzzled.

"Anyway," he said, draining his tea and straightening his wide tie, "just wanted to wet me whistle. I'll be orf now."

"What time will you be back?" Carolyn asked.

"See me when you see me," he called, picking up a small suitcase by his side and heading out the door.

Carolyn turned to me and rolled her eyes. "Between you and me, I don't much like him," she confided. "He never gives a straight answer. He's a bit of a spiv."

"Hmm," I murmured. "I can see."

"But Charlie says he's down on his luck and he needs a hand until he's back on his feet."

Needed more than a hand to get him back on his feet, if you asked me, but I kept my opinion to myself. I was just the nanny, after all.

That night I tossed and turned in bed. I thought of Bill, who had made so many sacrifices for his country. Now this dreadful war was over he was trying to make the best of this situation, following his heart and calling to Jesus. I daresay he had little money, but this was the age of austerity and he was knuckling down and getting on with it like the best of us. And then there were men like Bob, no doubt pulling scams and dabbling in the black market. Ducking and diving and living above garages. What a strange existence.

This was turning into a very odd place to work indeed! And it was about to get stranger.

Soon after shifty Bob's introduction another even more peculiar character arrived.

Carolyn had warned me about her brother. "He's a musician," she'd said. "A—well, how can I say—colorful character. He does rather tend to turn up when he pleases. You know what musicians are like—they don't keep the same hours as us."

Soon after, I was in the twin's nursery, dusting. Grandpa was asleep next door, and Mr. and Mrs. Sacks were out.

"Alwight, darlin'," boomed a loud voice up the corridor.

Jumping in shock, I managed to upend my polish and drop my duster.

I whirled round and gasped.

Standing before me was a vision in polyester. This must be Trevor the musician.

He was a tiny man, as slight as a sparrow and just as twitchy.

A head of thick dark hair had been slicked back with pomade. A tight, bright, yellow shirt was unbuttoned, revealing a thick bush of chest hair. Nestling in the bushy forest twinkled an enormous gold medallion.

Everywhere one looked, gold seemed to twinkle. Even his fingers were dripping with gold rings.

"Trevor's the name and music's me game," he chirped. "And what's your name, darlin'?"

I bristled. I most certainly was not his darling.

"I am Nurse Ashford, the children's nanny," I replied.

"Course you are, darlin'," he said, beaming. "What's a fella got to do to get a cuppa round these parts?" he said, planting his hands on his hips. "Me tongue's hanging out."

He was like nothing I'd ever come across before. I supposed he was embracing the modern trends I kept hearing about. Rock and roll hadn't been invented at that stage, but the music being played was the forerunner to it.

Turned out, Trevor played bebop jazz and boogie-woogie blues on the piano in pubs. "You should come and see me play tonight," he said, grinning, then heading to the kitchen.

"I can't," I said. "I'm working." In any case I couldn't bear the smell of beer and never set foot in a pub.

In the coming months, Trevor turned up sporadically and never with any warning. I began to feel like I was in a comedy of errors. Between the alarming Trevor and shifty Bob, I was living in a most peculiar household.

Trevor would sneak up behind me and frighten the life out of me with a booming "alwight, darlin'."

His outfits grew more outrageous with the passing months. No combination of clothing was off limits. From Day-Glo shirts teamed with bright patterned trousers to cocked fedoras and loud wide ties, Trevor could always be relied on to add a garish splash of color to the house.

From his tight shirts worn unbuttoned to his wide ties, he always seemed so casual and thrown together.

What Miss Whitehead, who was a stickler for a properly turned out uniform, would have made of this young man, goodness only knows.

Between Trevor and shifty Bob, who seemed to jump out of the shadows and scare me half to death, I was a bag of nerves.

What effect all these comings and goings were having on the children was anybody's business. It was most disconcerting.

On the whole, though, thanks to separate day and night nurseries, the children didn't seem too put-out by the mayhem created by these bizarre characters.

Children by and large are fairly resilient and not easy to shock. They took these sketchy men in their stride. As ever in 1940s households, the children were confined to certain areas of the house, such as the day and night nursery and the kitchen and garden. They would no more play on their hands and knees with their trains in the living room than I would. This meant, luckily, they mainly saw only their mother and me.

With four children under five I had to run that household with a meticulous eye for detail and a consistent routine.

While the elder children were playing with their toys and the twins were napping, I washed and ironed their clothes, washed bottles, or did any of the countless tasks that seemed to make up my day. I was forever looking ahead (not to mention left and right) to see what tasks I could complete to save time and confusion. Carolyn cooked, so I didn't have to make their meals, but keeping all four entertained, fed, watered, and happily playing was most certainly a full-time job that involved a high degree of stamina.

I couldn't take my eye off the ball for a moment. If I did, you could be sure chaos would break out. One afternoon I was trying to change the twins' diapers when I heard the most terrific din downstairs.

Trevor was doing a full-throttle rendition of a jazz number on the piano in the room below. It sounded like a stray cat was being strangled.

"Really," I muttered, securing Violet's terry cloth diaper with a large safety pin, "this is quite intolerable."

"Don't leave the room, boys," I ordered to the older two and, after making sure the twins were safely in their cots, I stormed downstairs and told Trevor in no uncertain terms that his playing was above the acceptable limits of tolerance for my ears.

On the landing I dodged Bob, who was just going out—or was he returning? One never knew—and let myself back into the nursery, shut the door, and fell back against it with a big sigh.

My relief was short-lived.

"What on earth?" I gasped.

The boys had somehow managed to get hold of a pot of Trevor's pomade and had smeared it all over their hair and faces, and tried on every piece of clothing they owned. Pullovers were bundled over shirts and they had socks on their hands.

The twins were an eager audience to this hectic scene and were sitting up in their cot, giggling and banging the cot bars with the pomade lid.

"We're putting on a show for the twins, Nanny," piped up the older boy.

By the time I had cleared up the mess I was quite exhausted. Thank goodness poor old Grandpa was bedbound. It was far and away the safest place for him to be!

With days such as these, scarcely did an evening pass when my head did not hit the pillow and I was sound asleep by 10:00 PM. Even if I had wanted to watch Trevor showing off on his piano down the pub, I would never have had the energy to stay awake.

And throughout all this bedlam Mr. Sacks still kept conveniently forgetting to pay me my wages on time.

One morning, about five months after I started, I had had enough.

He was late paying me again and yet only the day before I'd seen him counting a big wad of money. "I shall need paying promptly each week," I said sharply.

"Nurse Ashford," he said smoothly, "don't fret. I won't see you short."

That evening he arrived home late from London, with the oldest boy. As I was helping the boy into his pajamas I asked, "Where did you go today? Anywhere nice?"

"I played the piano at Harrods," he replied.

"Oh," I said. "Were you trying one out to buy?"

"Oh, no," he replied. "Dad and I just go all over."

Suddenly, it dawned on me that the image of the professional city gent that Mr. Sacks had presented to me all those months ago in Fortnum & Mason was totally at odds with reality.

I very much doubted whether the slippery Mr. Sacks worked at all. They'd probably only moved in here for somewhere bigger to live, nothing to do with a fraudster care assistant.

More likely than not he was gambling, which would explain his erratic hours and why sometimes he had money and other times not.

I resolved to say nothing. It wasn't my place to question my boss and I had grown fond of Carolyn and the twins, but a sense of mistrust had settled in my heart toward Mr. Sacks and his dubious associates.

Even I was surprised at what he did next. One spring morning Carolyn's father died. It had been in the cards. The poor old man couldn't even get out of bed.

Carolyn, of course, was distraught, and I vowed to help her as much as I could to take the burden off.

I was just taking the twins out one morning, when I saw Mr. Sacks acting suspiciously by the door, packing things into boxes.

When we returned from our walk, I paused in the hallway. Something was different. Then I realized: the duck egg blue china tea set was gone, as were most of the paintings. A faint line of dust outlined where they used to hang on the wall. In fact, anything of value was missing.

"It's all right," said Carolyn, walking in and seeing my concern.

"Charlie has stored them in next door's cellar to avoid probate."

Life could be so puzzling. Mother and Father had brought me up to tell the absolute truth at all times. Behaving in this deceitful way was against everything I held dear. Bill would never dream of behaving in such a way.

The only upside was that Bob hadn't been seen around lately and seemingly had vanished off the face of the earth. I'll admit it, I felt relieved now that he wasn't sidling around the place.

Around the same time I received a phone call that saddened me to the core. It was my friend Mary, who I had to thank for introducing me to Bill.

Nothing had happened between Bill and me, but I had so enjoyed that wonderful day in Cambridge.

"Did you know Bill has decided to become celibate?" she asked.

She paused and her words hung in the air.

I felt my heart sink like a stone in water. "Celibate?" I choked. "N-no," I stuttered. "No, I didn't know that."

"Yes," she went on. "Apparently he has decided to give himself to the Lord completely."

She carried on talking but I had stopped listening. I found I had a sudden lump in my throat. Despair engulfed me. I had thought so fondly of Bill, had even half hoped I might fit into his future plans somewhere.

Now it seemed only one person featured in his life—Jesus!

First Henry and his betrayal and now this. I wasn't having much luck with men.

Fortunately, my job meant that I was so busy I didn't have much time to think about Bill.

The twins were coming up to a year old now and were toddling all over the place, their toothy little grins enchanting me every time I looked at them.

I had seen every stage of their life so far, and what changes indeed!

From newborns who cried, slept, and ate on demand to five-month-olds who suddenly seemed to wake up to the world, charming me with dreamy smiles, frantically kicking little legs, and curious deep blue eyes that never left mine.

Those smiling mouths were set in total determination when they reached ten months or so and realized that those same pudgy legs that are so perfect for kicking were actually quite good for standing up on, too.

Each month brought its own set of challenges, from colic to teething to the joy of discovering they could crawl and then walk.

Of course, all children change and evolve all the time and at their own rates, but there seem to be more miracles to savor in the first year of a child's life than at any other stage. That is the wonder of children. I urge people to remember that when they are despairing over a child who won't sleep or who is cutting her first painful tooth. Everything is just a stage and it won't last long. Try not to despair or wish it away, as something else is always waiting round the corner to whip the rug from under your feet or charm you senseless. We can never freeze time, but we should appreciate every delicious moment of a child's life, for as we all know, they grow up so fast.

All mothers are privileged to go on that journey with their child in that first precious year. Every time I have a tiny baby in my care I consider that journey to be an absolute honor. I've been asked so many times over the years what my favorite age is and I always say the same thing.

The tiny helpless newborn infant.

There really is nothing so awe-inspiring as holding a fresh young life in your arms.

How lucky I was back then to have added twins to my experience of care. Double the work, it's true, but also double the fun! Seeing the world through their excitable eyes was enormously satisfying.

"You clever things," I said, grinning, one morning in the nursery when they pointed jubilantly with pudgy little fingers to the open window.

"Brr . . . brr," squealed Violet, jumping up and down on her bottom in excitement.

"Yes, poppet, a bird." I smiled. "Shall we look at the birdies outside the window? There's blackbirds and blue ti . . ."

As I gazed out the window, my voice trailed off.

"What on earth?" I gasped.

There, crawling through the rhododendron bush, were three of the most suspicious-looking youths I had ever seen.

They wore trilbies pulled down firmly over their faces, and, what's more, they were crawling straight to the front door.

"Mrs. Sacks," I shrieked, "come and look at this."

She rushed in, took one look out the window, and paled.

From downstairs we heard the sharp rap of the front door knocker and froze like startled rabbits.

"I don't like the look of that one little bit," I whispered.

"It's all right, Nurse Ashford," she said. "I'll go."

She rushed downstairs, and I realized my heart was thundering in my chest.

"Stay here, children," I said, softly shutting the door and straining over the banister to listen.

"Does Bob live here?" said a gruff voice. I could tell by Mrs. Sacks's voice she was scared.

"Yes," she said. "He lives over the garage but we haven't seen him around for weeks."

With that she shut the door with a bang and hurried back up the stairs.

From my vantage point I could see the men scurry back onto the path, furtively glancing this way and that.

"Well, what on earth was that about?" I gasped.

Carolyn shrugged, mystified.

Nothing that happened round these parts surprised me anymore.

An hour later the door knocker went again, and Mrs. Sacks answered.

This time it was two policemen.

"We are looking for three youths who have absconded from a remand home," said one, looking past Carolyn into the hallway.

"They raided the warden's office and stole a sum of money from him. We have reason to believe they may have come to this address. They are friends with a former resident, a man who goes by the name of Bob. Do you know him?"

Oh dear, oh dear, oh dear. This was getting worse by the moment.

Carolyn ushered them into the living room and softly closed the door. I heard a muffled exchange of voices and a short while later she came out.

"Nurse Ashford," she said, "they are looking for people who saw anything to give a statement." Enough was enough.

"I am not getting involved," I replied firmly. "What would the Norland say? I am horrified at the thought of getting embroiled in a police investigation. The scandal, imagine?" I blustered.

"Of course," she soothed, returning to the policemen. "Don't worry, I understand."

By the time the local constables had taken their leave, I had already made up my mind. "I'm sorry, Mrs. Sacks," I said, "but I can't continue to work here any longer and I am handing in my notice."

Bombs, disease, rockets, evacuees, and East End mothers I could handle. But this? Shady goings-on, men crawling about in bushes, and musicians in medallions?

Far too much scandal for my stomach, thank you very much.

And so with a heavy heart and a cuddle for Violet and Peter I took my leave.

I was twenty-five and, thanks to Bill's newfound celibacy, no closer to finding love and starting my own family; but thanks to this large and hectic household, my confidence as a child carer, and in my calling, was now absolute.

I may not have had the love of a man, but I had the love of many children to warm the recesses of my soul.

Of course I was disheartened to have lost out on the potential of a relationship with Bill, sadder even than I'd been when I discovered that Henry, a man I actually *was* in a relationship with, had cheated on me. But what doesn't kill you makes you stronger, and it was time for me to move on to new pastures.

If this was how postwar England was shaping up to be, it had seemed, perhaps not safer, but at least more normal during wartime!

Dramatic changes were sweeping the whole world and it was not a place I recognized anymore.

Bikinis went on sale in Paris and the seeds of rock and roll were being sown in America.

Women's lives had radically altered even in the time I had been with the Sackses.

Women were increasingly being employed in what were once men's jobs, not just in manual labor but in skilled positions, and the Trade Union Congress pledged itself to equal pay as a principle.

Women were drafted into work in key jobs in nursing, civil defense, government departments, and transport, and at the same time hundreds of nurseries were being established. The Post Office and Civil Service had scrapped the marriage bar, meaning that they would employ married women for the first time. Female teachers were no longer banned from marrying and universities increasingly became open to women.

Women's talents were being recognized at last, and they were entering the Royal Society as female fellows, starting their own organizations, and opening doors that were previously shut to them. They were taking on men at their own game!

Thanks to all this out on the streets I saw more and more women wearing trousers. Even the Church of England was relaxing its dress code and no longer required women to wear hats to attend services. In 1946 the BBC first broadcast *Woman's Hour*, and women marched about in stark utility-style clothes.

I never frowned on any of these dramatic changes; rather I looked on them like a bewildered bystander. As a Norland trained nurse I was ahead of the game in some respects, though, and at long last child care methods were coming into line with my own outlook.

In 1946 United States pediatrician Dr. Benjamin Spock published *Baby and Child Care*. This book was a bestseller in the United States and Britain and was hugely influential in changing attitudes to parenting. It challenged methods based on strict discipline and replaced spanking with communication and respect for children: a way I had been working for the past seven years, of course in my own quiet fashion. It was a huge step forward for children and their future care.

But the big question remained: with the world changing at such a rapid and bewildering pace, could I change with it?

TESTIMONIAL

Nurse Brenda has carried her responsibility with the highest degree of skill and devotion to which the remarkable progress and robust health of her charges now bears testimony.

It is with deep and profound regret that we now release her to return to her own home. Her generous and invaluable service is sincerely appreciated and her cheerful presence in the household will be greatly missed by all.

—MRS. SACKS

Nanny's Wisdom

TAKE TIME TO CHEER PEOPLE UP.

As a nanny I didn't just regard child care as my sole duty. I am a human being first and a nanny second. When Mrs. Sacks was terribly down and suffering with baby blues, I made time to treat her kindly and attempt to cheer her up. I do so wish people would take the time to look around them at the people in their lives and see who could do with cheering up. Throughout my career I have always advised parents and children to pick a little bunch of flowers or make a card for a friend, partner, mother, or for anyone in their life whom they love and who is troubled by something. It's the little things that count in life; and for many people, just to know they are in someone's thoughts will cheer them up no end. Giving is infinitely more rewarding than receiving.

PREPARE THE QUEENS PUDDING.

All my charges, the Sacks's children included, loved it when I cooked my mother's recipe for the Queens Pudding. I adored it as a child and I still cook it today. It's very cheap to make but a real treat and smells delicious when it's cooking. Nothing says I love you like warm meringue and jam. Serves four to six people.

1¾ cups fresh white bread crumbs
2 tablespoons sugar
1 teaspoon grated lemon zest
1½ cups milk
2 tablespoons butter

2 egg yolks

2 tablespoons apricot jam (but you can use any other flavor)

MERINGUE TOPPING

Four egg whites

⅔ cup sugar

Preheat oven to 320°F.

Put bread crumbs, sugar, and lemon zest in a bowl and toss lightly together to mix.

Pour milk into a saucepan, then add the butter. Gently heat until butter melts.

Pour milk mixture onto the bread crumbs, stir well, and leave to stand for 30 minutes.

Beat the egg yolks until fluffy. Stir into the bread crumb mixture.

Spread the mixture into a well-greased medium-sized oven-proof dish.

Bake in the middle of the oven for 30 minutes, or until firm and set.

Remove dish from the oven. Leave to cool for ten to fifteen minutes, then while bread crumb base is still warm, spread your favorite flavor jam evenly over the top.

Make the meringue topping. Using an electric hand mixer, beat the egg whites. Gradually add the sugar, beating until the whites form nice stiff peaks.

Cover the bread crumb base with swirls of meringue, then sprinkle with more sugar. Return to the oven and bake for a further 20 minutes until the top is pale gold.

Serve pudding warm with cream.

CHAPTER II

THE CIRCLE OF LIFE

THE BARCLAY RESIDENCE
HERTFORDSHIRE, ENGLAND
[1947, AGE TWENTY-SIX]

Itsy Bitsy spider climbing up the spout.
Down came the rain and washed the spider out.
Out came the sun and dried up all the rain.
Now Itsy Bitsy spider went up the spout again!

—NURSERY RHYME

Schedule

7:00 AM: Washed and dressed myself before waking the three girls.

7:30 AM: Assisted in washing and dressing the girls.

8:00 AM: Breakfast.

8:30 AM: Took two older girls to school.

9:00 AM: Home and played with Pippa in nursery.

10:00 AM: Down to the farm with Pippa. Collected eggs and helped milk Buttercup.

10:30 AM: Made butter with Pippa.

11:00 AM: Pippa down for nap before lunch. Cleaned nurseries and did washing, ironing, and sewing.

12:00 PM: Lunch with Pippa and then quiet reading time.

2:00 PM: Washed her hands, took her to toilet, and then out for walk in fresh air. Picked flowers and talked about nature. Took dogs to barn to catch rats.

3:00 PM: Collected girls from school. Gave them snacks of fresh fruit and milk and oversaw homework.

5:00 PM: Took girls down to the farm and walked the dogs, collected eggs, and visited horses. Fed Mr. Wiggles, the goldfish.

5:30 PM: Light tea of bread and homemade butter.

6:30 PM: Bath and teeth cleaning for girls, then read them a story.

7:30 PM: Girls bedtime.

7:30 PM TO 10:00 PM: Sewed, washed, darned, read, or attended dance class and then bedtime.

THE CONTRACTIONS WERE COMING hard and fast, and by the way missus had clenched her eyes shut and was gripping the bedsheets for dear life, another one was on its way.

The sound, almost feral, was terrifying. "Get. The. Doctor. Nowwwwww," she howled.

The contraction exploded within her, and the pain almost seemed to lift her clean off the bed.

The scream was so loud, I swear cows in the neighboring field stopped chewing and stared, puzzled, at the window.

"This baby is coming," she hollered, her eyes bulging as she clutched my hand like a vise.

"We've called the doctor out, Mrs. Barclay," blustered the elderly maternity nurse, feverishly wringing a towel in her chubby hands. "He's on his way."

The nurse looked at the door, then shot me a worried look. I knew just what she was thinking: Would he get here in time?

He'd only come out to examine her not half an hour ago and, as nothing was happening, he'd gone off to have his lunch. What's more, he hadn't seemed best pleased to be called out again so soon.

"Aaaarrrrghhhh," she screamed again.

"Hang in there, Mrs. Barclay," I said more calmly than I felt. "You're doing absolutely marvelously."

Her face screwed up in pain, and I felt so helpless as she collapsed back, exhausted, on the pillow.

"That's it," I soothed. "Gather your strength for the next one."

Looking at her face now, I was in no doubt. This baby was coming, doctor or no doctor!

When I'd started here two weeks previously, I hadn't planned on actually witnessing the birth. The lady of the house should have given birth by now and by rights I should have been nursing a little baby, not mopping the fevered brow of a laboring woman. But then life has a funny way of turning out how you least expect, doesn't it?

Jean and Percival Barclay were wealthy pillars of the community here in their home in a pretty village in Hertfordshire. They had two children, Jane, six, and Penny, three.

Their sprawling farmhouse was set in acres of beautiful grounds. As Jean was mad keen on animals, they owned horses, pigs, and cows galore.

After the chaos of the Sackses' household and conmen crawling through the bushes, I found the peace and quiet of this tranquil countryside most welcoming.

Percival Barclay was a reticent but terribly clever chap. We didn't see him for much of the week, as he had a very important job as chairman of a newspaper group in London.

Percival was typical of the men of his era. It was 1947 and he seemed to live in a pin-striped suit. Weekends were spent with his golfing buddies or locked away in his study. Even now, at the moment of his third child's arrival into the world, he sat downstairs, puffing on a pipe and doing the *Times* crossword. He would no more dream of being in this room than he would walk to the moon. It simply wasn't done. Men weren't to be subjected to the gruesome realities of childbirth.

In 1947, though just around the corner, the NHS hadn't even been formed, so it was left to a maternity nurse and doctor to ensure that everything ran smoothly. An emergency C-section simply wasn't an option.

Just then the door burst open and in bowled a frightfully put-out doctor. His mustache was quivering with rage as he dumped his black leather bag by the bed.

"What do you mean by calling me out again, nurse?" he bristled. "I was in the middle of my lunch."

"We hate to disturb your lunch, Doctor," I said smoothly, "but it would appear Mrs. Barclay's baby is unconcerned at whether you've eaten. She's coming now, you see."

The red-faced doctor looked from me to Mrs. Barclay, who was bearing down with a dogged determination and starting to push.

"Aaah, okay," he blustered. "Right, you," he said, pointing to me, "fetch me some hot water and towels."

I raced downstairs and filled up as many bowls of hot water as I could.

In the kitchen Mr. Barclay glanced at me over the top of his paper and nodded stiffly.

By the time I got back in the room, the doctor had scrubbed up, slipped a sterile sheet under Mrs. Barclay's buttocks, and was examining her. Mrs.

Barclay, meanwhile, wasn't waiting for anyone and was pushing with all her might, a vein on the side of her head throbbing as she bore down and grunted with the effort.

"Delivery imminent," said the doctor with a sigh, probably still thinking of the half-eaten steak and kidney pie growing cold on his kitchen table.

In a split second, the atmosphere in the room changed from one of panic to absolute focused calm.

Mrs. Barclay had stopped screaming and had almost seemed to turn in on herself, perhaps preserving every drop of energy for the arduous task ahead.

"Little pushes," said the doctor as he crouched down and gently maneuvered her onto her side. "That's it, nice and slowly. Breathe deeply."

Suddenly, the room fell under a magical spell and time seemed to freeze. The baby's head was crowning.

"Not too fast," said the doctor. "Pant, don't push—this baby is going to be a big one."

I could see it. I could actually see it. With the next contraction the head started to push through.

"Oh," I breathed, wide-eyed with wonder. "She's coming."

Suddenly, the head slithered out and I gasped. What on earth?

"Oh, you're lucky," squealed the maternity nurse. "She's born in a caul."

I'd only ever heard of babies born in their amniotic sac, and I had heard a child born this way was said to be possessed of remarkable luck or intuitive powers. Who knew whether it was simply an old wives' tale? But it was fascinating to observe.

As the rest of the baby's body slid out effortlessly onto the sheet I was stunned to see she was entirely encased in a bluey-white transparent bag. We could just make out her little face gazing out bewildered from inside her veil.

"Boy, girl?" cried Mrs. Barclay.

"It's a healthy girl," said the doctor. "And she'll be fine."

Working quickly, the doctor deftly made a small incision in the membrane by the baby's nostrils so she could breathe and then gently peeled back the rest of the sac from her skin.

I stood rooted to the spot, utterly spellbound. It was like watching the most precious present of all being tenderly unwrapped.

And what a gift! Now that the sac had gone I could see a wriggling little pink bundle. She was perfect, from her chubby little clenched fists to her curled-up toes. She was now a separate being.

I had just witnessed birth, in all its brutal splendor.

"It's a miracle, Mrs. Barclay," I breathed.

I felt my eyes begin to mist over. "Towel," barked the less sentimental doctor.

Minutes later the cord was clamped and the maternity nurse weighed her.

"Ooh, she's a big one," she said with a smile, "nearly eleven pounds."

With that Mrs. Barclay went as white as flour and collapsed back against her pillow. The effort of delivering an eleven-pound baby born in a caul seemed to entirely swamp her.

The nurse wrapped the baby in a towel and, seeming to sense that Mrs. Barclay needed peace as the doctor delivered the placenta, handed her to me instead.

Holding the precious bundle like it was the most fragile lace, I breathed in that incredible musky smell that all newborn babies seem to have and sighed in wonder.

Walking with her over to the window, I gently peeled back the towel so I could get a better look.

Her little face may have been covered in blood and mucous but quite honestly she was the loveliest thing I had ever clapped eyes on.

Just then she made a slight snuffling sound and her deep blue eyes opened just a fraction for the first time. A tingle ran the length of my body as I realized I was the first person in the world she had set eyes upon.

"Welcome to the world, sweetheart." I smiled. "You're a big girl, aren't you."

Her blue eyes gazed curiously at me and for a split second I felt an instinctive understanding run between us.

"I'm your nanny," I whispered, softly stroking her furrowed little brow with my finger.

Her skin was as soft as satin.

Not since David's birth all those years before had holding a baby affected me quite so profoundly. I had witnessed the miracle of her birth and had the honor of holding her just minutes after she was unpeeled from her caul. It was a moment I shall treasure always.

Seconds later she let rip a ferocious and indignant cry.

"Nothing wrong with baby's lungs, then." The maternity nurse chuckled.

Baby Pippa and I formed a strong bond created in those powerful minutes after the birth. Little Pippa and I were as close as close can be. For eight blissful years she was my be-all and end-all.

As Pippa and the rest of her fellow baby boomers grew up and took their first unsteady steps, the world was a rapidly changing place.

On July 5, 1948, nine months after her birth, the National Health Service Act was passed and the NHS was formed, pledging free health care for all. It was a momentous achievement and everybody wanted the new service to work.

We may have still been war-weary, accustomed to austerity, and had rationing still in place, but it was a sign of good things to come. Prior to this law only people who could afford expensive private health insurance—mainly men—could be guaranteed health care.

In those days we were happy with the simple things in life. There was no television set at the Barclays', so we contented ourselves with plenty of walks in the fresh air or listening to plays on the radio. Life was certainly a lot less complicated, competitive, and fast-moving, and all the better for it, if you ask me.

Foreign travel was out of the reach of most people, so the British seaside and Butlin's camps became magnets for pleasure seekers.

After the carnage of war, life was looking up. Britain and the Western world were recovering.

Father's business, while not exactly booming, was at least surviving, and now Christopher helped him out. Michael was starting to train for a career in the theater; and Basil was working abroad for a timber firm.

Mother, still at a loss after her beloved evacuees left, had bought herself a dog, a delightful little whippet she called Bambi, to fuss over and care for.

The baby boom was keeping midwife Kathleen rushed off her feet, and she seemed to spend all of her time delivering babies in Surrey.

Important steps were being made in child health, and thanks to the Children Act of 1948 their welfare was being taken seriously.

I marveled at how lucky and privileged we were to suddenly have access to vaccines and medicine that before just simply weren't available to the masses. Little Pippa and her sisters wouldn't have to go through the pain of so many childhood illnesses like I had suffered. The pharmaceutical industry was creating a flood of new drugs. Penicillin, polio vaccine, better anesthetic agents, cortisone, drugs for the treatment of mental illness such as schizophrenia and depression, diuretics for heart failure, and antihistamines all became available.

The war had created a housing crisis—alongside postwar rebuilding of cities, the 1946 New Towns Act created major new centers of population that all needed health services.

Newly rebuilt towns had to put the family first and consider the welfare of schools, nurseries, and parents. And so it seemed that innovation could be born from times of crisis.

It was on one such visit to a new NHS baby clinic for a checkup for Pippa that I realized perhaps I was in danger of being viewed as an outdated relic, a prewar dinosaur.

I was sitting in the clinic, holding Pippa in my lap. She was dressed ever so smartly in her little wool coat and cap, I was in my Norland uniform, and the older girls were playing happily nearby pulling a little wooden duck on wheels about. Jane and Penny were so good and on the whole were content to sit and paint pictures; do coloring in; or, as now, to play with whatever toys were available.

A mother sitting nearby looked at me and sniffed. "You one of those Norland nannies?" she asked.

"Yes, I am." I smiled. "Have you heard of them then?"

"Oh, I've heard of 'em all right," she said with a laugh. "Out of touch they are, with all their highfalutin ways."

"What do you mean?" I asked, feeling my cheeks flush at this sudden attack on my profession.

"What's the good in having a Norland nanny?" she went on. "They don't work—they don't like to get their hands or their uniform dirty. I mean to say, it's ridiculous. Who needs a nanny in a cape?"

I sat, gobsmacked, staring after the woman as she was called in to see the doctor.

Was that really how she saw me? How the world saw us? As work-shy snobs?

Furious, I took the girls, tucked them up in their coach pram, and marched home.

"I have never been lazy in my whole life," I muttered as I strode down the road.

"What's wrong, Nana?" asked Jane.

"Nothing, darling." I smiled brightly.

But do you know what I did as soon as I got home?

I took off my uniform, folded it up, put it away, and then changed into a plain blue overall dress.

Rightly or wrongly, I didn't want to be seen that way.

I am sure Mrs. Whitehead would have had a blue fit, but the world had changed so much since 1939.

As we entered the 1950s a nanny in a uniform seemed strangely outdated.

Society was changing, and I had to be seen to be changing with it.

I could get my hands dirty with the best of them, and there and then I made a vow. I could only truly call myself a proper nanny if I did everything that a mother would do.

In the case of the Barclays that meant getting my hands really dirty!

Mrs. Barclay went out to their small holding every day to ride her beloved horses and feed her animals.

I used to love taking the girls out to the farm to pick buttercups and make daisy chains.

But now I realized we could all do more. "Can I help with the animals?" I ventured one spring morning, after nearly four years on the farm.

"Well yes, Nurse Brenda, that would be lovely," Mrs. Barclay said, handing me a pail. "You can start by milking Buttercup. The relief milker's sick."

Buttercup was what was known as a house cow. Half Guernsey and half shorthorn, she provided all the fresh milk for the household. Her delicious milk was used in Mrs. Barclay's morning coffee and the children's cereal, as well to make cream and cheese.

Buttercup was staring dolefully at me. I gulped.

A nanny who milks. Well, one has to be adaptable in these changing times.

The children giggled as I sat on the milking stool, took a deep breath, and gently prodded her swollen udders.

Two seconds later milk sprayed everywhere, and the children were in fits of giggles. "You're supposed to get it in the bucket, Nana." Jane laughed as it dripped off the end of my nose.

"Practice makes perfect," I said, diving in again.

Poor Buttercup. She stared at me patiently with those big brown eyes as I wrestled with her udders.

By the time I'd finished I'd managed half a bucket and I was thrilled.

"Well done, Nana," the children cried. After that we had the most magical day. We fed hay to the animals, helped muck out the horses, and then together we skimmed the cream off the milk to make butter.

Everyone helped out. Even their two dogs, an Alsatian called Beau and a whippet called Jester, worked as a double act.

Thanks to the new buildings nearby, hundreds of rats had been disturbed and decided to take shelter in the barn and outhouses.

Beau raced in and sniffed out the rats, and as they ran for the door, the whippet was waiting to catch them.

"Look," I cried delightedly to the children. We watched them for hours until finally dusk sneaked in over the fields.

"Come on, children," I said, taking their hands. "Time for tea."

As we headed home across the fields, the light of the farmhouse spilling out across the countryside, I felt a warm flush of happiness.

Country life suited me. There was no time to feel regret at my lost loves or lament not having time to find a new man. My heart was fulfilled and I loved my job with a passion. Surely that was more important?

"I've had a lovely day, Nana," three-year-old Pippa said with a smile, her little hand warm in mine.

"Me, too," I trilled.

Sitting down in the kitchen, eating toast and jam at the end of the day spent with the children in the fresh air, I realized what a truly important lesson I was teaching them. A sense of responsibility and caring for others isn't easily taught: it has to be demonstrated.

That night I tucked the children up in their beds, planted little kisses on their heads, and wrapped their feet up in soft blankets so their toes didn't get cold, as my own mother had done all those years before.

"Sweet dreams, girls." I smiled.

"I think you're a super nana," whispered Penny sleepily under her eiderdown.

Later I was snuggled up in my own bed. I may have been alone but suddenly, with a jolt I realized, I didn't care!

I was nearly thirty now with no husband or a child to call my own, but for some reason it didn't seem to matter. The need to find a man didn't drive me in quite the same way as being the best nanny that I could possibly be did.

Being on my own wasn't actually the end of the world.

From what I could see, men were nothing but trouble anyway. Perhaps I was wise to leave the heartache to others?

After that, every spare minute was spent down on the farm, helping out, watching the beauty of the changing seasons, and observing the centuries-old traditions of farming.

One such tradition was that of Buttercup's yearly baby. Poor cow, every year she had to be artificially inseminated and have a calf to keep her milk supply going. The baby boom was nothing new for this sweet old cow.

When I'd been at the Barclays' for nearly four years, Buttercup gave birth to a frisky young black-and-white heifer. This heifer was quite mad: she ran round the field like a bucking bronco, charging anyone who dared come near her.

It wasn't just the heifer. Half the animals on this farm seemed quite, quite mad. The geese used to chase the horses round the fields and Percy, the enormous boar, regularly broke free from his sty and rampaged round the farm.

The war nursery and caring for Jimmy and the evacuees seemed tame in comparison!

I woke one morning on my thirtieth birthday to find the girls had made me a card. I was quite touched and looking forward to the day.

Mrs. Barclay had other ideas.

"Brenda, would you mind feeding Buttercup's heifer?" she asked over the breakfast table. "The relief milker's not shown up."

I wasn't surprised. He was scared out of his wits of that mad creature. Even the local gravedigger who came on occasion to help out refused to go in the field to lay out her hay.

But what sort of message would I send to the girls if I said no?

"Of course," I agreed.

"Thanks, Brenda." She smiled, returning to her paper. "You are a treasure."

With the girls lined up, watching safely from the other side of the fence, I picked up the stack of hay and quietly opened the gate to the cows' field. The mad heifer was grazing at the far end of the field. If I sneaked in, she may just not notice me. "You are brave, Nana," piped up Pippa, her nose pressed against the wooden gate.

Brave or stupid.

Venturing farther into the field I started to stealthily scatter the hay, hardly daring to breathe.

Just a few more minutes and then I'd be home and dry. Suddenly, I felt a hot breath on my neck. "Er, Nana," cried Jane. *"Run!"*

Turning round to find myself face-to-face with the mad heifer, I leaped to my feet. Not since the German planes had flown overhead had I felt such adrenaline pump through my body.

I hurtled through that muddy field toward the gate like a woman possessed, the mad heifer in hot pursuit.

"Run!" whooped and hollered the girls. "She's gaining on you. . . ."

"I'm nearly . . ." I started to yell, until "urghhh," I grunted. An almighty thud hit me in the back and I felt the air rush out of my body.

Suddenly, I realized I was airborne! Flying through the air I landed face-down in the mud with a splat.

Tossed into the mud by a mad beast? Some birthday this was turning out to be!

Limping back to the house with the girls supporting me, head to toe in mud, I had to laugh. Children were definitely easier to deal with than animals. To everyone's relief Buttercup's wayward daughter was sold shortly after, but it had certainly made it a birthday to remember.

Most people these days seem to spend their thirtieth birthdays in some riotous fashion, hosting a party or going on a holiday. I daresay on mine I was tucked up in bed after I put the girls down and was sound asleep by 10:00 PM, as I was most nights. I did some reflection on my life. Thirty is rather a milestone, isn't it, and one does tend to take stock at these times.

Jane was ten, Penny seven, and Pippa four, and caring for these three little angels was my life. If I wasn't collecting or dropping the older girls at school or helping them with their homework, I was caring for Pippa, and life was certainly most busy. There was not so much as a whiff of a man on the scene and quite honestly I didn't seem to find the time nor the inclination to go looking for one.

Was I unhappy about that fact? Honestly, if I searched deep inside my soul, I would have to say no. Child care had always been my calling. I had answered this call, and every day brought its own rewards. Okay, I might not have had a man, but I still had plenty of love in my life. I was doing perfectly well on my own, thank you very much.

You'd have thought we'd have learned our lesson about working with animals from the mad heifer incident, but sometime later at a local fair the girls won a goldfish.

"Can we keep her, Nana?" pleaded Pippa. "Can we, please?"

Staring into her beautiful cornflower blue eyes, how could I refuse my Pippa anything?

"Go on, then." I chuckled. "But only on the proviso you all look after her."

Bless them. They were so proud of their little fish, Mr. Wiggles, they carried him or her all the way home in a water-filled plastic bag.

Back in the nursery he soon had a new home in a glass tank.

"Mr. Wiggles can only stay if you all clean him out once a week and remember to feed him every day."

They were ready for the responsibility of caring for an animal, and a goldfish was the perfect place to start.

The girls nodded their heads and promised faithfully.

True to their word, they did. Except one week Penny was carrying the bowl out of the nursery to the sink when disaster struck.

"Nana," she screamed.

Mr. Wiggles had made a break for freedom and had splashed right out of the bowl and was flipping about on the nursery carpet.

Pandemonium broke out. "Help Mr. Wiggles," cried Penny.

Oh, crumbs. Getting down on my hands and knees I frantically tried to scoop the fish up, but he was too slippery—no sooner had I got him than he flipped out of my hands.

"He's going to die, Nana," yelped Pippa, tears streaming down her sweet little face.

Eventually, I got hold of him long enough to get him back into the bowl of water.

"Thank goodness." I sighed, sinking back against the door to catch my breath.

There was just one problem. From that day on Mr. Wiggles never swam straight again. He swam on his side!

Mr. Wiggles survived, but unfortunately, in the countryside, where there's livestock there is also dead stock, as I learned to my cost one day.

"Brenda," called Mrs. Barclay one morning, after I'd dropped the older girls at school and settled Pippa for a nap. "You wouldn't be a dear and come and help me with something, would you?"

As a nanny you hear that sentence uttered by the mouths of mothers an awful lot. From collecting something from the shop to making sure you are in for a deliveryman, you are often called upon to do things outside your job description.

On one memorable occasion I was even asked to put out a blazing incendiary bomb with a cowpat after it set fire to a boss's field! I never was asked to carry coal or eat with the servants, as the Norland stipulated was against the rules in my handbook, but every day, mundane tasks were often asked of me. I always agreed. I don't say this to sound like a martyr, but I was there to support the mother and so I needed to be prepared to roll up my sleeves and help out. Although even I could see what was asked of me now was pushing the boundaries somewhat.

Following her out to the farm I was intrigued to see Fred the local grave-digger huffing and puffing as he attempted to dig a grave in a nearby field.

It had been an icy cold night and frost coated the fields like a white blanket.

"Ground's as tough as rock," he muttered. "And me tongue's hanging out for a cup of tea."

"No time for that, Fred," snapped Mrs. Barclay. "Keep digging."

She seemed unusually tetchy and when we reached the sty I saw why. Her prize sow Susie was lying dead, frozen solid to the floor of the sty. "She died last night. Vet reckons swine fever." She sighed. "Highly contagious. We've got to bury her quickly and disinfect the whole farm before any of the neighboring farms get wind."

"But how will we get her out?" I gasped. "She's frozen solid to the floor."

"Only one thing for it," she said. "Go and start boiling some kettles. We'll have to defrost her."

Shaking my head I scuttled back to the house and returned soon after with a steaming hot kettle.

"Tea?" asked Fred hopefully, as I ran past with the kettle.

"Keep digging," I called.

Back in the sty I winced as we poured boiling water over the dead pig. Gradually, she defrosted and Mrs. Barclay was able to move her a little.

But there presented our next problem. "She weighs an absolute ton," she huffed.

"Can't we just call the vet?" I asked.

"No, Nurse Brenda," she said. "He won't come out for fear of contamination. This is down to us."

Last I heard, this wasn't in my job description, but it didn't seem to be the time to start quibbling.

"I've an idea," Mrs. Barclay said, her eyes lighting up. "Go and get the children's sled."

Shaking my head, I did as asked and returned with a large toboggan. "Now," she said, "you push and I'll pull."

With an almighty grunt, I pushed; but as the pig was still a bit icy, she just shot straight on the sled and off the other side, landing with a thud by Mrs. Barclay's feet. "Oh this is ridiculous," she cried, pushing the slippery sow and sending her ricocheting back over to me.

Suddenly, the humor of the situation hit me and I started to laugh. It started as a little chuckle but soon my body was racked with laughter and tears streamed down my face.

"This is absurd," I screeched.

"It is rather, isn't it?" Mrs. Barclay said, her mouth starting to twitch.

Soon we were both in hysterics. How we got that frozen pig onto the toboggan and out across to the field I'll never know, but the sight of two cackling women pulling a dead pig on a sled was too much for poor Fred.

"Queer folk," he muttered, putting his spade down and getting out of there as fast as he could.

Fortunately, he had dug enough of a hole for us to fit her in.

"On my count of three, tip her in," said Mrs. Barclay. "One . . . two . . . three, heave ho."

We lifted the sled and with a thud the sow landed half in and half out the grave, her little pink trotters poking out the ground.

"Oh, this is ridiculous," I cried. "There's only one thing for it."

I jumped down in on top of her and with a slither she landed in the bottom of the grave.

Without exchanging a word Mrs. Barclay pulled me out of the grave. Working quickly, we covered Susie in a sack of quicklime, filled in the grave, and hurried back to the house.

We never spoke again about the dead pig incident. I have done many bizarre things in my career as a nanny, but that may well go down as one of the oddest.

But while I was grappling in graves with frozen pigs, my contemporaries in Britain and America were spending their time in a no-less-energetic way.

Across the Atlantic in America, rock 'n' roll had been created. With its roots in blues, jazz, and gospel music it exploded on the scene in Britain in the mid 1950s.

The leading figure of this and the "king of rock and roll" was one Elvis Presley.

Women went crazy for his gyrating hips and men tried to emulate his cool.

Across the pond women danced and strutted their stuff in full skirts, colorful heels, and nylon stockings.

While many my age started wearing denim jeans—the symbol of the teenage rebel in TV shows—cropped pants, and halter-neck dresses to local dances, I stuck resolutely to my cotton dresses nipped in at the waist with a belt.

Children didn't simply become young adults at thirteen, they now became teenagers; and while they may have been taking over the world in other places, here in the small Hertfordshire village where I lived, country music was the only sound that rang out.

It was less shake, rattle, and roll and more do-si-do.

Every Friday night in the next village along from ours in the village hall they held country-dance lessons.

After the children went to bed I would get the bus.

I wasn't going to meet a man, more because I loved to dance. But if there happened to be a man as lovely as Bill, then that would be rather nice, too, thank you very much.

Sadly, when I pushed open the creaky door to the drafty village hall my heart sank.

The place was full of couples and I was on my own!

I was just about to turn on my heel and head for home when the instructor spotted me. "Oh, don't go," he said. "I'm Keith. I'll partner you."

Keith's eyes roamed over my body like a cheap suit as he took me by the waist and guided me to the dance floor.

"We don't get new faces here often, Brenda," he said, pressing his face so close to mine I could smell what he'd had for dinner. "A woman like you needs special attention."

I smiled awkwardly.

Keith ran the weekly country-dance lessons and was fairly adamant that I needed extra tuition. Unfortunately, Keith was what you might call the sexy type and his hands were forever wandering to places where they shouldn't have ventured.

No matter. I'd dealt with a few frisky animals back at the farm. I could deal with a harmless letch like Keith.

Week after week Keith insisted on partnering me, leaving his poor wife, Kathy, sitting at the side. Keith seemed to have more arms than an octopus and could seemingly swing me round, do the do-si-do, while letting one slightly clammy hand run down the small of my back.

At the end of one class Keith managed to wheedle out of me that I had that Sunday afternoon off. "Oh, you must come for tea," he oozed. "Kathy and I would love to have you."

I couldn't see the harm in it. His wife would be there, after all. I felt bad refusing, too; besides Keith was a man who didn't really seem to be able to take no for an answer.

I called Mother. "You don't mind if I don't come home this Sunday afternoon, do you?" I asked.

"Of course not, darling," she exclaimed. "I have Bambi to keep me company, and your father and I are going to take him for a long walk."

That Sunday afternoon, instead of returning home to the warmth of my family, I brushed my hair, splashed water on my face, and headed to Keith and Kathy's with a small bouquet of daffodils.

Keith answered the door. Two things struck me immediately as I followed him into the lounge: the overwhelming stench of Old Spice and the distinct absence of any wife.

"Kathy had to go out." He smiled as he sat down on the settee and licked his thin lips. "Her mother's sick. So afraid it's just you and me."

He patted the seat next to him. "Come and sit next to me."

Perched on the edge of the sofa, I felt as out of place as Mr. Wiggles the goldfish must have done when he found himself floundering about on the carpet.

As I nibbled on a crab paste sandwich and mentally planned my escape, it appeared Keith had other things on his mind.

"There's a big competition on in London soon." He smiled, his eyes glittering with mischief. "You know you're good enough to enter, Brenda, with some extra tuition from myself, of course."

With that he laughed heartily and clamped a hand down on my thigh. Dropping my sandwich, I jumped to my feet.

"I won't get the time off, Keith," I blustered.

A loaded silence hung in the air. "Well, it's been lovely, and I'm so sorry to miss Kathy, really I am, but I best be getting back to the farm," I said.

"Shame." Keith sighed. "I'll run you home."

"Really," I said. "It's no bother."

"I insist," he said, smiling and staring at my bosom.

As he got his coat, I looked round at the sitting room of the small semidetached house. Pictures of Keith and Kathy on their wedding day looked down from the walls.

What was wrong with some men? Did he honestly think I would fall into the arms of a married man? What did he take me for? He was as fake and cheap as the nylon shirt he was wearing.

As we bumped along the roads back to the Barclays in Keith's Ford I had an ominous feeling I knew what was coming. He pulled to a halt outside the farmhouse.

With no streetlamps it was pitch-black inside and outside the car, but I could see the whites of Keith's eyes.

Suddenly, he lunged across the car and pressed his thin lips on mine.

"Oh, Brenda," he groaned, his hands snaking over my body.

"Oh no, you don't," I snapped, disentangling myself from his clammy embrace.

I shot out of the car like my heels were on fire and ran like a whippet up the drive.

Once inside, I dashed upstairs to the landing window, my heart thumping in my chest. I heard Keith gun up his engine and speed down the country road. Of all the disgusting, slimy . . .

In bed I undressed and stared at the ceiling.

What was wrong with me? I wasn't a bad person. Why did I have the worst luck with men?

"I give up." I sighed. The only man I ever really felt anything for had promised himself to Jesus and all the rest seemed to be fickle cheats.

After that I had less and less time off. Mrs. Barclay, suffering with a kidney problem after a nasty kick from a heifer, more often than not took to her bed when I was due a day off.

Finally, after seven years on the farm, I started to get itchy feet. This place had been wonderful. I simply adored my charges, and my hands-on approach with the animals had made for some memorable occasions, but I felt instinctively that it was time to move on.

The magical wind of change was blowing my way, making me restless and uprooting me. There were babies being born everywhere, babies who needed my care.

I had done my duty here. I had even earned my badge of merit from the Norland in 1953 for more than five years of faithful service to one family. It was the same year that Her Royal Majesty Elizabeth was crowned queen. She had found her vocation and I mine.

Now, in 1955, Pippa was seven, and even though she was the apple of my eye, I could see she needed me less and less. Jane, now fourteen, and Penny, ten, were just as distraught.

"Please don't go, Nana," they cried, when they heard I had handed my notice in. "Who will help us milk Buttercup?"

"I'm sorry, my darlings," I said sadly. "We will always stay in touch."

I had had a riot at the Barclays', but it was time to move on.

As I dried the tears from Pippa's blue eyes I thought back to the magical moment I first saw her open them and gaze back at me. What a very special journey we had been on together. Sadly, Pippa's journey was to end before my own.

We did indeed stay in touch, Pippa and I, and she grew up to be a fine young woman, with two daughters of her own. I visited her many times in her own home and reveled in watching her grow as a woman and as a mother. I have always tried my hardest to stay in touch with all my families and visit them as often as time and circumstances permitted. If I couldn't visit, I always put pen to paper and wrote, and so was the case with Pippa.

Tragically, though, she was diagnosed with breast cancer and died in 2007 aged sixty.

As I sat at her funeral and watched her coffin lowered into the ground I was struck with a deep sadness.

I had been privileged to witness her entry into the world and now I watched bewildered as she left it.

I had gazed in awe as she had emerged from her mother's womb, heard her first words, witnessed her first steps, tended her grazed knees, and dried her tears. And now she was gone.

"Ashes to ashes, dust to dust," cried out the minister's voice, and I bowed my head in respect.

I had witnessed the full circle of life, from birth through to death.

Life on the farm taught me a great many things: that our journey through life can be fleeting and we none of us are masters of our destiny.

We are just as fragile as the snowdrops that push up through the soil in spring. We owe it to ourselves to live each day on earth as if it is our last.

TESTIMONIAL

Nurse Brenda has been in entire charge of my three children. Her care of the baby during infancy is beyond all praise and her management of all three children is admirable. It is with a feeling of real loss that she has left us to return to babies. Not only is she an outstanding nurse but her kindness and devotion to our family is beyond praise. She holds a unique place in our family life and will always be considered a member of it.

— MRS. BARCLAY

Nanny's Wisdom

APPRECIATE THE PASSAGE OF TIME.

When we are young we think we will remain that way forever, that somehow we have escaped the aging process. Working at the Barclays' made me appreciate the passage of time, the passing of the seasons, and that time doesn't stand still for anyone. We aren't invincible or ageless; we are but just tiny specks on this great planet and we must strive to make our mark on it any way we can. More important than anything, we must appreciate this life and not waste a single precious moment of it. It is a cliché, but life really is a gift. Don't overplan it or complicate it by forever thinking of tomorrow. Enjoy today, for what else is there?

MAKE YOUR OWN BUTTER.

Few people realize how easy it is to make butter, as we did at the Barclays'. When the girls and I used to make it, we churned it by hand using Buttercup's fresh milk and then squeezed it into shape on butter pats. Nowadays it's even easier.

Simply pour four pints of heavy cream into a bowl and whisk until thick. Continue whisking until the whipped cream collapses and separates into butter and buttermilk. This should take about five minutes. Turn mixture into a sieve to drain off the buttermilk, using a spoon to push the mixture down and force out the fluid. Return the butter to the bowl and beat until more buttermilk separates. Drain and repeat. Mix in some salt if you like the taste. Wash the butter in very cold water, shape into a pat, wrap in wax paper, and chill in fridge. Homemade butter is absolutely delicious on hot toast.

CHAPTER 12

TROUBLESHOOTING NANNY

LONDON AND THE HOME COUNTIES, ENGLAND
[1956, AGE THIRTY-FIVE]

Horsey, horsey, don't you stop,
Just let your feet go clippetty-clop.
The tail goes swish and the wheels go round.
Giddyup, we're homeward bound.

—NURSERY RHYME

Schedule

6:00 AM: Arrived at house. Mother and baby were often still in hospital, so I was shown to my room by staff or granny. Unpacked and put my uniform on.

6:30 AM: Tidied room and checked I had all my equipment.

7:00 AM: If there was an older sibling, I would get toddler up, washed, dressed, and ready for a breakfast of bread with butter and jam, or cereal. Grace would then be said at the end of the meal. Once toddler had requested to get down from the table, he would be allowed down.

8:00 AM: Potty time. I always have set times for potty training. If managed, I expressed great delight and encouragement. If not, then I said, "Better luck next time."

8:30 AM: Teeth cleaned and hands washed. I played with toddler on my hands and knees in nursery.

9:00 AM: Mother arrived home. Encouraged mother to rest, and I took her tea and breakfast in bed.

9:30 AM: Sleeping baby was gently placed in new cot in my bedroom.

9:00 AM TO 10:00 AM: While baby asleep, mother resting, and toddler happily playing I made beds, did laundry, washed nappies.

10:00 AM: Fed baby. If toddler old enough and anxious to help, I allowed toddler to help nurse the baby, with my supervision of course.

10:30 AM: Baby fed and put in his or her pram and placed in garden to sleep in fresh air; if wet out, then in cot. District nurse may visit (they visited every day for ten days). After that, responsibility handed over to me and I would take baby to clinic to be weighed and measured.

11:00 AM: If no cook, then I prepared lunch and sterilized used bottles. Gave toddler drink of milk, then put down to rest in bed for an hour. Most toddlers would sleep for an hour until lunchtime. I then made up feeds for the next twenty-four hours, did the washing and ironing, and cleaned the nurseries and bedrooms.

12:30 PM: Lunch.

2:00 PM: If fine, I took both children off for a walk, fed the ducks, or collected different colored leaves, picked blackberries, collected acorns and wildflowers.

3:00 PM: Fed baby. Mother may have woken by now and come to feed baby, too, and spend time in nursery with toddler.

4:00 PM: Ate a simple meal: jam sandwiches, slices of cheese, milk to drink, followed by sponge cakes and jelly. Encouraged toddler to eat a piece of ripe apple after every meal. Toddler washed hands.

5:00 PM: Toddler and baby with visitors or parents for the hour after tea, while I prepared for the children's bath time.

6:00 PM: Bathe toddler and top and tail baby. After bath, toddler into nighties or pajamas and I read to him or her. Then I encouraged parent to read a second story while I tended to the baby and fed evening bottle.

7:30 PM: Children asleep, so I caught up on ironing, sewing, and mending.

10:00 PM: Took baby through for parents to do last feed of the evening.

11:00 PM TO 6:00 AM: If baby still under three months, I would do three to four hourly feeds through the night, but for babies older than three months and getting sufficient feeds through the day I would just offer a drink of water or a pacifier and settle baby back to sleep, to wean off milk feeds through the night. I usually had most babies sleeping through the night by six months.

IT WAS 7:30 AM, AUGUST 1956. Courtfield Gardens, South Kensington, London, in the royal borough of Kensington and Chelsea.

I had just arrived at my new home and was about to report for duty. What a magnificent place to lay my hat!

The beautiful Georgian period town houses arranged in a square around a private garden spoke of money and refined elegance—a thoroughly British abode, a stone's throw from Buckingham and Kensington Palaces and the smarter districts of Mayfair and Knightsbridge.

The Clean Air Act had just been passed in Parliament in response to London's Great Smog of 1952, which killed twelve thousand poor souls, and for the first time in years the air felt clean and fresh.

Just a few years ago you might not have even been able to see the lampposts that dotted the square through the pea soup fogs that cloaked London in a thick green layer of smog.

It may have been August, but a light drizzle fell over the square and it felt most refreshing on my face.

Setting down my leather case on the white stone steps leading up to the mansion house, I shook out my umbrella and sighed happily.

The Conservatives had won back power from Labor in 1951 and taxes were low.

London was booming and industry was thriving for the first time since the war. British factories churned out cars in their millions, steel and coal production was soaring, and further to the east of London the docks employed thousands of men all toiling ceaselessly.

Huge oceangoing vessels loaded with produce sailed majestically in and out of the bustling docks.

London felt like the center of the world.

Women continued to gain in power and strength around the world with more and more countries granting them the right to vote.

The National Childbirth Trust (NCT) had just been established in 1956. Up until then women were given little or no information about pregnancy and birth and just blindly followed their doctor's instructions. Now, for the first time, they had support, advice, and guidance. Ultrasound scans were just around the corner and a woman didn't have to suffer needlessly with a life-threatening birth. She could have a cesarean section instead! The Americans were stirring things up, too!

Sexual Behavior in the Human Female by American author and sex therapist Alfred Kinsey was published in 1953 and caused huge controversy.

Here in South Kensington, however, there were no sexual revolutions, civil rights movements, or record-breaking attempts made that I knew of! Genteel peace and prosperity prevailed. The only sound was the clanking of glass milk bottles as a milkman tootled past standing up inside his refrigerated truck.

"Good morning to you, ma'am," he said with a smile, politely tipping his little white cap.

"And a good morning to you, too, sir." I beamed back. People were so polite and courteous in those days and it was commonplace to greet a stranger like a friend.

From the inside of the mansion, however, a different greeting drifted down the steps to meet me. The distinctive mewing cry of a newborn baby rang out and I smiled.

Before I knocked on the imposing door I took a moment to pause and reflect on my purpose here.

I was to be nanny to two-week-old twin girls and their poor exhausted mother.

I was here to make this the happiest home it could possibly be.

Since leaving the Barclays' fifteen months previously, I had already stayed in four private homes, caring for young children in three, and in the fourth looking after two young boys so their parents could go on a skiing holiday. With each job I had become aware of a growing need inside me.

I started in a home where the mother was frazzled, burned-out, and in dire need of help. I left behind me, I hope, a happier and more fulfilled home.

I can't have been doing too badly, as word had got round that I was open to short-term bookings, and now I was booked solid with short placements for new mothers for the next nine months!

This was my new calling. Nowadays you would call it troubleshooting, but back then I liked to call it good old-fashioned common sense.

Going from home to home to get new mothers on their feet was teaching me so much. With each home and family I worked for, I realized what I loved more than anything was getting the family on their feet and creating the happiest home I possibly could. Sprinkling a little of the magic that I had experienced in my own childhood was proving most gratifying.

I had enjoyed a blissful childhood and home life filled with love, laughter, and rich cooking smells.

I had puzzled many times over the ingredients for such a perfect recipe for a happy home. It needed to be a place with parents who worshipped their offspring. Throw in some stability, a dash of routine, and respect. Sprinkle some fun and imaginative games and stir well.

A vital ingredient in this recipe I had since concluded was the mother. As long as the mother is happy, the household will be happy. The mother truly is the heart and soul of a family.

So why, I reasoned, couldn't I re-create that recipe in homes around Britain?

I wasn't alone in my thinking. Magazines in the 1950s were full of articles encouraging women to return to their traditional roles as homemakers. They promoted the idea that feminine virtues were most important and that motherhood was the most important role a woman could occupy. I agree with this.

I am all for a woman working if that is what her heart desires—one must follow one's heart, after all. But whether a mother is in a part-time or full-time role, she must be happy if the home is to be content and full of love.

After all, the world would be a much happier place if people tried to fill their houses with love.

Some people just needed a little reminding, that's all.

With that I rapped the heavy black lion's head knocker twice on the mansion door.

The man of the house was one Mr. Gordon. He was a consultant obstetrician and gynecologist. Mr. Gordon was a man of few words, but as I was later to find out he was possessed of a kind heart, which would come to my rescue.

"Do come in," he said gruffly. "Babies this way."

He led me through to the day nursery, where the new mother was sitting with her twins.

"Oh, I say," I breathed. "Aren't they beautiful. You must be so proud."

"Yes," murmured the quite clearly exhausted woman.

"Now." I smiled cheerfully, taking off my summer coat, folding it carefully, and putting it out of sight. "Let's get one thing straight right away. I don't know what you've heard of Norland nannies, but I am here to do whatever you need me to do. Whatever you would do in the house, I must be prepared to do. Be that wiping down the kitchen, doing the ironing, feeding the baby, or making a cup of tea. I am here to serve you. 'Happy mother, happy babies,' I always say."

Her eyes suddenly grew as wide as saucers. "Really?" she gasped. "Oh, what a relief."

"And we'll start now," I said, rolling up the sleeves of my white summer overall dress. "What would you like me to do?"

"Well," she said, her face wrinkling into a frown, "I'm getting in a muddle with their feeding times. It's so hard to keep track of it. This beastly baby brain. I can't make head nor tail of things at the moment."

"Don't worry." I laughed. "You're not alone."

I wasn't the least bit surprised to hear this. All new mothers struggle with getting their babies into a regular feeding pattern.

I pulled out a notepad and pen.

"Four hourly is the best way from my experience. As it can be so tricky to keep track of, particularly with twins, we can write it down here. Are you breast- or bottle-feeding?"

"Oh, bottle-feeding," she exclaimed, as if there couldn't possibly be any other way.

I wasn't much surprised to hear that either. Most of the mothers I came across these days seemed to want to bottle-feed instead of breast-feed. I encouraged them to try breast and if they didn't like it to use the bottle, but I never pushed it either, especially not if they were adamant. That wasn't my job; besides, as every good nanny knows, you aren't there to comment or judge. Women make their own decisions, the ones they feel are right for them.

I had a sneaking hunch it had something to do with the war. During those terrible years women lived with so many restrictions hanging over them, rationing, followed by blackouts and conscription. Life was one long rule book.

Now the war was over and women had been enjoying their freedom. They wanted to be out at coffee mornings, bridge clubs, golfing with their friends; and breast-feeding does curtail you somewhat.

"I'll show you the twins' nursery," said Mrs. Gordon, leading me up the corridor.

Back in the 1950s parents never slept with their babies. Co-sleeping simply didn't exist, and babies were mainly put straight into their own nurseries from birth. Nowadays, the thinking is drastically different, and experts recommend that babies sleep with their mothers in the same room for the first six months. Parents didn't worry as much and monitors, alarms, and video linkups hadn't been dreamed up. I didn't worry about the child in another room, but I was concerned I might not hear her when she woke.

"If it's okay with you, I'd rather have them in with me," I said. "That way I can hear them when they wake for a feed."

"You'll feed them in the night?" she asked, simply agog.

"Like I say, I must be prepared to do whatever you do. I do think it's best for mother to do the last ten PM feed, though, with the father. It's so important for bonding—and often the only time father sees the child if he works—but I am happy to do the rest of the feeds."

She nodded enthusiastically.

"And now," I said with a smile, "how about we make you a nice cup of tea and you go back to bed for a nap. New mothers need their rest, you know."

Gratefully, she handed me the twins. "Thank you, Nurse Brenda," she said.

"Just doing my job," I replied. And so at Courtfield Gardens, South Kensington, we all settled into our new roles.

Over the coming days I hung back, watched, and listened. Every new mother is different; and using my instincts I try to get the feel of the house so I can be supersensitive to its balance and rhythms.

I am always thinking . . . thinking and watching.

In many ways a good nanny must be like a mind reader.

What does mother like? How does she like to do her washing, fold her clothes, hold her baby?

Does she want me in the room or is she craving space to bond with her baby?

And the same goes for babies. No two babies, including the twins I was caring for now, are alike.

Some love to be stroked; others are supersensitive to touch and would rather be left alone. Some will sleep at the drop of the hat; others I will have to push round in the pram to get them to go down.

Each household is so different, and part of the thrill of a new job was sussing out the lay of the land so I could support the mother.

New mothers all have something in common, though: aside from exhaustion they are all sensitive. With so many hormones raging around their bodies it's little wonder.

That's why I made sure never to take over or appear to be telling them what to do.

What's worse than an interfering nanny in the house telling you what you're doing is wrong? I should find myself out of favor rather quickly.

If a mother is floundering with changing a nappy or can't get baby to take the bottle, I would never say, "Don't do that" but rather "Have you tried doing it this way?"

Eye contact, gentle encouragement, smiles, rest, and support are all that is needed to get a new mother up on her feet.

Soon Mrs. Gordon and her twins were flourishing, and we had a lovely little routine in place.

The color was coming back into Mrs. Gordon's cheeks, and even Mr. Gordon seemed relaxed when he returned home from the hospital to find a hot home-cooked meal waiting in the dining room.

The way to a new mother's heart might be through gentle support and sleep, but the way to a new father's heart is definitely through home-cooked puddings.

Steamed suet pudding with apple and custard usually hits the spot, but from my experience spotted dick or bread-and-butter pudding works just as well.

I quickly realized Mr. Gordon was like all men, my father and brothers included. Place a bowl of something hot, stodgy, sticky, and smothered with custard in front of him and he'd stay quiet and content for hours.

"Damn fine pudding this, Nurse Brenda." He'd sigh happily, scraping up the last bit of custard from the plate.

"Eat up, eat up." I grinned. "New fathers need their strength, too."

This house was shaping up to be a very nice, happy household indeed.

I'd only been there a few weeks when I took the twins out to the gardens in the square for some fresh air so the Mrs. could get her afternoon nap. Sitting on a bench, I got chatting to a fellow nanny.

When I'd joined her, she'd been staring into the middle distance with her eyes glazed instead of watching the two young children in her care. A "park nurse," Mrs. Whitehead would have called her—untrained and undisciplined.

"Don't you mind not having a social life?" she grumbled with a sour face. "It's Saturday night tonight and I'm stuck in again. I never get out in the evening."

"I don't mind really," I replied, tucking the blanket up under the twins' chubby little faces.

I often saw nannies huddled together chatting, possibly trading secrets, but I preferred to keep myself to myself and watch over and interact with my charges instead. I was quite certain Mrs. Whitehead had long since retired and would no longer be pedaling the streets of Kensington, spying on errant nannies, but still, I had to make a good impression, and one couldn't do that by sitting gossiping.

As I parted from the disgruntled nanny and pounded the streets of Kensington, the children fast asleep in their pram, I thought about it.

Did I mind not having much of a life of my own? Did I mind spending tonight, Saturday night, like every other night? In bed . . . on my own with only two babies to keep me company.

I thought long and hard. Honestly, no. This need inside me to create a perfect home life for others was so strong it was all consuming. I just wanted to replicate my happy home life in as many places as I possibly could.

The enjoyment and satisfaction I got from my work far outweighed the need to go and socialize.

So far I had received more love from little babies than I had in my own, somewhat disastrous, encounters with men. But as I was busy building a home full of love and stability in Kensington, dark storm clouds were building overhead.

Unbeknownst to me, twenty miles away in Surrey, my own home was being torn apart. All that I cherished and held dear had been destroyed in one single, devastating moment.

The call came just after I'd put the twins down to sleep and a short while after Mr. and Mrs. Gordon had left for a dinner party.

I was looking forward to catching up with some correspondence, but the ringing phone distracted me.

"Gordon residence," I sang.

"Brenda Ashford?" came the unfamiliar and serious voice.

"Yes, this is she," I said quietly, a sinking feeling creeping over me.

"I'm calling from Kingston Hospital. I'm afraid to say your mother, father, and sister have been in a car accident."

I froze and gripped the hall table for support. "A-are they okay?" I stuttered.

"We need you to come in immediately."

"Are they okay?" I begged, my voice rising.

"Please come in and speak to the doctor immediately," replied the woman.

The phone slipped from my hand and in a daze I replaced it in the cradle.

This could not be happening. This simply could not be happening.

The phone rang again and I grabbed it. Perhaps it was the nurse again, ringing to tell me it was all just an awful, dreadful mix-up.

I would have done anything to turn the clock back just five minutes.

"Nurse Brenda," said Mr. Gordon's voice. "Is everything okay?"

Why he chose to ring remains a mystery to this day; perhaps he had a hunch all was not well.

"Not really," I whispered. "I've just been notified that my parents have been in a car crash."

"I'm on my way home now," he said calmly.

I stood rooted to the spot until he and Mrs. Gordon burst through the door.

Gently, he put a coat around my shoulders and, still wearing his dinner suit, he led me to his car outside. "The twins . . . ?" I said, snapping out of my daze.

"Will be okay," he said firmly. "They're with Mrs. Gordon."

I stared out the window in a trance and watched the rain-splattered streets of London speed past in a blur of neon light. Everywhere people went about their business.

Elvis Presley's first film, *Love Me Tender,* had just opened, and queues of giggling girls stretched down the street. Courting couples ran shrieking with laughter to shelter from the rain. Friends drank and chattered in bars. London was alive and throbbing.

With every mile that passed, fear clutched my heart. I knew nothing would ever be the same again.

At the hospital Mr. Gordon made an imposing sight as he strode down the corridors in his dinner suit. The hospital was his world, a place where he felt confident and in charge.

"Dr. Gordon, consultant obstetrician and gynecologist," he boomed when we reached the reception desk. "I demand to see a doctor."

Saturday nights were obviously a busy time at Kingston A&E, and the receptionist didn't take kindly to being bossed about.

"Take a seat," she snapped.

"No," he said, irritation rising in his voice. "This lady's parents have been in a car crash and we need to see a doctor immediately."

She slunk off and two minutes later returned with a doctor.

"Please, follow me." The doctor beckoned gently to a side room.

My heart sank. I knew without him telling me, I would go into that room and never come out the same again. I wanted to run screaming from the hospital.

Instead, I felt Mr. Gordon's arm on my shoulder, guiding me to my fate.

"I'm afraid to say the car accident was serious. Your mother didn't survive and your father is terribly ill. We don't know yet whether he will pull through. Your sister, Kathleen, was also in the car and has also sustained injuries."

I opened my mouth to say something, but nothing came out.

Suddenly, I felt quite small, and all alone in the world. "I want to see my father," I squeaked. "I need to be with him."

"Of course," said the doctor. The room was filled with the sound of scraping chairs, and my body seemed to move of its own accord.

As we walked I could hear a strange voice and muffled sobs, and realized in surprise they were my own.

The tears were still streaming down my face when we reached Father's room.

Father lay as still as stone in his bed. He had a tracheotomy tube in his neck so he could breathe and his face was a sickly gray.

Wires snaked over his body, pumping oxygen into him.

The blood in my veins turned to ice. "Oh no . . ." I choked. "No . . . no . . . no."

There was an awful stillness in the room that turned my heart over, the only sound the beeping of machines. I clutched Father's cold hand in mine and cried until I thought my heart might break.

Mother was gone and my father was fighting for his life.

Already I felt the loss of my mother to the bottom of my soul.

A mother is the linchpin, the heart and soul of a family, and now ours had been ripped out. She had only been sixty-eight. Far too young to die.

Who would I confide my hopes and fears in, over a cup of tea in the kitchen?

Mother was a permanent fixture in our home, as central to the house as a stove is to a kitchen.

Her loss was simply unimaginable and unspeakably horrific, not just to me but to every member of my family.

Little did I know it then, but the tragic events of that day were to shape my life in ways I couldn't yet imagine.

Eventually, the doctor pulled me to one side.

"Your father is very weak. He has broken every single one of his ribs and lost a lot of blood. It's imperative when he regains consciousness that you don't tell him of your mother's death. That could push him over the edge."

I nodded dumbly.

Next I visited Kathleen. She was conscious and wearing a patch over her right eye.

"They think I'll lose my sight," she whispered.

"Oh, Kathleen," I sobbed, hugging her. "What happened?"

Her voice was barely above a whisper. "We were driving up to some traffic lights and Father was slowing down, when suddenly there was an almighty smash. The lorry in front had turned his lights off and Father didn't see him until too late."

I choked back a sob.

Please God. Don't let Mother have suffered.

Eventually, Mr. Gordon drove me home to Kensington. I didn't sleep that night, just kept turning the awful events of the night over and over in my mind.

Thoughts whirled round my shattered brain at breakneck speed. But they always came back to the same dilemma. What should I tell Father?

The next day I visited the minister of a local Baptist church and confided in him.

I drew strength from the quiet and stillness of the darkened church.

The minister said nothing as I shared the whole story.

"Please, minister, what do I do?" I sobbed. "I've been brought up to never tell a lie. How can I lie to my father?"

"Just tell him that she's happy now," he said softly.

The next two weeks passed in an exhausted blur.

The Gordons were beyond magnificent and Mr. Gordon in particular so kind.

"Please don't worry about us," he said every time he drove me to the hospital.

On one visit the doctor pulled me aside. "Your father has regained consciousness and it would appear he is on the mend, but remember what I told you. This is a vital time in his recovery."

My heart sank and the minister's words rang in my ears.

Just tell him that she's happy now.

Father managed a weak smile when I walked in to see him.

"Oh, Father," I cried, rushing to his side. "You gave us quite a fright, you know."

His tracheotomy tube had been removed, but he struggled to speak.

He fixed his kind blue eyes on mine and gave me a look so bewildered it broke my heart.

His mouth was dry and his first word when it came was rasping and barely above a whisper.

"Mother?" he croaked.

I closed my eyes and summoned every ounce of my willpower and strength.

I smiled. "Mother is happy now," I said softly.

A light went out in his eyes. He folded his hands slowly and leaned back heavily against the pillow.

I squeezed back a tear. *He knows.*

Weeks later Father was to recall that he knew she was gone the instant he came round, and in many ways I wasn't surprised.

"You sense these things," he confided in me.

They had been married for thirty-eight years and in all that time had never spent a day apart. They thought the same, felt the same. In many ways they were the same person, their souls so tightly entwined after years of love and companionship.

A fierce love like that burned so brightly. It was almost inconceivable to have one without the other.

None of my brothers or Kathleen dared voice our fears, but we all felt it the day we buried Mother.

How would he breathe without her?

At the crematorium we all stared dumbfounded at Mother's coffin.

As it started to slide toward the red velvet curtains and disappear, I closed my eyes.

I didn't want to remember Mother in a coffin vanishing behind a set of curtains. I wanted to remember her for the kind, vibrant, loving woman she was.

With my eyes closed I could picture her clearly: with her knitting on her lap, her family gathered around her, humming along to Henry Hall on the wireless or laughing as Father made her close her eyes.

"For you, Bobby." He'd laugh as he popped a bag of sugared almonds in her hand and planted a gentle kiss on her cheek.

I conjured up a wonderful afternoon we'd had, where as a treat for being accepted into the Norland, Mother took me to London to buy some smart shoes and had even bought me an ice cream sundae at a fancy tea shop. Hadn't I felt grand, sitting in such a smart establishment, where the waitresses wore black-and-white uniforms, each table was covered in a linen tablecloth, and an orchestra wearing tuxedos had serenaded us? I'll never forget the look of pride that shone in Mother's eyes as she delicately sipped her tea. What a memory to cherish always.

But most of all I remember the sweet sensation of her kisses, the softest down on her cheek that tickled as it brushed against mine.

I touched my cheek as if trying to bring the memory to life.

"I love you, Mother, and I always will," I whispered.

When something as awful as that happens, you wonder how life will ever return to normal, but somehow it does.

Poor Bambi, Mother's dog, who was also in the car, had to be put down, as he never recovered from his injuries. In some ways it was a small comfort. Mother would at least have her beloved dog by her side.

Father and Kathleen recovered from their injuries. Kathleen regained the sight in her damaged eye and went back to delivering babies, but from that day on she never spoke a word about the accident.

She pretended it was the concussion, but I knew she remembered everything. I never pushed her, though.

The trauma of that fateful day had affected her in ways I would never know. She and I made a pact to take it in turns to spend weekends with Father back at the bungalow he and Mother had shared in Surrey.

My time at the Gordons had come to an end, too. "I will never forget your kindness in my time of need," I told them as I packed my bags.

"We should be thanking you, Nurse Brenda," replied Mr. Gordon, a little less gruffly than usual. "You have been the most wonderful help."

I left Kensington an older, sadder woman than when I had arrived.

But the mission I was on burned brightly, if not brighter than before.

My own home life had had the heart ripped out of it, but I owed it to Mother to carry on as before. After all, had it not been for her love and wisdom, where would I be now? No, I couldn't crumble. I had to remain strong.

As I gathered every ounce of my reserve Britain rose from the ashes.

"You will see a state of prosperity such as we have never had in my lifetime—nor indeed in the history of this country," said the then prime minister Harold Macmillan. "Indeed, let us be frank about it—most of our people have never had it so good."

In my darkest hours I never felt lucky. I felt consumed with grief. I missed Mother so much it was like a physical pain in my chest.

But my siblings and I kept our pain hidden, for Father's sake.

I went about my business in my own quiet way. Traveling from home to home, Scotland to Essex, Hampstead to Chelsea. Rarely staying longer than three months but usually just a few weeks. Just enough time to get the mother on her feet and a good routine established.

Then my feet grew itchy and I became restless.

I daresay, some of the mothers wanted me to stay—many offered me permanent positions in their homes—but I had no interest in putting down roots. I just wanted to pack my bags and be on my way.

Months turned to years, but still my energy never waned.

"Many more houses to help," I told myself.

Did I miss not having a home to call my own? Not being able to settle in one place? Get to know the area, the community, make permanent friendships, or even establish myself within the local church community? Perhaps a little. But the stronger urge within me, to help as many mothers as I could, drove me on.

Was I running from my pain? Keeping myself busy to ignore the dull ache left by Mother's absence? Maybe I was, but I also owed it to her memory to keep going, to replicate the home life she had given me over the length and breadth of Britain.

"But you're Norland trained," one nanny gasped when we got chatting in the park. "Why don't you work for royalty or diplomats?"

"I don't give two hoots for that kind of world," I replied smoothly. "I'd rather stay here on British soil."

By 1960 I realized I had been troubleshooting for five years and had even managed to pay back my bursary to the Norland.

I had traveled many miles, yet still the road felt less traveled to me. I was exhausted from waking every four hours the majority of the time but a long way from being burned out.

I was approaching forty and laughter lines had crept over my face, but I still felt full of stamina and open to learning. And what rich experiences!

With every home I passed through I learned something new about the complicated job of caring for little folk and balance within the home. Keep the mother happy, and the home will always have harmony. Listen, really listen, to a child by getting down to his or her level. As for the babies? Keep them to a four-hour-feed routine and lavish them with plenty of cuddles and they should flourish, too. It's not so complicated.

The arrival of a baby into a family is a momentous occasion and for siblings not always a happy one. All children bar none experience jealousy driven by their extreme love for their mothers when a new baby arrives on the scene.

"I can't stop him clinging to me when I'm feeding the baby," wailed one desperate mother about her three-year-old.

"Gentle persuasion," I replied calmly. "Your older child will need a lot more attention in these coming weeks than your baby, believe it or not."

And with that I got down on my hands and knees to talk to the put-out toddler.

"I see you've been having a tea party with your teddy." I grinned. "Who else is coming to tea?"

The toddler's face lit up. "Well, mummy teddy and daddy teddy, too."

"Oh, how marvelous," I cried, clapping my hands.

Tantrum diverted, we had a perfectly lovely game after that. Children love to be with adults who understand play at their level. It doesn't have to be a teddy's tea party either. It can be pretending a cardboard box is a train and going on a marvelous adventure to painting a picture or simply reading a book.

The more attention and love you lavish on that child, the less he will feel isolated from his new family unit. But if diversion tactics didn't work and the older child still insisted on clinging to his or her poor mother's knee, then I would try to get the child involved.

"Why don't you help mummy feed the baby her bottle?" I would say, helping him or her to feed the baby.

"Aren't you doing wonderfully, you clever thing."

Soon the aggrieved child would have quite forgotten her jealousy and be basking in the glow of praise.

I passionately believe there is no problem that can't be solved by immersing yourself in a child's world. Get down to their level, see the world through their eyes.

This works particularly well in my opinion with children prone to tantrums. We've all been there and seen the red mist that always descends before a good old wobbler.

Often tantrums can be avoided by changing the way we speak to our children. Don't just say no without offering explanation. Intelligent children will always need to know why they can't have more sweets, go on the highest slide, or not run when they should walk. Don't automatically say no; talk it through instead. If no really does mean no, then try not to use the word all the time. You'd be surprised how many times the word no is said to a small child.

Instead of saying "No, you can't watch television," just think about it and rephrase: "Yes, when you've tidied up your toys." Instead of "No, you can't go and play with your friend," suggest: "Yes, of course you can, but at the weekend so you have something to look forward to."

If that doesn't work and a full-blown wobbler develops, never, ever raise your voice. You will have lost control if you do that. My mother never shouted at me, and I hope I have never shouted at a child in my care.

Instead, remember to breathe deeply, count to ten, and give your child a cuddle. If the tantrum continues, then explain that his or her behavior will not be tolerated and he or she will be removed.

If the screaming continues, then the child must be taken to his or her room. Not a naughty step—which is a designated step, chair, or area nearby—where he or she will continue to be seen and heard, which is surely exactly what he or she desires, but out of sight and earshot in his or her bedroom, until he or she has calmed down. And when he or she is sufficiently calmed down to return to the room, reward him or her with a hug.

Things I will simply never tolerate are bad manners, fussy eaters, and untidiness. If you can't get a child to put away his toys completely at the end of the day, at least get him to tidy up.

"A place for everything and everything in its place," I always say. And lead by example. "Always hang your things up when you come in. The floor is the untidy child's table."

Manners are so vitally important. I can't abide it when children don't say please and thank you. It's such a little thing but it means the world.

I love this little poem as there is so much truth in it.

> *Hearts, like doors, will open with ease*
> *To very, very little keys.*
> *And don't forget that two of these*
> *Are "Thank you, sir" and "If you please."*

—AUTHOR UNKNOWN

Isn't it lovely?

As for fussy eaters? I don't stand for it.

In the late 1950s, when rationing had all but died out, I started to see many mothers indulge fussy eaters and start giving them options.

This is a mistake in my book.

Maybe after my public showdown when Miss Whitehead insisted I eat all the beetroot on my plate I have taken a hard line on fussy eating. "This is a home, not a restaurant, and you will jolly well try it before you turn your nose up at it," I would say. Children shouldn't take for granted having a well-stocked larder and fridge.

By the late 1950s, with more access to imported exotic ingredients, cooking Mediterranean food was all the rage; but when I had to cook I stuck to the good old-fashioned foods of my childhood like pies, puddings, and roasts.

It was a brave child who turned his nose up at Nanny's cottage pie! So many children and adults lived on relatively little throughout the war and certainly didn't have the luxury of choice, but everyone got by and no one starved. Be grateful for the food on your plate, for you are lucky it is there at all.

Maybe I sound old-fashioned, but sticking hard and consistently to these principles has always improved children's behavior in my care and in a short space of time, too.

The biggest thing I think I learned from the Norland, and which I hope I brought to every home I passed through, was to encourage the mother to spend time playing with her child.

A child needs love and attention. Even if it's a thirty-minute game once in a day, every child just wants to spend time with his or her mummy, basking in her sole attention. I do wish parents would put down their cell phones and laptops and make their children the sole recipient of their time and love for a part of their day.

Some mothers, of course, are simply too tired or busy and have forgotten how to play with their children. I wouldn't tell them what I was doing but by demonstrating, I was secretly showing them how to play.

Every day I read books to children. Reading creates such a lovely routine and helps a young mind to blossom. Or we'd let our imagination run wild. Any old box can be a pirate ship or a sheet draped over two chairs a secret den.

Let them create secret worlds. Give them your undivided attention; laugh and join in, and they will love you for it. Their childhood will last that much longer, too.

After so many years in other women's homes, it was inevitable that I would come across a mother who resented me. But I like to think it was just the one home.

Mrs. Lillian Schaffer and her husband, Neil, were wealthy and lived in a large open-plan house in North London with all the latest mod cons including a fridge and washing machine.

When I arrived, it took me all of two minutes to realize that their oldest child, Jennifer, had a ferocious temper and was horribly spoiled. "Take her off somewhere and give her sweets," snapped Lillian to her husband. "She has been screaming so loudly all day I can't hear myself think."

Jennifer was dragged kicking and screaming to her bedroom.

"She's a terribly behaved kid," she told me, sighing. "I don't know how I'm going to cope when this one arrives."

With that she placed a hand on her large bump. "She'll just have to get used to it, I suppose."

Annoyance bristled inside me. Kids are baby goats. Jennifer was a child. It showed such a lack of respect.

I didn't have a terribly good feeling about this appointment.

Suddenly, we both became aware of a commotion overhead.

I stared up to a large mezzanine balcony overhead, and my jaw flopped to the ground.

A door had flown open and there was Mr. Schaffer, striding stark-naked along the corridor without a care in the world . . . and I had a bird's-eye view. "Oh gracious," I said, averting my gaze.

A second later he was in the bathroom and the sound of the shower went on.

I looked flabbergasted at Mrs. Schaffer, but she didn't raise so much as an eyebrow.

I could see this was going to be a most peculiar house to work in.

A few days later Mrs. Schaffer was taken into hospital to give birth, and I was left alone with the stripping husband and their truculent child.

Jennifer was like most naughty children. She needed discipline and more love, not the hearty slap Mr. Schaffer would have me issue.

With some gentle coaxing and firm encouragement I had soon engaged her and gradually she began eating all her tea and playing a little better.

One night I had just retired to bed when Mr. Schaffer burst into my bedroom. I pulled the bedsheets up around me, quite alarmed, but he plonked himself down on the end of my bed like it was the most normal thing in the world. "I've just got back from the hospital," he said. "My wife's not very happy with you."

"But why?" I gasped.

He smirked. "I told her how well behaved Jennifer's being now that you're here."

Oh thank you very much.

That was quite sure to enrage her. Sure enough, when she returned she was very frosty toward me and when my two weeks came to an end I was most relieved to go.

With each passing job I quickly realized though, with the exception of Mr. Schaffer's blasé attitude toward nudity, very little shocked me.

Women were changing and transforming. By 1960 the wealthy ones that I worked for had luxuries I could only have dreamed of.

So many labor- and time-saving electric appliances had been invented in the 1950s, the decade of domesticity: washing machines; stoves, toasters, kettles, vacuum cleaners, and—oh glory of glories—the electric iron. No more wrestling with a hot flat iron that needed heating over an open stove.

I thought back to my days of training at the Norland in Pembridge Square and how all the girls in my set and I had sweated and toiled on laundry days.

As I watched mothers in the 1960s glide their new steam irons over their husbands' shirts and have them pressed in a jiffy, I could only shake my head in amazement. If only they knew.

I always bit my tongue of course—no one likes to hear someone harp on about what it was like in their day—but there were occasions when I found it hard to resist.

Especially when I heard a new mother grumbling about changing her child's diaper. Thanks to modern technology, women had been freed from the backbreaking task of scrubbing countless soiled terry cloth nappies, now that disposable ones were so readily available.

"You should have seen the ones we had to wash when I was training," I said with a chuckle when I saw a young mother wrinkling her nose in disgust. "At least you can just throw them in the bin."

In many ways, women didn't realize how good they had it. They had freedom and choices.

Some called it the greatest scientific invention of the twentieth century. I don't know about that, but there is no doubting the pill changed the lives of women forever.

The contraceptive pill became available worldwide in 1961. Suddenly, women could have their cake and eat it, too. They weren't confined to the home and raising an ever-expanding family. They could choose to start their families later and pursue further education and a career on their own terms.

Gradually, I began to realize that many of the women I worked for were leaving the nursery to go back to work or start interesting careers. I saw them fly planes, run businesses, begin exacting jobs, or even in one case have a planned cesarean so she could go off on a skiing holiday for a fortnight, leaving her baby with me. They were liberated in a way my mother's generation could never have dreamed.

My father witnessed all this, too, but increasingly this new modern world just washed over him. He moved about as if in a dream world.

As we feared, he never recovered from Mother's death.

I visited him as often as I could but increasingly found him sitting sadly on his own. It was as though he was just going through the motions.

He still went to his office as often as he could, but even there he couldn't escape Mother's memory. "You won't believe what his secretary told him," hissed Kathleen, when I visited her one afternoon. Kathleen looked terribly upset and whatever it was it had clearly rattled her.

"She told him that she was a clairvoyant and she'd been contacted by Mother with a message she simply had to pass on."

"What on earth?" I blustered.

"Yes, apparently she said that Father's not to worry about the silver thimble. She has one now."

I stood silent as I allowed her words to sink in. We knew that some time ago Father had had a terrible job finding Mother a silver thimble that she had wanted. "Does he believe it?" I asked.

"Yes, I think so," she fumed. "I mean, it's outrageous saying things like that to a widowed man. It's not natural to dabble in things like that."

I didn't know what to make of it, but it left me with a strange feeling in my tummy.

Soon after, and two years after Mother's death, I was working for a family in Micheldever in Hampshire. It was slightly strange, as the man of the house had a hook instead of a hand. I never asked why—it would have felt most impolite. He and his wife were lovely, though, and had two beautiful children and a new baby. The hook did nothing to curtail his life and he managed to drive, dress himself, go to work, and cradle the baby with his good hand.

The call had come one Sunday morning and I was due to drive over and see Father and Kathleen later that day. A nagging feeling of unease had stalked me all day.

Had Father really received a message from beyond the grave? Was he to believe a so-called message from Mother about a silver thimble?

When Kathleen called, I knew what she was going to say before the words were even out of her mouth.

"I have to tell you," she said quietly, "Father's died."

"I know," I said simply.

"How do you know?" she gasped.

"I don't know—I just do," I replied.

Funny how in our society death is much feared, discussed, and obsessed over; but in my father's case everything continued just as before. Time didn't stand still.

By the time I reached his bungalow, Kathleen, ever the professional nurse, had called everybody and the funeral parlor had even come and collected Father's body and taken him to the local mortuary. She was so organized and efficient. There was nothing left to do except sit down and talk.

"What happened?" I asked.

"Father went out to mow the lawn after lunch," she said. "The first I realized that something was wrong was when I saw the lawn mower go past the window on its own.

"I rushed outside and found him dead on the ground. "Too early to tell yet but a suspected heart attack," she went on. "It would have been quick."

We sat in silence as I digested the information. Father had been seventy and had lasted twenty-four months without his beloved wife.

The kitchen clock ticked, next door's cat strolled across Father's half-mowed lawn, the kettle flicked on for the cup of tea Father liked after gardening came to a boil.

I could feel pain clawing my heart—first Mother, now Father—but I suppressed it.

"Well." I sighed. "It was a glorious death."

Kathleen nodded in agreement.

I don't mean to sound flippant. My father avoided being blown up, shot, or going insane in the trenches in World War One, and served his country again throughout countless enemy raids during World War Two.

A peaceful and mercifully quick death among his beloved roses was the best he could have hoped for.

"He's with Mother now," said Kathleen softly, "the reunion he had been dreaming of."

I nodded. "Bet they're both up there now." I smiled sadly. "Mother knitting a baby's bonnet, Father sipping a stout, Henry Hall playing in the background."

Suddenly, I realized, and one by one the hairs on the back of my neck had stood up. Father had died on a Sunday afternoon. . . . Mother and Father's hallowed time together! They had always insisted on having Sunday afternoons on their own together, with us children sent out to play.

Even when they were caring for evacuees during the war, nothing had interrupted this tradition.

Father had gone to join Mother during "their time." Now they would be together for eternity.

TESTIMONIAL

Nurse Brenda has been with us for five weeks in charge of our twin girls. She has been a wonderful help in every way and we are very sad she's leaving. Her very high professional skill has been coupled with a great ability to fit in with the ordinary day-to-day life of the family. It is with a great sense of regret that she's leaving.

— MR. GORDON

Nanny's Wisdom

KEEP A HARMONIOUS HOME.

I know it's hard in this fast-paced, frantic, modern world, but I do wish people would try harder not to let stress and anger into the home. If families treated their homes as a sanctuary, then the people in it would remain calmer. I could never believe it when I heard people bickering in front of their children. Why, oh why, would parents subject them to that? Children learn so much from their parents, so when they hear arguing, it normalizes it and teaches them that shouting is perfectly acceptable behavior. It is just so damaging for children. I never heard my own mother and father raise their voices to each other, not once, and as a result we respected them. If they said no, we listened and we did what they told us. We grew up knowing the difference between right and wrong.

FOLLOW A ROUTINE WITH NEWBORNS.

All newborns need a routine. The correct equipment supports that routine. As a rule of thumb this is what a newborn requires: four nightgowns, four vests, four matinee jackets (cardigans), diapers, one dozen muslin nappies, large shawl, two blankets for pram, and cot covers, three pairs of bootees, two fitted waterproof sheets, four cotton sheets, pram cover, cotton wool, two soft towels, nappy rash cream, baby soap, baby hairbrush, nail scissors, baby sponge, bucket for soiled nappies, baby feeding equipment, bottles, sterilizer, six bottles, brush for cleaning bottles, nipples, dried milk for bottle-fed babies.

I aimed to feed baby every four hours, not on demand. If a baby screamed for food between those feed times, I would try to give cool boiled water. Hungrier babies will need to be fed every three hours To help keep track of feeding times, I jotted them down in a notepad. Newborn babies tend to sleep a lot, and I always encouraged that. Daytime naps should be taken where possible outside in the fresh air in a cot or pram. I discouraged their sleeping past 5:00 PM and always tried to keep baby awake with a little kickabout play on a mat. If they are still napping past 5:00 PM, they will not fall asleep at 7:00 PM.

In many ways newborn babies are very straightforward.

They cry if they are hot, cold, hungry, wet, or overtired. I always considered all the possible causes when I had a baby who was crying a lot and not just assume he or she was crying for milk.

I've noticed that a lot of new mothers panic and use milk to try and soothe a crying baby, when most of the time the baby needs a change, a burping, or even just a little walk round the garden. Too much milk can be a bad thing for a baby's tiny tummy.

All children are different, so I always told mothers not to be scared to use their intuition and let the baby guide them. Watch and listen carefully and try to work your child out. Have a routine in mind, but don't be a slave to it.

Some babies I cared for suffered from dreadful colic and screamed the house down. Unfortunately, this usually coincided with the return home from work of father. If gripe water didn't work, then I drove baby round in the car, as motion settles colicky babies, or otherwise a pacifier helped. I don't really encourage the use of a pacifier, but babies who suffer with colic or reflux, or a terribly sucky baby—one who is very oral—will on occasion need it.

INCLUDE NEW FATHERS.

I do so feel for new fathers when a baby comes on the scene. Often they are quite forgotten in the flurry of excitement that a new arrival brings. Everything, quite rightly, is focused on the mother and baby. But when I saw an anxious new father hovering at the nursery door, I welcomed him in and tried to include him in the duties. Fathers need time and space to bond with their babies, just as much as new mothers do, in fact sometimes more so. A mother can feed her baby and do so much for him, but a father can quite often feel like a spare part and if not included can grow resentful. Some of my favorite times were showing new fathers how to change diapers and seeing the wonder in their eyes when they realized they had done it all by themselves. I do wish people would remember that a father is a vital cog in the wheel and as such every effort should be made to include him.

CHAPTER 13

COMING HOME

THE GORDON RESIDENCE
SURREY, ENGLAND
[1965, AGE FORTY-FOUR]

Pat-a-cake, pat-a-cake, baker's man,
Bake me a cake as fast as you can;
Pat it and prick it, and mark it with B,
Put it in the oven for baby and me.

—NURSERY RHYME

Schedule

7:00 AM: Got twins and Susanna up. Twins washed and dressed themselves while I fed Susanna her bottle.

7:30 AM: Twins have breakfast.

8:00 AM: Twins got ready for school while I changed Susanna.

8:45 AM: Twins to school. Put Susanna down to sleep, outside in fresh air if fine, inside if wet.

9:00 AM TO 10:00 AM: Chores.

10:00 AM: Woke Susanna for a feed. She was a very easy, contented baby; and most times I loved to just sit with her snuggled in my arms, watching her coo and gurgle.

10:30 AM: Visit from district nurse or took Susanna to NHS clinic for checkup.

11:00 AM: Prepared lunch, and sterilized used bottles. Made up feeds for the next twenty-four hours, did the washing and ironing and cleaned the nurseries and bedrooms.

12:30 PM: Lunch.

2:00 PM: Susanna out for afternoon nap in fresh air under shade of a big oak tree at the far end of the garden. While she slept I did housework.

3:00 PM: Fed Susanna. Twins returned home from school; and they loved to help feed their little sister.

4:00 PM: A simple meal for the twins: jam or Marmite sandwiches, slices of cheese, milk to drink, followed by sponge cakes, jelly, fresh fruit.

5:00 PM: If home, the girl's father visited while I prepared for the children's bath time.

6:00 PM: Twins bathed and I topped and tailed Susanna. All girls to be dressed for bed.

7:00 PM: Fed Susanna her bottle, then she went to sleep in her cot like a dream.

7:30 PM: Supervised twins' bedtime and ensured lights out when they had finished reading to themselves.

7:30 PM TO 10:00 PM: I spent my evenings catching up on ironing, sewing, mending. I scarcely had time to read a novel or socialize in the evenings. Mr. Gordon had dinner parties once a month, so I cooked for him and then washed and cleared up after.

11:00 PM TO 6:00 AM: Woke every four hours through the night to feed Susanna until she was three months old.

"GOOD TO HAVE YOU BACK," boomed Mr. Gordon, opening the door to the spacious Surrey home. "Come on in and meet the new arrival."

It was 1965 and many years had passed since I first worked for Mr. Gordon and his wife. Nine years to be precise since that fateful job in Kensington when Mother had passed away. Were she still alive, she wouldn't recognize London from the place where we had taken tea in the Lyons Corner House all those years ago.

Now the Beatles were dominating the charts; women's hemlines had risen to almost indecent levels; and there was a revolution in fashion, music, and sexual behavior fueled by the pill.

Girls in Mary Quant miniskirts and go-go boots strode down the King's Road in London's Chelsea. Nowadays people shopped in supermarkets; ate sliced bread; watched soap operas; and bought mass-market, low-quality disposable products. Would Mother have approved? I'm not sure.

I had returned to the Gordons' on a number of brief occasions since the twin's birth but never stopped for more than a few weeks each time.

My quest to work for as many families as I possibly could had spurred me on; and even now, one day after I had turned forty-four, I had not the slightest inclination to stop.

I must have cared for nearly one hundred children but still the itch wasn't yet scratched.

I had long since given up on finding a man: that boat had sailed for me and with acceptance of it came a kind of freedom I could never have imagined.

While my contemporaries were taking the pill, forging new careers, and traveling more than ever before, I was now firmly entrenched in the nursery. But I was at peace with my decisions, a stronger, more confident woman than ever before.

A decade of troubleshooting, of living in other women's homes, and caring for their offspring does that to you.

"Can't we tempt you to stay longer, Nurse Ashford?" said Mrs. Gordon. "The twins are eight and now I have a new baby, we really could do with your help." I'd heard this kind of plea before from many a mother, but I was adamant.

"I'm afraid not." I smiled. "I'll stay for six weeks until you're up on your feet."

She sighed. "Oh well, perhaps you better meet your new charge."

Suddenly, the twins, Belinda and Fiona, rushed in.

"Oh, Nana," they said, laughing and wrapping their arms round me and smothering me in kisses. "You've come back."

"Gracious." I chuckled, untangling myself from their sticky embraces. "It's so nice to feel wanted."

"Do you want to meet our new baby sister, Susanna?" Belinda blurted, eyes shining. "Do you? She's very little, just like a real doll."

"Oh yes, please." I laughed. "I should like that very much indeed."

Just then the door to the drawing room swung open and in walked Mr. Gordon, carrying the nearest thing I had ever seen to a real-life little doll.

"Oh my," I breathed. "May I?"

"Of course." He laughed, gently placing her into my arms.

Not since David's birth thirty-five years previously, nor Pippa's eighteen years ago, had such a little baby had such a profound effect on me.

Everyone else in the room just seemed to melt away as I locked eyes with this precious pink bundle. "She's so tiny," I marveled. "Just a little scrap."

"She was a month premature," said Mrs. Gordon. "Just five pounds."

She may have been the size of a tiny porcelain doll, but she was perfect in every single way. I was so filled with wonder I could scarcely take my eyes off her.

Each exquisite slender little finger was complete with a minuscule little fingernail, and her tiny little cheeks were as soft as satin.

Little dark lashes curled out from tiny eyelids as she slept soundly in my arms. Only her little lips, like petite rosebuds, twitched in her sleep. Suddenly, something startled her and her eyes shot open in surprise and her arms and legs jerked backward.

I sensed the twins take a step back.

"It's all right," I whispered. "She's quite okay. It's called the Moro reflex—she was just startled."

Baby Susanna gazed up at me with serious deep blue eyes. Then she snuffled, her eyes gently closed, and she snuggled down into my embrace. I felt quite overwhelmed with love.

How could anything so tiny be so perfect?

I had held countless babies in my arms before, but none touched my heart quite like this little girl.

Holding her tenderly, I was suddenly reminded of every child who had made an impact on my life.

It had started with the wonder of seeing my baby brother David, but so many children had influenced me and made me the person who I had become: the Ravenshere boys who taught me the importance of family life; the helpless yet tremendously brave children at Great Ormond Street who fought a daily battle with pain; the irrepressible Bethnal Greenies at Hothfield, separated from their parents but making the best of each and every day. Then there were Benjy and Peter, my darling first charges who never stopped smiling even when the bombs rained down; bewildered Gretel, the Jewish girl forced to flee her country by the Nazis; Jimmy the sweetheart brought up in dismal poverty; the Sacks twins, who helped me in my journey; and Pippa, whose first moments on earth I so gratefully shared—not to mention countless others who have entered and then left my life again, leaving their own indelible mark on my heart.

Those children were all unique in their own ways, but they all shared a robust and brave resilience, all sparkled with fun, and had an endless capacity for love. That is what is so precious about childhood. Love and cherish a little person and you will receive love back tenfold. What other relationship on earth promises so much magic? Was it any wonder I chose to spend my life surrounded by children and not with a man?

I learned so much from all these little folk: how to be organized, fair, loyal, patient, consistent, reliable, energetic, fun-loving, and resourceful, not to mention tenacious. As I sat cradling this new tiny soul I was overcome with a rush of devotion for my profession. As a nanny my love hadn't been squandered. Twenty-six years ago, in 1939, I had received a calling to help overturn the tyranny of the nursery. How grateful was I that I had answered it?

Maybe it was this, or maybe it was because Susanna was so tiny and so vulnerable, but holding her in my arms was having a powerful effect on me.

Love flooded my body. I imagined this must be what a new mother feels like holding her baby for the first time.

In the weeks that followed the bond between us grew and intensified. It was most extraordinary. Susanna yelped when strangers tried to hold her and clung to me. Even her own father in his smart dark suit got short shrift, but nestled in my arms she was as good as gold.

As far as I was concerned she was the best thing since sliced bread. And when six weeks was up, could I leave? Nothing on earth would have dragged me from her side.

Bonds between humans are a most mysterious thing. Why then, after years of holding babies, did such a powerful bond form between Susanna and me? What chemistry ran between us that made me feel compelled to break free from my wandering ways?

Why then, after all these years, did I feel the need to settle down?

The urge to nurture and protect is the most powerful instinct in mankind. Perhaps there was something about her fragile little body that tugged at my heartstrings and made me vow to remain by her side. But remain by her side I did. I unpacked my bags and, when six weeks was up, not one word was said by either side. It remained an unspoken agreement.

I'm so glad I did. For shortly after Susanna turned nine the relationship between Mr. and Mrs. Gordon sadly broke down and they made a decision to divorce.

I had tried not to get involved, but living cheek by jowl with them as I did, I could tell all was not well. "Mrs. Gordon is leaving to live in London," Mr. Gordon informed me. "Please, will you stay on, Nurse Brenda? Susanna and the twins need some stability and continuity in these difficult times."

"Of course," I reassured him. "You can count on me." It was even written into their divorce agreement that I would stay on to care for Susanna. She was such a sensitive little girl and I felt sure she would feel it deeply. After her mother left, I found little notes under my pillow: *Please don't leave, Nana.*

As if I could. Instead, I stayed. I took over the running of the house and tried my hardest to provide stability, love, and reassurance for all its occupants.

I stayed because I realized that finally, after all these years, after losing my parents, I had found the closest thing to a family to call my own. My mission was over. I had come home.

TESTIMONIAL

Nana was my rock. She was always there for me, when I was tiny, when I was growing up, and when I was old enough to know better. Never questioning, always supporting. Her total love and kindness to me were those of a mother. I never knew any different. And so it has always been and is still now, and the most lovely thing for me is that my children love her just as I have always done. Truly inspirational, with a love of babies that enabled her, even at the age of eighty, to get up in the small hours to care for them. She just has a way with them that is impossible to put into words, they just respond to her. "I can't" is not in her vocabulary. Always there to help and love, through good times and bad.

—SUSANNA MORRIS

Nanny's Wisdom

GIVE CHILDREN SECURITY.

All children need consistency and continuity in their lives. It's vitally important in order for them to feel secure, confident, happy, and good about themselves. It was very painful for Susanna when her parents divorced and sadly not uncommon. Divorce rates seem to be skyrocketing, I'm not sure why, but perhaps another good reason that I never actively pursued a relationship.

I'm so glad it was agreed that I stay on to care for her after her parents parted. It meant I could really be there to ensure she didn't suffer. A mother may not have been living with her any longer, but I could provide consistency of care. Susanna and I didn't talk about the divorce much; the main thing was I was there, and I could lavish her with love and cuddles whenever I sensed she was down. I think all parents who are going through a difficult divorce could do well to remember that. It's not what they say—it's what they *do*, their actions, that count. Families rocked by a breakup need to be fair, reliable, consistent, but above all physically be there with a ready supply of cuddles and kisses. Painful separations can be soothed if both parents put their children's emotional well-being first.

PUT BLACK BACK.

Some children do seem to react strongly to color. Susanna absolutely yelped whenever anyone, even her own father or godmother, came near her wearing a dark-colored suit. Some babies find dark colors intimidating and frightening. I never wore black, only white, pastels, or on occasion royal blue, and I know babies reacted better to it.

Epilogue

CLIFTON COURT RESIDENTIAL HOME
OLNEY, BUCKINGHAMSHIRE, ENGLAND
[2013, AGE NINETY-TWO]

Star light, star bright,
The first star I see tonight,
I wish I may,
I wish I might,
Have the wish I wish tonight.

—NURSERY RHYME

I AM ETERNALLY GRATEFUL FOR the love that I was able to give and receive in return from Susanna and her family. We don't share blood but a powerful all-consuming love flows through my veins for her.

I left Susanna when she turned fifteen and went to boarding school, then carried on working until well into my seventies, when I finally retired.

Not once did I lose my enthusiasm or my total devotion and love for the job. "Why don't you retire?" my brothers asked when I turned seventy. Why? I shrugged. Being a nanny wasn't a job as far as I was concerned. It was my vocation—my calling—and everyone knows you can't simply retire from love. Children leave you; you don't leave children. That's the natural order of things. As long as I had breath in my body and the will to go on, I would.

The fresh, unlined face that I started with at eighteen grew more wrinkled over time, and my brown curls faded to silver. But each laughter line told a story—the creases round my eyes, furrowed deep from years of laughter spent in the company of children. I'll admit, there were times when my back ached and my knees throbbed. Bending down to a child's level was certainly more of a challenge as the years rolled by, but I ignored the aches and pains because the passion in my heart and the fire in my belly urged me to keep on, day after day, child after child, year after year.

I only eventually stopped in my late seventies, and that was because Kathleen, my elder sister, had retired as a midwife and then promptly had a breakdown. Poor Kathleen, she always wanted something or somebody to feel they belonged to her, but she never found love or had children. Like me, she spent her life in service and so never found the time to have her own family. Unlike me, it affected her so deeply and, I suspect, in part led to her breakdown.

Kathleen always loved Yorkshire in the north of England, so I felt it my duty to move with her and keep her company; she was family, after all, and one must put family first. So I retired and we moved in together in a little bungalow, two elderly spinsters together. A nanny and a midwife with about 120 years' experience between them of delivering and caring for babies. Dinner table conversation certainly did tend to revolve around baby stories.

And that would have been that, the end of the story. Except then Susanna, whom I had always stayed in touch with, fell pregnant and asked for my help. I was absolutely thrilled to come out of retirement at age eighty to help care for Susanna's two children, Felix first, in 1999, and then Jemima a year later, in 2000.

Such joy I didn't know existed. Felix and Jemima are my "grandcharges" and as every grandparent knows, that is a unique relationship like no other on earth. When I held them both in my arms, as I had done all those years before with their mother, Susanna, I marveled at the glory of life and birth. My baby had had her babies—what an unbelievably astonishing moment. "You clever thing, you." I smiled when she first brought them home from hospital.

Just like that, I knew I had to go on, and suddenly, with renewed vigor, I became the nanny I was all those years before; getting up in the night to feed them, pacing the bedroom with Felix when he decided to try his little lungs out, or just sitting snuggled with them on my lap.

With each child, I stayed for six weeks to help Susanna get up on her feet, and then I decided to move back down to the south of England to be closer to them and my brothers.

That was my last job and perhaps my proudest. Today, Susanna is forty-eight, and I love her, care for her, and worry about her as you would a daughter. She visits me regularly; and she is so good, picking me up and having me to stay at Christmas and Easter. When I was confined to hospital recently after a fall, she rushed to my side and told the doctor she was my daughter. What a lovely, warm feeling it gave me to hear her say that.

Felix is fourteen, and Jemima is thirteen; they are both splendid children who have me in fits of giggles regularly. Jemima adores my chocolate cake, and cheeky Felix makes me laugh so. Last Christmas we went to church, and it was so packed we all had to squeeze into the pew. Felix slid off the end of the pew and pulled a hilarious face when no one was watching. The naughty thing kept nudging me until I had tears streaming down my face. What a scream! His voice is breaking and he seems to have grown six inches every time I see him. He towers over me, and I'm so proud of the fine young man he's growing into. Jemima is a beautiful, intelligent, affectionate, young lady who is forever giving me cuddles. "I'm your last baby, aren't I, Nana?" she says all the time. Bless her, she is so terribly proud to be my last charge.

The last time I stayed with them, they had picked me the most wonderful bunch of flowers and put them by the side of my bed in a vase. I was so touched.

They both call me Nana, just as Susanna still does. What a privilege and honor to have earned that name.

Sadly, my sister Kathleen and brothers Basil and Michael have passed away, but David, now eighty-three, and Christopher, now eighty-five, are very dear to me. They ring me every Sunday and visit regularly to check I am okay. To me they'll always be my baby brothers.

As for me? Today, I am ninety-two, and I can look back on a wonderful, rich, and rewarding life crammed full of adventures and love.

And what adventures! From ducking flying shrapnel to caring for illegitimate children and running war nurseries with rockets whistling overhead.

During World War Two, I encountered German Luftwaffe pilots, draconian hospital matrons, doyennes of England's oldest nanny school, East End mums, and lords and ladies, but surviving the war was only part of the story.

I've had my heart broken and battered, been betrayed and bombed, but I've kept smiling throughout. Being a nanny is not for the fainthearted, you know! It's a calling, not a career, that's for certain.

But I owe my profession a debt of gratitude. Looking after babies and children has kept the sparkle in my eye and the spring in my step.

They say caring for children keeps you young. Perhaps that's why I was able to come out of retirement at eighty years old, meaning, I am proud to say, I've been a nanny for sixty-two glorious years. Surely that makes me Britain's longest serving nanny?

There has never been a dull moment. Children have moved me from extremes of despair and heartache to sheer joy and helpless giggles.

I never dreamed when I graduated from the Norland Institute at eighteen that I'd still be looking after babies when I was eighty!

Which just goes to show that if your heart is full of love for little children, your body will keep on going.

I never did find true love or have a child to call my own. There were simply too many babies who needed my love.

Yes, I sacrificed my dreams of finding love and having my own family to care for the offspring of others but I have not one single regret.

I've seen child care trends come and go, but the only thing any mother need really do is to give her whole heart over to love. If she does this, the rewards will be endless.

In sixty-two years I hope I have imparted a little of that love, magic, and wisdom. I am still in touch with many of those children today and every year at Christmas and birthdays I am rewarded with many letters and photos from my "babies" all grown up.

These days, my life is a little less eventful. I live in sheltered accommodation, and I still find it a surprise to be called Brenda. I'm so used to being called Nanny, you see. But I have the memories of a thousand cuddles from chubby arms. Those smiles and the magical sound of a child's laughter will keep me going for a few more years yet.

I daresay as a Norland nurse I could have worked for royalty or diplomats and traveled the world. But I didn't. I'm proud to say I stayed on British soil and did my duty.

It's funny, the word *duty* is almost regarded as a dirty word these days, but for me it means being proud to be associated with a cause in which you believe, proud to be in the service of children.

In 1953 our queen had the responsibilities of a nation placed on her twenty-five-year-old shoulders when she was crowned in a spectacular coronation, in which she promised to be a "servant to my people." An onerous promise for one so young. The same year I was awarded my badge of merit from the Norland for more than five years faithful service to one family. I daresay our duties are a little different, but our intentions are the same.

Today the queen is eighty-seven and I am ninety-two, and we can both look back on a long and happy life spent in the service of people who depended upon us.

I like to think I did my little bit to help secure the safety and freedom of our children, and I found love by the bucket load along the way.

The Norland motto is "Love never faileth." I hope I never have failed a single child.

More than anything, I hope I have lived my life nobly, bravely, and with honesty, virtues I hold dear. I never made much money being a nanny, but I don't give two hoots for that. I can't take it with me, so what is the point of having a well-stuffed bank account? Instead, I have something far, far more valuable—sixty-two years in the service of children, and that, in my opinion, is priceless. Children should be cherished, loved, adored, and nurtured every day and at every stage of their lives. At ninety-two, of course I am now at a stage in my life where I start to reflect on my passing, but I don't fear it; oh no, I know exactly where I am going.

In heaven I will be able to look down and watch over all my babies. Until then, I thank each and every one for a truly magical and blessed life.

AUTHOR'S NOTE

I FOUND THE FOLLOWING HELPFUL during the process of writing *A Spoonful of Sugar:*

The Hothfield History Society; Geoff Webb, author of *A Redbourn Commoner*; Katherine Stone of the War Studies Department, Kings College, London; Penelope Stokes, author of *Norland: The Story of the First One Hundred Years, 1892–1992*, published by the Norland College in 1992; Susan Briggs, author of *Keep Smiling Through* and *The Home Front: War Years in Britain, 1939–1945* (London: Weidenfeld & Nicolson Ltd., 1975); Kevin Telfer, author of *The Remarkable Story of Great Ormond Street Hospital* (London: Simon & Schuster, 2008); and Richard Holmes, author of *Tommy: The British Soldier on the Western Front, 1914–1918* (London: Harper Perennial, an imprint of HarperCollins, 2004).

ABOUT THE AUTHOR

Brenda Ashford is a graduate of Norland College, a world-famous institute for British nannies. For sixty-two years, she cared for more than one hundred children, making her Britain's longest-serving nanny. She lives outside London and still regularly bakes chocolate cake for her many former charges who visit her weekly.

ABOUT THE CO-WRITER

Kate Thompson is a freelance journalist with more than fifteen years' experience. Previously, she was deputy editor of the award-winning *Pick Me Up* magazine, helping to launch it in 2005. She writes for *Marie Claire*, the *Sunday Mirror*, and *The Daily Mail*, among others.